A Mathematics Wizard in Different Eyes

Second Edition

A Mathematics Wizard in Different Eyes

Second Edition

Editors

Dr. Haripada Maity
Shri Manmatha Nath Das
Prof Ranajit Kumar Nayek
Shri Balailal Das

ALLIED PUBLISHERS PVT. LTD.

Noida • Mumbai • Kolkata • Chennai

ALLIED PUBLISHERS PRIVATE LIMITED

D-5, Sector-2, **Noida**–201 301
Ph. Nos.: 0120-4320295/2542557/4352866
E-mail: delhi.books@alliedpublishers.com

17 Chittaranjan Avenue, **Kolkata**–700072
Ph.: 033-22129618 • E-mail: cal.books@alliedpublishers.com

15 J.N. Heredia Marg, Ballard Estate, **Mumbai**–400001
Ph.: 022-42126969 • E-mail: mumbai.books@alliedpublishers.com

No. 25/10, Commander-in-Chief Road, Ethiraj Lane (Next to Post Office)
Egmore, **Chennai**–600008
Ph.: 044-28223938 • E-mail: chennai.books@alliedpublishers.com

Website: https://alliedpublishers.in

First published 2023
Second edition 2025

ISBN: 978-93-48699-28-2

Published by Sunil Sachdev and printed by Ravi Sachdev
at Allied Publishers Pvt. Ltd., D-5, Sector-2, Noida–201 301

THE RAMAKRISHNA MISSION INSTITUTE OF CULTURE
(A Branch Centre of Ramakrishna Mission, P.O. Belur Math, Dist. Howrah, West Bengal 711202)
GOL PARK, KOLKATA - 700 029, WEST BENGAL, INDIA
Phone : 033 - 4030 -1200, 2464 -1303, 4030 -1263 ; Fax : 033-2464-1307
E-mail : rmic.secretary@gmail.com, golpark.rmic@rkmm.org; Website : www.sriramakrishnqa.org; YouTube : rmicgolpark

June 20, 2025

Foreword

'A Mathematics Wizard in Different Eyes', a very significantly titled book on Prof Jagadis Chandra Misra, is by his associates of whom some are holy persons of the Ramakrishna Mission, Belur Math, some are renowned persons, his peers, teachers, the majority being students he created mainly during his teaching career at the IIT Kharagapur and some are his relations—all joining hands to convey their gratitude and appreciation to this towering personality, a veritable banyan of formidable vastness. I am not the person with any capability to fathom his greatness as a true human being bordering on the divine or to appreciate his scholarship as a man of Mathematics. But I can candidly appreciate the exquisite demeanour he carries with him wherever he goes and I was impressed by his humanness when he first entered my office one morning probably a year ago and presented me with his autobiography. He could be my teacher as well since some of my college teachers were his contemporaries at the Vidyamandira college. I, out of curiosity, turned over a few pages and felt he was an affectionate human being almost nonpareil. By the time, I glanced through a few more pages I felt the book is a gem. I suggested that Professor would do well to translate it in English for wider readership. I think he did it. Meanwhile a fresh command came that I would have to write a foreword for a new book on him. This very book on him is spread over four sections as per classifications of the status and identity of the contributors. Here is a fascinating man who manifested multi-faceted dimensions of his character without desperately trying to impress his supremacy upon others. He brought to the outer society the very affectionate touch of a family spirit or a Paribar-Chaitanya. Articles on him reflect on his rare ability to convert every arrogant intellect into a first class obedient disciple. He is neither an ignorant baby nor an omniscient Lord. He is little or nothing but life pure.

The secret behind this illustrious life is that the formative period of his life was spent in the spiritual ambience of the Belur Math. Apart from his Principal, Swami Tejasanandaji Maharaj, he was blest by innumerable senior Swamis of the Belur Math and received Mantra Diksha from Swami Shankaranandaji Maharaj, the 7th President of the Ramakrishna Mission. On this solid foundation of inner poise, he erects the edifice of his sacred human personality. They all filled his little bowl with their bounties regardless of his need. Truly, he was ahead of his peers with abundant surpluses of life.

For all this and many more, I salute him and his teachers, his parents, his relations and peers. I convey my special regards to Prof H.P. Maity, Sri Manmathanath Das and others who edited the book for many a bud to bloom. His life shall provide the beacon light to a generation aspiring for excellence. I am grateful for being chosen by Prof Misraji to write the foreword of such a book. I pray to the Holy Mother Sarada Devi that the book might evoke new possibilities of fulfilment, sing a new saga of courage and hope and pave the ground for new ventures, now and always.

Swami Suparnananda
Secretary

Editorial Note

A towering tree, though a child of Mother Earth, spreads its countless branches far and wide, hoisting the flag of its grandeur across the vast sky. Naturally, we bow before such magnificence in awe and reverence. Like any other being, it has been nurtured by the love of the soil, the essence of water, air, and sunlight. As it grows, it surpasses the ordinary with its vitality, extending its glorious branches adorned with leaves and blossoms toward the heavens. Yet, in its greatness, it provides shelter to innumerable creatures—offering cool shade, luscious fruits, and a haven of comfort to all. Despite its extraordinariness, it becomes one of our own, dear and familiar. Overwhelmed with gratitude, we express our love and admiration in songs of praise.

Professor Dr. Jagadis Chandra Misra is such a towering figure in the realm of mathematics and science. Surrounding him, we are countless individuals, diverse in education and achievements, yet united in love and respect for him. A few among us have come together to compose this tribute—a collection of reflections and admiration—which is now presented in the form of this book, *"A Mathematics Wizard in Different Eyes."* While only a handful initiated this endeavour, we firmly believe that in spirit, we all shared this sentiment. Thus, this book is truly the collective expression of all its contributors. We extend our heartfelt gratitude to our esteemed writers and warm wishes to all involved.

One might ask—what is the significance of publishing such a book? To answer, let us pose another question—why has our tradition, for centuries, honoured great trees like the banyan and the peepul? The answer lies in humanity's profound gratitude for their invaluable contribution to our world. Similarly, Dr. Misra's erudition, exceptional teaching, skilled administration, and extensive research in mathematics and science have left an indelible mark, not only on academic institutions but on society as a whole. Furthermore, despite standing on the pedestal of great achievements, he has consistently demonstrated a deep love for all—setting an extraordinary example of a compassionate heart. This publication serves both as a humble acknowledgment of his invaluable contributions and as a token of society's deep respect for him. Recognizing and expressing gratitude is, after all, a hallmark of civilization.

One more thought—ideal individuals are the driving force behind the progress of civilization. *"The path trodden by the great is the path for all."* However, such exemplary figures are not born in abundance across all times and places. In such instances, books chronicling their lives become their true representatives. We believe that this book on Professor Misra's life will serve as an educational guide for both present and future generations. Reading it may not necessarily turn a student into a scientist or mathematician, but it will certainly impart invaluable lessons in dedication, perseverance, resilience, and the pursuit of true humanity. Through this book, Professor Misra's vision and wisdom will extend beyond the confines of the classroom, illuminating the paths of many lives near and far. With this profound belief, we embarked on this editorial journey, offering our heartfelt tribute, admiration, and best wishes to the distinguished scholar, Professor Dr. Jagadis Chandra Misra.

We want to put on record our deep sense of gratitude to Srimat Swami Suparnananda, Secretary, Ramakrishna Mission Institute of Culture, Golpark, Kolkata for his kind encouragement in bringing out this Second Edition (English version) of the book in the interest of wider circulation among the future generation of students and young faculties and for kindly writing a befitting "Foreword". This is an updated version and is further enriched by several new articles contributed by some more distinguished personalities.

We wish to extend our sincere thanks to Shri Jagdish Singh and all his team members at Allied Publishers Pvt. Limited, Noida for their meticulous efforts in printing and publishing this book. We also acknowledge with deep respect the generous support of Dr. Misra's family, whose contributions have been instrumental in making this publication possible.

Finally, we eagerly look forward to readers' thoughts and suggestions on this book.

With humble regards,

Dr Haripada Maity
Shri Manmatha Nath Das
Prof Ranajit Kumar Nayek
Shri Balailal Das

5th December, 2025

About the Editors

Dr. Haripada Maity born on 2nd September, 1947 in Ektarpur, Bhagabanpur Police Station. Later settled in Contai. After teaching at Palpara and Moyna College, he became the Principal of Mugberia Gangadhar Mahavidyalaya. He is the author of books like *Medinipur in the Freedom Struggle (Vol. 3)*, *Martyr Khudiram in the Era of Fire*, and others. He has edited numerous works including *Anannya Abha, Gandhipathik Swadhinata Sangrami Bishwapada Jana*, among many more. A leading figure in various cultural initiatives, he has served as a direct inspiration for the endeavours of many. He is also well known for his eloquence and engaging speech.

Manmatha Nath Das born on 3rd Baishakh 1349 (Bengali calendar) in Mangalchak, under Patashpur Police Station. Later settled in Bhupatinagar. He taught at Chakrasul and later at Mugberia Gangadhar High School. After retirement, he served as Principal of a private primary teacher-training institute. An active organizer and editor of literary journals, he is also the author of stories, poems, biographies, and books on local history. Of particular note is his compilation *Medinipur Charitabhidhan* (2 volumes), a biographical index of over two thousand notable people from Medinipur.

Ranajit Nayek born 9th October, 1945. Village Bansgora, P.O. Brajalalchak, P.S. Chandipur, Dist. Purba Medinipur. Later residence at Village & P.O. Bhupatinagar. Qualification: M.A. LLB. Served Mugberia Gangadhar Mahavidyalaya as Lecturer in English from 1968 to 2005. A writer of Poems, Short-Stories, and Literary and Religious Essays. No. of Books written is 17. His most notable book is '*Sansarbritte Dharmacharan*". A Rabindra *Sangeet* Singer and Reciter. Interested in Social and Cultural Service.

Balailal Das born on 20th July, 1942 in Pania, under Patashpur Police Station. He taught for a brief time at the village school, then at Goura Sonamui High School, and finally at Panchagram Shiksha Niketan. He is the founder of *Sonali Sangha* and has held leadership roles in several cultural and service-oriented organizations. A contributor to various journals and magazines, he is also an enthusiast of travel and culture.

Dedication

To all the Well-Wishers,
Colleagues, Students,
Research Scholars of His Group
and Compassionate Family Members
Who Have Been Part of
Professor Dr. Misra's Resolute Journey.

Contents

Page

Foreword *v*

Editorial Note *vii*

About the Editors *ix*

Dedication *xi*

SECTION I

Peers and Teachers

CHAPTER 1: Our Jagadis Da 3
Swami Devarajananda

CHAPTER 2: A Few Words about My Dear Student Jagadis Chandra Misra 6
Dr. Sachindra Kumar Baksi

SECTION II

Students

CHAPTER 3: My Research Guide, Prof. J.C. Misra—A Tireless Crusader 11
Dr. S.K. Pandey

CHAPTER 4: Professor Jagadis Chandra Misra: A Remarkable Personality 17
Dr. Gopal Chandra Shit

CHAPTER 5: Professor J.C. Misra, as I Found Him 20
Dr. Santwana Mukhopadhyay

CHAPTER 6: Prof. Jagadis Chandra Misra: A Remarkable Example of Cooperation and Compassion in Research 22
Dr. Subhash Chandra Samanta

CHAPTER 7: As I Found Sir 26
Dr. Gopal Chandra Bera

CHAPTER 8: Prof. J.C. Misra: Memories Filled with Gratefulness 28
Dr. Sukumar Chandra

CHAPTER 9: Recollections of the Past 30
Dr. Sushil Kumar Ghosh

CHAPTER 10: My Association with Prof. J.C. Misra 36
Dr. G. Radhakrishnamacharya

CHAPTER 11: Respected Sir 38
Dr. Aniruddha Sinha

CHAPTER 12: A Bright Star in the Sky of Mathematics 41
Dr. Saktipada Nanda

CHAPTER 13: Professor Jagadis Chandra Misra in My Eyes 43
Dr. Mrityunjay Kumar Patra

CHAPTER 14: Reminiscences of My Association with Prof. J.C. Misra 46
Dr. Narayan Chandra Chattopadhyay

CHAPTER 15: My Esteemed Doctoral Supervisor 48
Dr. Biswajit Mallick

CHAPTER 16: Prof. J.C. Misra, as I Saw Him 50
Dr. Bijay Kumar Sahu

CHAPTER 17: Some Memories from the Past 52
Dr. Sukhendu Bikash Kar

CHAPTER 18: The Guiding Light of Our Lives 55
Manasi Nanda Raut

CHAPTER 19: From the Pages of Memory 59
Dr. Namita Mahapatra

CHAPTER 20: My Experience with Professor Jagadis Chandra Misra 64
Dr. Motahar Reza

CHAPTER 21: A Distinguished Son of Bengal 67
Smt. Gita Misra

CHAPTER 22: Remembering with Deep Gratitude 69
Dr. Sanchita Dandapat (Sikdar)

CHAPTER 23: Dr. Jagadis Chandra Misra: Some of My Personal Insights 71
Ashish Panda

CHAPTER 24: Prof. J.C. Misra—My Research Guide 72
Dr. Somnath Maiti

SECTION III

Classmates, Colleagues and Educationists

CHAPTER 25: Prof. Jagadis Chandra Misra, A Celebrity Among Contemporary Mathematicians 77
Dr. Biswanath Das

CHAPTER 26: Shaping Lives Touching Lives: The Profound Impact of Prof. J.C. Misra 80
Dr. Tapas Chatterjee

CHAPTER 27: Jagadis Chandra Misra: A Friend from the World of Mathematics 82
Dr. Dhiman Ganguly

CHAPTER 28: Our Friend Jagadis 84
Prof. Nitya Niranjan Kundu

CHAPTER 29: Bow Down in Reverence 88
Srabani Sengupta

CHAPTER 30: My Elder Brother 91
Dr. Subhash Chandra Mahapatra

CHAPTER 31: 'A Traveller in an Unknown Land' by Prof. J.C. Misra: Some Observations 96
Prof. G.P. Bhattacharjee

CHAPTER 32: Prof. J.C. Misra—My Former Colleague 97
Dr. Sudarsan Nanda

CHAPTER 33: A Conversation with a World-Renowned Mathematician 100
Dr. Haripada Maity

CHAPTER 34: Memories are Always Sweet: Recollections of Friendship 107
Dr. Purnendu Sekhar Das

CHAPTER 35: The Eminent Personality: Jagadis Babu 110
Manmatha Nath Das

CHAPTER 36: Dr. J.C. Misra—A Wonder 116
Prof. Ranajit Kumar Nayek

CHAPTER 37: My Schoolmate Jagadis Chandra Misra 118
Balai Lal Das

CHAPTER 38: In the Company of Jagadis at the Vidyamandira for Five Years 120
Dr. Kamalesh Bhowmik

CHAPTER 39: In Search of Old Memories 125
Ashok Bhowmik

CHAPTER 40: My Friend Sri Jagadis Chandra Misra—A Classmate of My Early College Days 128
Sibabrata Bagchi

CHAPTER 41: Jagadis Da, as I Saw Him at the Vidyamandira 130
Debiprasad Dutta

CHAPTER 42: Jagadis Da 132
Shyamal Chowdhury

CHAPTER 43: Jagadis Da, Our Revered Elder Brother 134
Swapan Bhadra

CHAPTER 44: Looking Back 136
Swapan Bhattacharya

CHAPTER 45: My Intimate Friend Jagadis 138
Paresh Manna

CHAPTER 46: Our Beloved Jagadis Da 140
Prof. Pranabesh Jana

CHAPTER 47: Prof. J.C. Misra in My Eyes 142
Saroj Narayan Misra

CHAPTER 48: As I See Prof. Jagadis Chandra Misra 145
Saktipada Giri

CHAPTER 49: A Few Words about Dr. Jagadis Chandra Misra 147
Dharanidhar Gayen

CHAPTER 50: The Song of Jagadis Chandra (Rhythm: Dadra | Scale: Ma-Ga) 149
Binod Bihari Jana

CHAPTER 51: Mathematician from Patashpur Renowned in Europe and America 151
Debmalya Bagchi

CHAPTER 52: Encourager of Children's Mathematical Pursuits 155
A Staff Correspondent, Anandabazar Patrika

CHAPTER 53: Banyan Trees of the Society 157
Mrs. Sonali Ghosh

CHAPTER 54: A Scientist Who Thinks for the Nation 158
Nikunja Bihari Ghorai

CHAPTER 55: Inspiring the Young to Love Mathematics 160
Correspondent, Teerbhumi Daily

SECTION IV

Relations

CHAPTER 56: My Brother, My Inspiration: The Story of Dada 165
Parames Misra

CHAPTER 57: My Younger Brother Jagadis 173
Durgarani Bhattacharya

CHAPTER 58: Prof. Jagadis Chandra Misra: Glimpses from a Different Perspective 176
Dr. Achintya Mukhopadhyay

CHAPTER 59: Honourable Shri Jagadis Chandra Misra 179
Sukdeb Chakraborty

CHAPTER 60: Arya Acharya Jagadis 182
Dr. Bishnupada Nanda

CHAPTER 61: Dr. Jagadis Chandra Misra: A Multifaceted Personality 183
Dr. Soumyadeep Mahapatra

CHAPTER 62: My First Interaction with a Bright Star 185
Dyutiprava Bhattacharya Mahapatra

CHAPTER 63: A Few Words about My Father 187
Dr. Subhas Chandra Misra

CHAPTER 64: My Father in My Eyes 190
Dr. (Mrs.) Sumita Mukhopadhyay (Misra)

CHAPTER 65: Our Father 195
Dr. Sudip Misra

CHAPTER 66: A Dedicated Karma Yogi in the Eyes of the Eldest Daughter-in-Law 198
(Mrs.) Sulagna Misra

CHAPTER 67: Our Baba in My Eyes 201
(Mrs.) Satamita Misra

Chapter 68: Bhaimoni 204
Devarati Misra

Chapter 69: Our Bhaimoni, as I See Him 206
Devadeep Misra

Chapter 70: My Paternal Grandfather 209
Devapratim Misra

Chapter 71: Bhaimoni 211
Devadrita Misra

Section V

Appendices

Appendix 1: Authors (in alphabetical order) 215

Appendix 2: Personal Details of Prof. Jagadis Chandra Misra 221

Appendix 3: Children 222

Appendix 4: Curriculum Vitae 223

Appendix 5: New Findings in Biomechanics 237

Appendix 6: Citation of INAE Outstanding Teacher Award 2013 239

Appendix 7: Glimpses of His Journey 241

Appendix 8: Slideshow 251

Section I

Peers and Teachers

CHAPTER 1

Our Jagadis Da

Swami Devarajananda
Joint Convenor, Ramakrishna-Vivekananda Bhava Prachar Committee, Ramakrishna Math and Ramakrishna Mission, Belur Math-711202

A rather unusual request came to me from a senior fellow-student. He, of course, mentioned that he was merely passing on a request from some other people. The request was simple yet profound—he wanted me to write about him as I had seen him. The reason behind this was that a certain organization, committed to instilling self-confidence among students, wished to introduce them to individuals who, despite being born in remote villages with limited opportunities, had managed to shape their lives merely through determination.

Writing about someone while they are still alive—especially if they are dear to you—is often an awkward task. However, I felt compelled to do so in the hope that it may benefit future generations. The person I am writing about is our beloved and revered Jagadis Da, Prof. Jagadis Chandra Misra.

The very mention of his name brings to mind a calm and composed young man, freshly graduated from college. I had the rare privilege of enrolling in the undergraduate programme at Ramakrishna Mission Vidyamandira (Belur Math) in 1965, and that is when I first met him. As far as I recall, he had already completed his undergraduate studies at the Vidyamandira in 1964 and was pursuing a postgraduate degree elsewhere. However, he used to frequently visit the Vidyamandira and pay homage at Belur Math.

Jagadis Da was a cherished disciple of Belur Math, very affectionate to many revered monks there. Our professors and hostel superintendents often referred to him as one of the ideal students of the Vidyamandira. At that time, I never truly reflected on why he was considered an ideal student. But later, when I delved into the writings of Swami Vivekananda, I realized that the qualities Swamiji envisioned in a Vidyamandira student were vividly reflected in Jagadis Da's life.

Here are a few such qualities:

1. A student must be pure, patient, and persevering. These three qualities—purity, patience, and perseverance—are essential for anyone striving for success.
2. A student must have deep respect for elders, teachers, and even himself. Their faith in their own abilities should remain unwavering.
3. The foundation of learning is concentration, which requires regular practice. By learning meditation techniques from a qualified teacher and dedicating a portion of the day to such practices, they can enhance their focus.
4. Students must have discipline and obedience toward the rules of their institution. Discipline should not be viewed as a restriction but as a guiding fence that helps prevent obstacles in their path to growth.
5. One major flaw of the youth is the tendency to mock traditional values. Those who genuinely aspire to build their character consciously strive to free themselves from this flaw.

These qualities naturally manifest in the ideal students of any educational institution run by the Ramakrishna Math and Mission. Their faces reflect the inner glow of such virtues. In the case of Jagadis Da, every action, every gesture of his exuded an aura of grace that evoked affection from elders and reverence from us.

I remember a photograph of him standing beside Swami Shantananda, a senior monk and a direct disciple of Holy Mother Sarada Devi. This image alone testifies to his character. During my three years at Vidyamandira, I saw Jagadis Da on numerous occasions. However, after my graduation, we lost touch for many years.

Much later, while visiting a former classmate's quarters at IIT Kharagpur, I learned that Jagadis Da was at that time a professor there. After a long time, I had the chance to see him again. To my amazement, his face still carried the same radiance I had seen back in the Vidyamandira. Age had done nothing to dim his glow.

He invited me to his residence for a meal. As we sat down to eat, I noticed that he kept looking at me with a thoughtful, affectionate gaze. Curious, I asked what was on his mind. With a sigh of nostalgia, he simply said, "Brother, what could have been and what has become…"—his words carried a hint of regret.

Jagadis Da in the Holy Company of Shrimat Swami Shantananda ji

It seemed as though the life he had once envisioned for himself, and the expectations others had for him, had not fully materialized. A subtle sadness filled his voice. Perhaps he was struggling to accept the ways of fate. However, in my eyes, he was living the life of an ideal householder. His family was united in harmony, reflecting the ideals of a devoted household.

And yet, there was a trace of unfulfilled dreams from his youth—perhaps the ache of an aspiration left unattained.

Nowadays, we occasionally speak over the phone. Each time, his affectionate greeting reminds me of the same old Jagadis Da, just as warm and inspiring as ever.

CHAPTER 2

A Few Words about My Dear Student Jagadis Chandra Misra

Dr. Sachindra Kumar Baksi
Professor and Head of the Department of Mathematics (Retd.),
Ramakrishna Mission Vidyamandira, Belur Math, Howrah

It gives me immense joy to write or speak a few words about my beloved student, Jagadis. He is one of those distinguished individuals who have brought great repute to Vidyamandira.

When I joined Vidyamandira in July 1962, Jagadis was a second-year student majoring in Mathematics. I still recall the names of some of his classmates—Ganes Das, Shailen Saha, Ashok Patra, Ramen Chatterjee, Jiben Chakraborty and Barin Bera. In the very first class of my teaching career, I began teaching them Hydrostatics. I was quite nervous and unsure of how well I taught. In their third year, I taught them Probability and Statistics.

Jagadis was an intelligent and hardworking student. He listened attentively and practiced the material repeatedly. Some students may be bright but lack sufficient practice—they often don't reach great heights. On the other hand, students with average intelligence but diligent practice don't fall behind either. Jagadis, however, was not only bright—he was exceptionally gifted—and he practiced thoroughly. It is this rare combination that has led him to great heights today.

He has earned both a Ph.D. and a D.Sc degree and has received numerous awards, among which the Rammohan Award is notable. Initially, he taught at Uluberia College for some time, and later served for many years as a Professor of Applied Mathematics at IIT Kharagpur. He was a highly successful teacher. His students learned not only academics from him, but also what it means to be a good human being.

Faculty and Students of B.Sc. Mathematics Honours, 1961–64

Sitting L to R: Dr. Sachindra Kumar Baksi, Dr. Pran Ranjan Sengupta, Prof. Aswini Kumar Lahiri, Swami Gokulananda (Principal-in-charge), Dr. Amiya Bhusan Roy and Dr. Dhirendra Nath Sarkhel

Standing L to R: Barin Bera, Ganes Das, Jiben Chakraborty, Nikhil Garai, Ashok Patra, Jagadis Chandra Misra, Sailen Saha and Ramen Chatterji

Another admirable quality of Jagadis is his devotion to spirituality. Vidyamandira is a residential degree college. The hostel where Jagadis resided was under the care of Swami Gokulananda (Govinda Maharaj), who was very affectionate toward him. Perhaps it was his influence that nurtured the spiritual inclination of Jagadis.

I sincerely wish Jagadis a long, peaceful, and fulfilling life.

SECTION II

Students

CHAPTER 3

My Research Guide, Prof. J.C. Misra—A Tireless Crusader

Dr. S.K. Pandey
Professor and Head, Department of Mathematical Sciences, IIT (BHU), Varanasi, U.P., India

Hijli had been an infamous site known for the execution of Indian freedom fighters during the British period, before the first and the largest Indian Institute of Technology was founded, in its vicinity, at Kharagpur. This was in order to provide engineering students with world-class education as we had an acute scarcity of engineers who could contribute to uplift the Indian face in terms of infrastructure and industrialization in an extraordinary way. Its inception not only brushed aside the infamous spot but also painted the face in vibrant colours. Mathematics is the queen of all sciences, so was there a department of mathematics founded right from its inception in 1950. In 1971, joined Dr Jagadis Chandra Misra, an applied mathematics graduate of Calcutta University and a doctorate of Jadavpur University.

Dr. Misra started his research career in thermo-elasticity; the young researcher, however, was soon fascinated with the hidden laws of biological systems. This was a turning point for the making of a new leader in the research frontier called mathematical modelling of biological systems. Biology and mathematics were traditionally considered different disciplines. The fact that physiological processes can be mathematically formulated, or in other words, mathematical formulas govern physiological processes, had been undermined. This thought process revolutionized the scientific world. Dr. Misra chose the mechanics of bio-systems to work on. Meanwhile, in 1975, he received the coveted International Humboldt Fellowship Award from the celebrated scientist Professor Werner Heisenberg, Germany. This early recognition paved the way for an endless expedition. It is hard to say whether he inherited consistency, or developed over the years, but it is an integral part of his exemplary personality.

His working hours start early in the morning and continue late in the evening. Age never mattered.

Living beings are the automated creations of the universe. Their decision-making ability is simply astonishing. Although humans are the best creations, the rest of the animal kingdom and even plants that grow and reproduce make the world amazingly beautiful. Reproduction is the key phenomenon that keeps the world youthful and attractive. All that is neither randomly done, nor is that no laws are taken care of. All biological systems follow some natural laws and hence their inherent mathematical formulations are a challenge for the scientists to unfold and discover the latent principles so that they learn the pathology of the health related issues, and replicate the knowledge for suggesting remedies and possible clinical corrections. His top class pioneering work in cardiac function that dealt stresses with pulse loading, poro-elastic spheroidal shell model, research in brain injury, rotational brain injury, effect of pulse loading on brain injury, human cranial system effect of solar radiation, etc fetched him a series of outstanding publications, and also added new dimensions to research in biomechanics. This was enough to bring him global recognition.

The biological laws are not straightforward as the laws of physics, nor are they as easy to experiment as chemicals in laboratories. Biological phenomena are interdependent and hence are quite complex to investigate. Numerous parameters make them an open system while only closed systems can be formulated. This left the researchers to compromise with some less significant parameters. Even some significant parameters had to be dispensed with to lay the foundation of formulation in the beginning. This process of formulation emerged in the scientific world in the name of mathematical modelling. It revolutionized the scientific world. Simulation together with mathematical modelling became a new path to scientific investigations.

This was not new to the scientific community; however, the momentum was built up somewhat late in the mid-20th century. Amidst the tremendous zeal for such explorations, a number of scientists across the world worked day and night; a few excelled, made phenomenal contributions and enriched the field enormously. Amongst them, as mentioned earlier, was Professor J.C. Misra as a bright star.

His group of scientists at IIT Kharagpur made industrious efforts in bio-solid mechanics such as fracture and remodelling of bones, thermal and piezo-electric effects on bones, wave propagation in bones, and compressibility of vascular tissues.

A tissue, in biology, is a bunch of cells, the tiniest units, in terms of structure and function of an organism. Thus the entire anatomical structure comprising bones, cartilages, muscles, etc. are made up of tissues of different kinds. Bones are primarily composed of hydroxyapatite, i.e. $Ca_{10}(PO_4)_6(OH)_2$, proteins such as collagens and non-collagens, and water. Collagens are amino-acid complex structures which form a flexible framework, offer tensile strength and resilience to the bone. Vascular tissues make vessels through which liquids such as blood pass. Cracks during sport-activities and when one grows older are often heard. Prof. Misra studied the intensified stress-field generated in the vicinity of cracks in patella and other bone specimens. Some of his theoretical contributions in bone biomechanics are landmark contributions to osteology and orthopedics, since bone compression assists physical activities and could be useful to arrest fracture to a large extent.

Prof. Misra and his team theoretically showed that vascular tissues are compressible (Misra and Chakravarty, Rheologica Acta, 1980). This was later verified at the Biomechanics Laboratory of the University of California, San Diego by a research team led by Prof. Y.C. Fung, the father of modern biomechanics.

Pierre and Jacques Curie (1880) discovered that some materials generate electric charges when mechanical stress is applied, and vice versa. This phenomenon is referred to *piezoelectricity*. Misra and Samanta [1983] considered the piezoelectricity of osseous material along with the electric and magnetic fields induced by the travelling torsional waves in tubular bones, and successfully bridged the gap between the theoretical predictions and experimental reports.

The National Science Foundation of USA, Imperial Press UK, and World Scientific Singapore appointed him as a member in their Expert Committees. The editor of Applied Mechanics Reviews invited him to act as a reviewer by joining their "carefully selected worldwide group of scientists and engineers". He was elected in 1981, a member of the International Society of Biorheology, New York. The next year, in 1982, Society of Applied Mathematics and Mechanics, Germany elected him a member. His outstanding contributions to mathematical biology fetched him the D.Sc. degree of Calcutta University in 1984, which is rarely awarded. His appointment to the post of Professor was a special offer from IIT Kharagpur in recognition of his academic excellence.

Much of Professor Misra's research work earned a place in standard textbooks. To name a few, I would prefer the following: Professor Ronald Glaser included his work on bone piezoelectricity in the chapter "Electric fields outside the cell" of the Biophysics Text Book published by Edward Arnold Ltd. London, 1989; and Professor Richard B. Hetnarrski, Rochester Institute of Technology, USA referred to his research publications in the chapter "Thermal Stresses in Plates" in the treatise "Thermal Stresses" published by North Holland in 1986.

Once his outstanding research contributions surfaced out, institutions felt pride to give him awards and felicitate. IIT Kharagpur felicitated him with Silver Jubilee Research Award in 1984. In recognition of his contribution and the impact of his work in theoretical physics, biomedical engineering and technology Professor Misra received several fellowship awards. The National Academy of Sciences, India elected him a Fellow in 1987, followed by Fellowships of the Institute of Mathematics and its Applications (U.K.) in 1988, the Institute of Theoretical Physics, Calcutta, the Royal Society of Medicine, London in 1989.

The other research areas enriched with his group's profound contribution are arterial blood flow in atherosclerotic arteries and peristaltic flows of physiological fluids. Atherosclerotic plaques develop in arteial walls due to fat deposition that retards flow in arteries, resulting into cardiac arrest in the case of coronary arteries.

Peristalsis is a pumping mechanism in the body for transporting fluid from one place to another without any possible contamination because of the absence of mechanical pistons. Several mathematical models developed by Misra and his associates uncovered a somewhat underrated role of peristalsis in vas deferens, which revealed it to be much closer to the experimental data. Another model of them designed for the propagation of contraction waves confined to the stationary boundary of oesophagus was a milestone that successfully brought about qualitative as well as quantitative corrections.

The American Biographical Institute Board of International Research selected him as "Man of the year 1997". Besides holding life membership of many academic societies, he was elected/nominated member of International Society of "Biorheology, New York", "Biomechanical Engineering Society, USA" in 1989, the "New York Academy of Sciences" in 1996. He received the Fellowships of the Indian National Academy of Engineering in 2000, the Royal Society of Public Health, London 2019, the Institution of Engineering and Technology, UK in 2019, and the Royal Society of Biology, London in

2020. He also received, in 2004, 'Rashtriya Gaurav Award' and Raja Ram Mohan Roy Prize for outstanding contributions to the field of Mathematics along with eminent astrophysicist Dr J.V. Narlikar who was awarded for Physics. That consisted of a cash prize of Rs. five lakhs, a memento, and a citation. Besides, he is a recipient of numerous awards including, but not limited to, CEGR Shiksha Gourav Purskar-2014, EET CRS "Best Scientist Award-2014", Lifetime Achievement Award-2015 of VENUS International Foundation, EET CRS Award for Research Excellence, 2017, by India International Friendship Society, New Delhi for meritorious services and remarkable research contributions in Mathematics. He was also a recipient of Dr. APJ Abdul Kalam Award for Lifetime Contribution in Science. In 2006, he was elected President, Indian Science Congress (Mathematical Sciences Section). He also figured in the list of top 2% Scientists in the world for six consecutive years from 2020 to 2025 according to studies conducted by a team of scientists at Stanford University, USA led by Prof. John P.A. Loannidis.

The distinguished Scientist Prof Misra delivered numerous invited lectures, plenary talks and keynote addresses throughout the globe. The prominent among them are the Platinum Jubilee Lecture in Mathematical Sciences at the prestigious Indian Science Congress in 2005, and talks at Courant Institute of Mathematical Sciences, New York, and at the Cornell Medical Centre of the New York Hospital, as well as at the fourth International Congress of Biorheology Tokyo. He also delivered P.L. Bhatnagar Memorial Lecture in 2001, and also an invited lecture at the international Congress on Computational and Applied Mathematics, Belgium, 2002, and many more.

He has to his credit over 250 publications in reputed international journals such as Journal of Mathematical Biology, Bulletin of Mathematical Biology, Journal of Biomechanics, Journal of Biomedical Engineering, Blood Vessels, Rheological Acta, Biorheology, International Journal of Solids and Structures, International Journal of Engineering Science etc. Besides, he edited twelve advance level books published by World Scientific, Singapore and Norasa, New Delhi. He also acted as the principal investigator of several sponsored research projects.

Professor Misra guided 30 Ph.D. scholars in different areas of mathematical and biological sciences. After superannuating from the Department of Mathematics, IIT Kharagpur, which he also served as the Head of Department, he remained active as a researcher publishing a large number of research articles apart from discharging administrative responsibilities as Pro-Vice Chancellor and Adjunct Professor at various universities and institutes.

Teaching and research is his passion which fetched him the INAE Outstanding Teachers Award-2013' of Indian National Academy of Engineering, New Delhi. The best job is a faculty position—he opines. Both of his sons are IIT-professors, the elder at Kanpur and the younger at Kharagpur, while his daughter has been working as a faculty at the Indian Institute of Engineering Science and Technology, Shibpur. She is a Fellow of the prestigious Institute of Engineering and Technology, U.K.

Prof. Misra's expedition continues even after decades of his superannuation. The prolific writer Prof Misra can work for hours at a stretch, ever ready to write and correct papers, no matter what the ambience is. Heat does not distract; cold never frightens; medicines he is not used to; journeys he loves irrespective of the class his ticket is booked for.

Despite all achievements, this great man of mathematics is recognized better by his humbleness. He is his friends' pride. They published two collections of articles on him. He used bicycle during the service at Kharagpur. The man in his loose shirt and paint, the belt above the navel, careless about the shoes or slippers he wears, speaks the least; the sentences are calculated; the voice is soft; the face adheres to humility; the dense eyebrows semi-surround the large eyes carrying love and natural compassion. The beholder is mesmerized! Successes lie at his feet; the shoulders are doubtlessly up; smiles play with lips; the face shines; the broad forehead glazes; and ideas run endlessly through the nerves! Great! Yes, it is the only word, which truly paints the personality of this living legend.

CHAPTER 4

Professor Jagadis Chandra Misra: A Remarkable Personality

Dr. Gopal Chandra Shit
Professor, Department of Mathematics,
Jadavpur University, Kolkata-700032

"*Education is not the learning of facts but the training of the mind to think.*"— The person who has truly inspired me with this philosophy is the esteemed Professor of Applied Mathematics at IIT Kharagpur, my research guide, Dr. Jagadis Chandra Misra. His personality embodies both the calm, profound wisdom of a dedicated teacher and the guiding strength of a mentor who nurtures his students like a guardian. That is why, in my life, he holds a very special place as an ideal teacher.

When I first joined IIT Kharagpur for my M.Sc. in 1999, I soon found myself overwhelmed by the immense academic pressure. With classes often running from 7:30 AM until the evening, followed by personal studies and assignments, I was struggling to cope. It was during this time that I decided to seek the guidance of our Head of the Mathematics Department, Professor J.C. Misra. That was my first interaction with him outside the classroom. Naturally, I approached him with some hesitation, but when I shared my concerns, he responded with a quote: *"The struggle you're in today is developing the strength you need for tomorrow."* That day, he motivated us by explaining that the tougher the journey, the greater the growth. Overcoming challenges, he said, leads to true joy in one's work. Initially, these words were difficult to grasp, but as life progressed, I realized their profound truth. His calm, patient, and student-friendly approach to problem-solving remains etched in my memory.

One of the most significant contributions, 'Sir' made to my life occurred after I completed my M.Sc. Although I had qualified for the CSIR-NET (JRF), financial difficulties at that time made me hesitant to pursue a Ph.D., so I took up a teaching job at a school. However, 'Sir', being deeply invested in the well-being of his students, took the initiative to check on me. Through a common acquaintance, he called me back and assured me of all the necessary support to continue my Ph.D. From helping me with the registration process to taking on the role of my Ph.D. supervisor, he guided me at every step of the way. That crucial moment of his mentorship changed the course of my life, enabling me to move forward toward what I am today. I consider myself fortunate to have done my Ph.D. under his guidance.

"A teacher takes a hand, opens a mind, and touches a heart."—This famous quote seems most fitting for an extraordinary teacher like him. His kindness, love, steadfast dedication to his students, and selfless commitment to their growth are truly inspiring.

Under his guidance, I embarked on multiple research investigations. But he was not just a guide—he was meticulous about every detail of our work. Many nights, I worked with him in the lab until late hours. Such was his dedication that he often forgot to take his food, while immersed in research. This relentless pursuit of excellence inspired me to strive for even greater achievements.

Those of us who were fortunate enough to be close to him often received warm invitations to his home, where *Masima* (Prof. Misra's wife) would treat us to home-cooked meals, saying it was to "refresh our taste buds." Their kindness and hospitality, along with the warmth of the heart, made us feel like family. Over the years, I have realized the immense value of the many pieces of advice and life lessons I received from Prof. Misra.

During my Ph.D., financial constraints led me to take up a job at a college. Even then, Sir advised me to stay near IIT so that I could continue my research effectively. His unwavering support at every stage of my academic journey has been invaluable.

Professor Jagadis Chandra Misra is not just a teacher; he is a mentor, a guide, and an inspiration—someone who has left an indelible mark on my life and the lives of many students like me.

I have always tried to follow every piece of his advice, and without hesitation, I can say that although the path was challenging, I found success by following the path he showed me. His relationship with his students was not confined to that of a teacher-student bond; rather, he provided a sense of guardianship under which I was fortunate to be nurtured.

Like many others, during my Ph.D., I aspired to pursue higher studies abroad, but a sense of fear and uncertainty held me back. Even in that situation, it was Sir who guided me. He encouraged me to pursue post-doctorate studies abroad and taught me how to turn my dreams into reality. Following his advice, when I was doing my post-doctoral research at the University of Paris-XII, France, he continued to check in on me through video calls, inquiring about my studies, health, and well-being. His relentless dedication to guiding his students on the right path is truly admirable.

For those of us who come from humble backgrounds and enter prestigious institutions like IITs, language barriers can often pose a significant challenge. I, too, faced this difficulty, but 'Sir' provided immense support. Through months of perseverance and his guidance, I was able to overcome this obstacle. His help extended far beyond my research activities; we could freely share our concerns with him, even about minor issues, and he would always offer us clear guidance.

One particular incident that I must mention occurred when my father suddenly fell ill. I was completely lost, but 'Sir' advised me to get him admitted to a hospital in Kolkata, which I did. Understanding my financial struggles, he went a step further—while I was trying to arrange money, he unexpectedly sent his daughter and son-in-law with a cheque to provide financial assistance. His empathy and fatherly support still move me to this day. This is a debt I can never repay, but I will always remain deeply grateful to him.

Currently, as a faculty member at Jadavpur University, I collaborate once a while with 'Sir' for some pieces of research. Even today, his dedication and patience towards his work leave me in awe.

The quote, "*One child, one teacher, one book, one pen can change the world,*" holds profound truth in my life. Sir has transformed my life's trajectory, reshaped my perspective, and played a crucial role in making me who I am today. His empathy, dedication, commitment to work, philosophy of life, and relentless passion for learning and teaching continue to inspire me. Following his ideals, I aspire to carry forward these values in my own journey as an educator.

CHAPTER 5

Professor J.C. Misra, as I Found Him

Dr. Santwana Mukhopadhyay
Professor, Department of Mathematical Sciences & Associate Dean (Academic Affairs), IIT (BHU), Uttar Pradesh

It is a great honor for me to have the opportunity to put on record a few lines about the distinguished personality, Professor J.C. Misra. I consider myself fortunate to have had the chance to come in contact with such a highly respected scholar with profound erudition.

My first encounter with Prof. Jagadis Chandra Misra in 1993 remains vividly etched in my memory. At the time, I was conducting research under Professor S.K. Roychowdhury in the Department of Mathematics at Burdwan University. Dr. Misra, a distinguished professor from the Department of Mathematics at IIT Kharagpur, had been invited to visit our department. Professor Roychowdhury entrusted me with the responsibility of receiving him from Golapbag of the University Campus.

I was already aware of Prof. Misra's extensive research and scholarly contributions. In fact, I had begun my research based on one of his published research works on thermo-elasticity. I recall waiting for him with a mixed feeling of excitement and nervousness. When I finally met him, I introduced myself, and to my amazement, he treated me with such warmth and kindness that my apprehension instantly disappeared. I soon found myself conversing with him effortlessly.

During our conversation, he inquired about my research work and future plans, offering invaluable advice that significantly enriched my academic journey. That memorable interaction at Burdwan University remains an unforgettable experience in my life.

Later, I joined the Department of Mathematics at IT-BHU (now IIT BHU) as a faculty member, which provided me with further opportunities to meet him through various academic programmes at IIT Kharagpur and

IIT (BHU). He once invited me, as a young researcher, to deliver an invited lecture at an international conference (ICRAMS) at IIT Kharagpur and later at a technical session of the Indian Science Congress. I felt deeply honored by these invitations. His invaluable counselling and encouragement for junior researchers has always been exemplary and inspiring.

Professor Misra's research contributions have been recognized both nationally and internationally. He has made significant contributions to the broad fields of structural engineering and bioengineering. His research papers on modeling and simulation in bio-fluid mechanics are regarded as pivotal in biomedical engineering research. His contributions to medicine and physiology are also noteworthy. With over 250 published research papers and several high-quality books, his work remains invaluable to aspiring researchers.

He has been honored with numerous prestigious awards and recognition, including Fellow of the National Academy of Sciences (FNASc), Fellow of the Indian National Academy of Engineering (FNAE), the "Outstanding Teacher Award" from INAE, and a Fellowship from the Alexander von Humboldt Foundation, among others.

However, beyond his immense scientific contributions, I have known him as a generous, responsible, and compassionate individual. A dedicated and sincere academician like him is truly rare.

He has visited our department (Department of Mathematical Sciences, IIT BHU) multiple times to conduct Ph.D. oral examinations and deliver lectures. His contributions to bio-mathematics are particularly inspiring. Moreover, the way he conducts Ph.D. oral examinations is a lesson in itself. Students always receive his encouragement and motivation.

I have never seen him lose his temper or become agitated, even in challenging situations. His ability to resolve complex issues calmly, yet firmly is a remarkable trait.

Since 1993 Prof. Misra has been playing the role of my academic mentor and well-wisher. I hold him in high esteem.

I sincerely wish that he continues to contribute to mathematical sciences and mentor young minds for many more years to come. I pray to the Almighty for his and Madam Misra's good health and long life. I offer them my heartfelt respect and humble regards.

CHAPTER 6

Prof. Jagadis Chandra Misra: A Remarkable Example of Cooperation and Compassion in Research

Dr. Subhash Chandra Samanta
Professor, Department of Physics (Retd.), Midnapore College

It was probably around 1978. By then, I had been teaching at Midnapore College for six years. I realized that some newly discovered scientific phenomena, previously confined to research papers, were soon to be included in undergraduate physics syllabi. To prepare for my lectures, I visited the library at IIT Kharagpur for some reading.

At the main gate of IIT, I unexpectedly met Jagadis-da after nearly 13 years. From 1962 to 1965, when I was an undergraduate student, I lived at the Ramakrishna Mission Kolkata Vidyarthi Ashram in Belgharia. After completing his bachelor's degree with Honours in Mathematics from Ramakrishna Mission Vidyamandira, Jagadis-da enrolled in the M.Sc. programme in Applied Mathematics at the University of Calcutta. During his M.Sc. Programme (1964–1966), he too resided at the same Vidyarthi Ashram. As per the tradition of the Ashram, he naturally became like an elder brother to me.

Recognizing each other at the IIT Main Gate didn't take long. I had heard that after completing his M.Sc., Jagadis-da was teaching at Uluberia College. I hadn't expected to see him at IIT Kharagpur, so I was a bit surprised. Once I got over our initial astonishment, he took me to his department. During our brief conversation, I learned that he had just returned from Germany after conducting research for a few years under the Alexander von Humboldt Fellowship. As we caught up on the past 13 years, he asked if I had completed my Ph.D. When I admitted that I hadn't, he suggested that I could pursue research under his guidance in some area of Mathematical Sciences.

In reality, I had never been particularly keen on earning a Ph.D. degree. After completing my postgraduate studies, I even received a fellowship to conduct research in spectroscopy at the Indian Association for the Cultivation of Science but chose not to pursue it. However, by then, Ph.D. had become mandatory for college faculty members. As a result, five of my colleagues had already taken leave from the Physics Department to pursue their Ph.D.s at IIT and other universities. Given this context, I couldn't outright refuse Jagadis-da's offer.

I hesitated, asking whether it would be possible to conduct research in mathematics with just an undergraduate-level knowledge of the subject. He encouraged me nonetheless. Before I left, he handed me some of his recently published research papers for study. Since they were closely related to physics, I didn't have much trouble understanding them. However, as mathematical derivations in research papers are often not fully elaborated, it took some effort to fill in the missing steps and grasp the essence.

When I later went to discuss my understanding of his papers, his first question was, "Why did it take you so long?" Without waiting for my response, he began narrating a story:

A novice student once approached his professor for a research paper. The professor handed him the paper and advised, "Pay attention to the references cited at the end. Don't just read this paper; carefully go through the cited sources as well, as they will be necessary for understanding the full context."

The student took the advice seriously and went to the library. However, once he went in, he never seemed to return.

After a long time, in the library the professor found the student still deeply engrossed in the research paper along with several other reference materials.

"Are you still reading the same paper?" the professor asked.

"Yes, Sir," the student replied. "You told me to trace the cited sources one by one. I've been following that trail backward."

Annoyed yet amused, the professor remarked, "Do you realize where you'll end up if you keep going backward like this? You need to balance moving forward with looking back. Otherwise, when will you progress?"

After hearing the story, I asked, "Does that mean I've taken too long?"

Jagadis-da laughed and replied, "Not at all! You've taken a reasonable amount of time. I was just joking."

And so, my research journey with Jagadis-da began.

Since I couldn't afford to take leave from my college duties—especially when five colleagues were already on leave, leaving the department understaffed—I decided to stay at IIT Kharagpur overnight for research. This arrangement gave me extended access to the library, which was crucial for my studies. Conducting theoretical research required mathematical analysis to derive results, which could then be validated in two ways—either through direct observation or by applying theoretical models to simulated scenarios. The first method, though ideal, was nearly impossible without a well-equipped laboratory. The second approach required access to a computer and proficiency in using it, but I had neither formal training in computing nor official permission to use the computers at IIT Kharagpur, since I was not an enrolled student there.

Fortunately, the head of the department was sympathetic and recommended for unrestricted access to the library, considering my acquaintance with Prof. Misra. More importantly, my association with Professor Misra worked wonders. At the time, he was supervising five research students, all of whom were respectful and welcoming toward me. When not in the library, I would spend most of my time in their research room, engaging in discussions that turned out to be incredibly productive for all of us. Our conversations revolved around our respective research topics, allowing us to understand each other's work and resolve challenges collaboratively. In fact, many of the research-related issues that might have reached Professor Misra's desk were often resolved informally during these discussions, significantly easing his workload.

This type of intimacy also helped me navigate my lack of computing skills. Despite the age gap, I bonded well with the younger researchers, who patiently helped me with all computer-related problems. Through me, Jagadis-da also kept an eye on his students' interpersonal skills and teamwork. Sometimes, he would join our discussions, which, when held in his office, took on the more formal title of "seminars." But not all our gatherings were about research—occasionally, we would head to a Chinese restaurant or celebrate special days at the IIT hostel, and Jagadis-da often joined us there too.

Among the many memorable academic moments, one incident particularly stands out. One of Jagadis-da's students was researching on the effects of head impact on the human brain. Since our skulls are not perfect spheres but rather slightly flattened at the poles—what is known in geometric terms as a "prolate spheroid"—his research involved mathematically analyzing how stress and deformation waves would propagate when an impact occurred at a specific point on the skull. Using complex mathematical techniques, he successfully derived analytical results. However, when he tested his findings on a computer, the calculations did not match the expected outcomes. Despite repeatedly verifying each step, he couldn't identify the error.

Naturally, when faced with such challenges, the students would first turn to me for help. But in this case, the mathematical intricacies were far beyond my expertise as a physics researcher. So, I expressed my inability. However, considering my close association with Jagadis-da, they assumed I was a student of mathematics (though I was unaware of this assumption). As a result, they did not believe that I was incapable of identifying the errors in the research paper. Consequently, I was somewhat compelled to get involved in the research problem.

Delving deep into the study was beyond my capability. Yet, I suddenly noticed an inconsistency among the various terms in a mathematical series. It seemed that the fundamental principle—"addition is possible only between like quantities"—had been violated. I realized that inserting a square root symbol in the right place could resolve the discrepancy. Without providing a detailed explanation, I simply suggested this correction to the researcher. As soon as this minor adjustment was made, the computational results aligned perfectly. The research outcome that Jagadis-da had envisioned and guided the student towards was successfully achieved. A valuable research paper was produced. I later heard that this paper was particularly useful in medical science as well.

My research work with Jagadis-da continued, lasting somewhat longer than usual for various reasons. However, this had both drawbacks and benefits. Thanks to his encouragement, I got the opportunity to work independently on some projects. At that time, besides his regular research students, there were several part-time research students like me. Jagadis-da entrusted me with some supervisory responsibilities for their research, which undoubtedly deepened my own understanding of the subject. As a result, after earning my Ph.D. from Jadavpur University, I was later entrusted with guiding two research students under the academic framework of the University. Eventually, they, too, earned their Ph.D. degrees. Needless to say, Jagadis-da provided immense support in this regard as well.

Many years have passed, and I have witnessed numerous events. Even today, reminiscing about my years of close association with Jagadis-da, our discussions on various research topics, and his generous and enlightened mind fills me with great joy and happiness.

CHAPTER 7

As I Found Sir

Dr. Gopal Chandra Bera
Principal, Midnapore College (Retd.), West Bengal

My respected research guide was Professor Jagadis Chandra Misra, former Head of the Department of Mathematics, IIT Kharagpur. He is not only an internationally renowned scientist and a popular teacher, but a deeply compassionate human being. When it comes to writing a few lines about such a towering personality, I find myself at a loss for where to begin.

On the advice of my Professors, I reached out to Dr. Jagadis Chandra Misra, Professor of Mathematics at IIT Kharagpur. Looking back, I believe that was the most significant turning point in my life.

At my very first meeting with Prof. Misra, I was deeply impressed by his firm yet kind manner. After listening to my entire situation, he agreed to guide me for my doctoral research. He advised me to also get in touch with Prof. Subhash Chandra Samanta of Midnapore College—himself a former Ph.D. student of Prof. Misra.

Prof. Samanta agreed to help me, as our research interests aligned perfectly—we were both working in the field of Mathematical Modeling. I started working under Prof. Misra's guidance, taking help from Prof. Samanta. However, I faced another challenge: staying in touch with Prof. Misra. With school duties from Monday to Saturday, it was extremely difficult to make time outside of Summer and Puja vacations.

Understanding my situation, Professor Misra came up with a solution. He told me that he would make time for me on Sundays. This alone speaks volumes about his empathy, sensitivity, generosity, and kindness. Despite his incredibly busy schedule, he would dedicate almost every Sunday to guide me. I would arrive at his house by 8 a.m. and return to my house in the evening, spending the entire day with him.

Lunch was always reserved for me. Mrs. J.C. Misra, or Boudi as I respectfully call her, was like Goddess Lakshmi in the house. She looked after me with great care, affection, and hospitality. I shall never forget her kindness. I offer her my heartfelt respect and pranam.

I was also fortunate to receive the affection of Prof. Misra's revered parents—his father and mother—whom I fondly referred to as Mesobabu and Masima. Just seeing them would fill me with reverence. Their kind and sincere words always left me touched, and offering them pranam brought me peace.

Then there were Subhas, Sumita, and Sudip—Sir's two sons and a daughter. They were very young at the time, perhaps in Class VI or VII or younger—I don't exactly recall. While Sir reviewed the manuscripts of my research papers, I would spend time chatting or playing educational games with the children—always careful not to disturb their studies. They were all incredibly well-mannered, cultured, and warm. Such was the beautiful environment in Sir's household.

If I had not received the wholehearted support of Prof. J.C. Misra and his family, I would not have been able to complete my Ph.D., and whatever success I have achieved today would not have been possible. For this, I remain forever grateful to every member of his family.

My research topic was *"Some Biomechanical Studies of Bones"*. Though my background was in Physics, my research focus was on Mathematical Modeling. Naturally, I had apprehensions whether I would be able to successfully carry on my theoretical research. But thanks to the unwavering support, cooperation, guidance and blessings of Prof. Jagadis Chandra Misra, along with the help of Prof. Samanta, I was able to complete my doctoral work.

I still remember the day my first paper was accepted for publication in an international journal. On that happy occasion, when I bowed down and offered pranam to Professor Misra, he smiled and gently asked, *"You're feeling happy, aren't you?"* I've never forgotten that moment.

And I distinctly remember the day of my Ph.D. viva, when Prof. Misra first addressed me as *"Dr. G.C. Bera."* I don't know why, but that moment filled me with immense pride and satisfaction. It felt as though Professor Misra himself was the embodiment of divinity. I have never forgotten that day.

Sir, I offer you my deepest respect and gratitude.

CHAPTER 8

Prof. J.C. Misra: Memories Filled with Gratefulness

Dr. Sukumar Chandra
Principal, Pingla College, Paschim Medinipur

My first meeting with the esteemed Professor, Jagadis Chandra Misra, dates back to 2006 when he was a faculty at IIT Kharagpur. As a Ph.D. scholar, I had the privilege of joining his research group and to conduct my doctoral work under his supervision and guidance. He was not only my research guide but also a mentor who played a pivotal role in my academic journey.

Later, Professor Misra took on the role of Pro-Vice Chancellor (Academic) at the Institute of Education and Research in Bhubaneswar, Odisha. So I had to frequently travel to Bhubaneswar to continue my research under his guidance. During my stays at Bhubaneswar, I was warmly welcomed into his home, where he and his wife treated me like a family member. His wife, whom I affectionately called 'Kakima,' took care of me like a mother, ensuring I was well-fed and comfortable. Professor Misra, too, was incredibly affectionate and supportive. Every time, he helped me find a place to stay at a reasonable expenditure.

It was only through my close association with such a distinguished scholar that I truly understood what it meant to learn with care and warmth. His profound mastery of the English language left me in awe, and his patience, even at the age of 65 and beyond, was remarkable. I often wondered how he could possess such immense perseverance, but then I reminded myself—this was the same man who, in addition to his Ph.D., had earned the prestigious D.Sc. degree, a distinction achieved by very few in the country.

His groundbreaking research focused on analyzing variations in human blood flow due to cholesterol deposits in the arterial lumen and exploring how magnetic, electric, or electromagnetic fields could be utilized in medical treatment. His pioneering ideas were published in reputed international journals as distinguished research papers. Thanks to his guidance, I, too, had the opportunity to publish my research in renowned international journals published by famous publishing companies, like Springer and Elsevier.

There were times when I felt disheartened, unable to find solutions to research challenges. But a single reprimand from him would rekindle my motivation, as if some unseen force was guiding me toward the answers. His mentorship provided me with a new perspective on academics and research, shaping the scholar I am today.

For all this, I shall remain highly grateful to him throughout my life.

May these cherished memories stay alive forever.

CHAPTER 9

Recollections of the Past

Dr. Sushil Kumar Ghosh
Associate Professor, Garhbeta College, Paschim Medinipur

It was 1991. I arrived at Nehru Hall of Residence to pursue my MSc in the Mathematics Department at IIT Kharagpur. The grand buildings, smooth roads, and massive hostels left me in awe. I was particularly impressed by the beautiful dining hall. For admission, we were called to the S.N. Bose Auditorium. At that time, the course was known as MSc (Lateral Entry).

After completing the admission process, we proceeded to the Mathematics Department on the second floor of the Main Buildings of IIT. It was customary for each batch to have a faculty advisor to assist students with admissions, subject selection, rules and regulations, academics, and grievances. In 1987, when M.Sc. first-year admissions took place, Professor J.C. Misra was the faculty advisor. Subsequently, he became our faculty advisor as well. That was my first interaction with 'Sir'.

During that period, we had a course on C-programming, and Dr. S. Roy assisted us. We fondly called him "Roy-da." He was from the Ghatal region of Medinipur and quickly recognized that I was also from Medinipur District. He told me that Professor J.C. Misra was also from Medinipur and was an exceptionally talented person. I often saw Sir in the Mathematics Department, engrossed in studies, writing, and discussing about research with scholars. On seeing him so dedicated, I felt inspired to do my Ph.D. under his guidance.

In my second semester, I enrolled in one of his courses. The academic environment in the Mathematics Department was excellent. By the fourth semester, while my studies continued, I successfully cleared the GATE exam. However, I was a bit unsure about my next step. Eventually, I decided to pursue research in bio-fluid mechanics.

When I met 'Sir' to discuss my Ph.D. aspirations, I felt encouraged that I could indeed achieve it. I directly requested him to be my supervisor, to which he assured me, saying, "It may be possible, but you will have to work hard." I then spoke to the head of the department, who advised me to prepare well for the interview.

As part of my preparation, 'Sir' asked me to meet him at 4:00 PM in the Mathematics Department to collect a book. I was overjoyed at the prospect of not having to return to my humble clay-roofed home after completing my M.Sc. Programme. Caught up in chatting with friends at *Tikka*, I completely forgot that Sir had asked me to meet him. When I remembered, it was already past 7 PM. I rushed there on my bicycle, only to find the main entrance locked. I sneaked in through the back stairs and found 'Sir' still engrossed in his work. With a feeling of nervousness I approached him. To my surprise, he calmly said, "I was waiting for you," and handed me Y. C. Fung's book on Bio-Fluid Mechanics, without showing the slightest sign of displeasure for my delay. From that moment, my respect, trust, and admiration for him deepened. That book became an invaluable resource for my research scholar interview and my entire research journey.

Now, I realize that Professor J.C. Misra was not just my mentor but also my guide, philosopher, and lifelong friend.

After about two months, I formally joined as a research scholar to pursue my Ph.D. Initially, we had coursework, and my colleague, Dr. Biswajit Pal, and I started working under Sir's guidance. He advised us not to meet him every day but to focus on our coursework and literature survey while contemplating research topics. One of his most remarkable qualities was that he never imposed a research problem on us. Instead, he gave us the complete freedom to explore our interests. This approach later helped me develop a creative mindset for blending traditional mathematical theories with modern engineering applications.

'Sir' set a routine, so that we could discuss with him our academic progress and the complexities of mathematical theories at least twice a week. However, he insisted that we remain present in the Mathematics Department and inform him if we ever left campus. 'Sir' was not only an experienced teacher but also an excellent administrator.

A couple of weeks later, Sir casually said, "Sushil, come over to our house someday—we can chat." Those days I was facing severe financial difficulties. I had no decent clothes and couldn't even afford to attend the convocation to collect my M.Sc. certificate. I had to mortgage my mother's small piece of gold jewelry to secure my Ph.D. admission. So, I told Sir, "At the end of this month, when I get my scholarship, I will buy a decent shirt and then visit your house."

I could say this because I had immense trust and respect for Prof. Misra. I knew he would not mock or belittle me but rather understand the harsh reality. The bond of respect, trust, and genuine emotions between us remains strong to this day. The relationship between Sir and me was not just that of a scholar and a guide—it transcended into something deeper and more meaningful. His words and demeanor exuded humanity, sincerity, and profound knowledge. I realized that the brilliance of great personalities is not just a myth. From him, I learned how to stay resilient in tough situations, seek the right path instead of giving up, and navigate challenges with determination.

There are countless incidents where I felt his kindness, generosity, and deep affection for his students. Let me share a few.

Sir's father, whom we fondly called "Dadu," was Shri Ganes Chandra Misra, a teacher at Tikrapara Higher Secondary School in the Patashpur region. He used to teach English to young students.

Whenever Dadu visited the campus, he would engage in discussions with us about the past and present of English education and the significance of language learning.

Once, Dadu fell seriously ill and was admitted to the railway hospital. He was unconscious when we visited, and after some time, Sir told us, "You should go back—you have your studies to focus on." So, Biswajit and I left. Meanwhile, Sir kept shuttling between IIT and the hospital, and we didn't check in on him or visit the hospital again. Two days later, we learned that Dadu had passed away. Sir had looked for us, but we were nowhere to be found.

When we later visited his house and heard about it, my heart ached with a feeling of guilt—we hadn't been there for him in his moment of grief. I couldn't say a word that day, but writing about it now brings me some relief. At that time, Sudip had just finished school, and Sir used to travel by bicycle. He truly needed our company, but we failed to be there for him. Even today, the matter fills me with remorse. Yet, not once did Sir express any anger or disappointment over our absence. This speaks volumes about his immense love and care for his students.

Dr. S.I. Singh, a scholar from Manipur, pursued his Ph.D. under Sir's guidance in Bio-Solid Mechanics. He came from an underprivileged background, yet his deep understanding of mathematics, discipline, excellent manners, and respect deeply impressed 'Sir'. He completed his Ph.D. in just three years and earned his degree. Unfortunately, he fell ill and sought treatment at AIIMS, Delhi.

However, fate was cruel, and he passed away prematurely. This incident left a deep scar on Sir's heart.

Later, whenever a new research scholar joined, 'Sir' would first tell them about Dr. Singh. He would recall his memories, offering advice with a choked voice and an air of melancholy. I had never seen a teacher so personally invested in his students before.

Once, 'Sir' had to go abroad for some academic assignment. Before departure, he had given us a specific date and time to meet him. But we completely forgot, caught up in watching India vs. Pakistan cricket match. 'Sir' came all the way to B.C. Roy Hostel looked for me and patiently explained everything that I needed to do during the period of his absence. At that moment, I felt ashamed of my irresponsible behaviour and regretted my carelessness.

Sir said, "The cricket match is on... Alright, take care of everything."

That day, his calm, composed, and kind demeanor became the harshest lesson for me. It taught me a profound lesson that eventually earned me the respect of my students in my professional life.

Professor J.C. Misra was not just my mentor in mathematics but also a guide in the discipline of brahmacharya. Throughout my Ph.D. journey, there was never any sense of distance between him and his scholars. If any scholar, even one with another guide, strayed from the right path or halted their research, he would personally check in, guide them, and ensure they completed their Ph.D. under his mentorship.

To me, Prof. J.C. Misra is a unique and unparalleled figure. He is truly great. Measuring the depth of his knowledge or the vastness of his humanity would be an act of arrogance beyond my own intellectual limits. However, I can say this: without his influence, it would have been impossible for a rural student, like me from a cultivator family background, to rise to the position of a professor in a degree college.

The days of the past seem to call me back...

Many days have passed like this—working on research manuscript corrections. We started at 3:00 pm. The work continued… and continued… Evening had set in. It was drizzling outside. The street lights flickered on. The mathematics department was silent, utterly still.

I felt hungry. But Sir was deeply engrossed in the depths of the research paper. I was restless, waiting for him to say, "Let's stop here now." But no interruption broke his flow of thought. Finally, I spoke up:

"Sir, shall we stop for today?"

He asked,
"Why? Are you feeling hungry?"
"Yes," I admitted.

Sir replied,
"Then go and have your meal. I'll continue till the revision work is completed."

I went to B.C. Roy Hall, had my dinner and brought some cake, biscuits, and water for him. He ate them with no sign of dissatisfaction.

This was Professor J.C. Misra—someone who could completely immerse himself in the world of his scholars.

That day, he revised the entire research paper. He demonstrated to me through his patience and dedication that perseverance leads to the desired goal.

Another day, at his home, a reading and discussion of *Sri Ramakrishna Kathamrita* was held. All the attendees were former students of the Ramakrishna Mission educational institutions—except me. During the introduction, Sir said, *"This is Sushil, my scholar, from Garhbeta College. In quality and capability, he is second to none here."*

Sir never belittles any of his students.

Many more memories flood my mind, but at some point, I must stop. I spent nearly 6–7 years in his close company. Countless lessons, endless guidance—they remain etched in my life like an indelible mark on the shores of time.

It has been nearly twenty years since I left IIT Kharagpur. Yet, it feels like just yesterday.

I recall the times spent at Sir's home, enjoying a tasty meal, served with all affection and chatting with grandparents (Sir's parents). The discussions on research, the encouragement to persevere, and the unwavering focus on goals—these lessons remain ever fresh and radiant in my mind.

Professor J.C. Misra was my research guide—this is my pride.

It fills my heart with immense joy to write about an internationally renowned scholar, a mathematician honored with numerous awards from across the world.

O Master of Mathematics—your contribution to the spread and advancement of mathematics is undeniable.

Your research, which applied mathematics to solve complex biological problems, has opened new horizons.

The impact of your work on human welfare will be eternally remembered by people worldwide.

You are celebrated not just for your intellect but for your extraordinary qualities. Your role in shaping my journey will remain etched in my memory forever.

With folded hands, I seek your blessings for my future. May you remain in good health and live a long life.

CHAPTER 10

My Association with Prof. J.C. Misra

Dr. G. Radhakrishnamacharya
Professor of Mathematics & Dean (Retd.), N.I.T. Warangal,
Andhra Pradesh, India

It is a matter of great pleasure for me to share a few memories of my long-standing association with Prof. J.C. Misra, whom I have known for about five decades.

I was at IIT Kharagpur from January 1975 to July 1978, pursuing my Ph.D. During this time, I had the privilege of associating with Prof. Misra—both academically and personally—for nearly two years, although he was away in Germany for some time on a Humboldt Fellowship. Later, during my tenure at IIT Kanpur from January 1983 to July 1984, I had another opportunity to interact with him more closely for two months, when he served as a Visiting Professor there. Since then, I have had the pleasure of meeting him on several occasions, including during his visits to NIT Warangal during faculty selection committee meetings, where he was invited as an external expert.

I fondly remember the deep and enriching academic discussions I had with him on numerous occasions. I was always amazed by his sharp intellect and profound knowledge in diverse areas such as fluid mechanics, solid mechanics, biological systems, and advanced mathematical techniques.

Though he was not my formal teacher, he has always been a great source of inspiration in my research pursuits, especially in the field of bio-fluid dynamics.

Despite being a stalwart in his domain, Prof. Misra was always supportive and encouraging towards my academic efforts. His genuine interest in mentoring young researchers, his patience, and his willingness to spend long hours in academic discussions are truly admirable. He is a *guru* in the truest sense—always ready to guide students and researchers selflessly, without expecting anything in return. I remain deeply grateful for his affection, encouragement, and generous support over the years.

Prof. Misra's prolific research contributions, numerous projects, awards, international recognitions, and visits abroad stand as testimony to his excellence and dedication to the field.

I also fondly recall my brief interaction with his son, Dr. Subhas Chandra Misra, a Professor of Industrial Management Engineering at IIT Kanpur during his visit to NIT Warangal. Although our time together was short, I was deeply touched by his humility, respectful nature, and warmth.

I consider it a privilege to have been associated with Prof. J.C. Misra. I sincerely pray to the Almighty to bless him with many more years of good health and active life so that he may continue to inspire generations of young researchers.

CHAPTER 11

Respected Sir

Dr. Aniruddha Sinha
Assistant Professor, Department of Mathematics,
Yogada Satsanga Palpara Mahavidyalaya, Purba Medinipur

"*Gurur Brahma, Gurur Vishnu, Gurur Devo Maheshwara, Guru Sakshat Param Brahma, Tasmai Shri Gurave Namah.*"

As a child, I understood this Sanskrit verse to mean that the Guru embodies Brahma, Vishnu, and Maheshwara, and is the very manifestation of the Supreme Being. Over time, as my journey progressed, the deeper meaning of this verse became clearer. Perhaps, I would have never realized its true essence had my path of learning not led me across various domains of knowledge.

Today, I wish to speak about someone who has played a pivotal role in my life—a special teacher, my research guide, Professor Dr. Jagadis Chandra Misra. I consider myself fortunate to have had the opportunity to learn under the guidance of such a distinguished scholar in Applied Mathematics at the prestigious Institution, IIT Kharagpur.

The well-known saying, "A true teacher is a friend, philosopher, and guide", finds its fullest meaning in my revered mentor. In him, I have always found the companionship of a friend, the wisdom of a philosopher, and the unwavering guidance of an exceptional teacher. His remarkable personality, compassionate nature, relentless dedication, and ability to create a deep bond with his students have been a boundless source of inspiration for me. His mentorship opened a new dimension in my life, instilling in me the qualities of a true teacher.

In 2006, after completing my M.Sc., I came to IIT Kharagpur on the advice of a Professor from the Department of Applied Mathematics of the University of Calcutta. At that time, with the absence of Google and social media dominance, I had very little knowledge about IIT Kharagpur. The only thing I relied on was my good academic record. A friend introduced me to Dr. Misra, and with a mix of excitement and apprehension, I met him for the first time at the

CTS Lab. Although he had a serious demeanor, his words and encouragement quickly put me at ease. He reassured me that he would give me the opportunity to pursue research under his guidance and would assist me with the admission process. Within a week, he arranged my interview, and after clearing it, he ensured that all formalities, including registration and medical procedures, were completed smoothly.

However, I soon encountered my first hurdle—I had no hostel accommodation in the beginning. Once again, Dr. Misra stepped in and arranged for me to stay at the 'VSRC' Hostel and later at the 'MMM Hall of Residence. Thus began my Ph.D. journey—a path filled with challenges, moments of despair, and unfulfilled aspirations. But at every step, I found him standing beside me as my mentor.

I still remember my first research assignment—working on blood flow through an arterial segment. The concept of research was entirely new to me. Dr. Misra guided me to read international journals and build my understanding. After months of relentless efforts, I completed my first project within a year. When he reviewed my first manuscript, I was astounded by his patience and meticulous approach—he took 4-5 days to check it thoroughly. Eventually, I revised and submitted the paper to JMMB, which was successfully published in 2008. Under his mentorship, I got the opportunity to work extensively in the fascinating field of Biomechanics.

A particularly significant incident occurred in 2009 when I was advised by my doctor to refrain from working in the lab due to asthma. In that difficult time, Dr. Misra supported me wholeheartedly and allowed me to carry on my research activities from the hostel. His empathy and unwavering support for his students were truly remarkable. Many times, even on holidays, he visited me at JCB Hostel, working with me for hours. His dedication and work ethics left an everlasting impact on me.

Sports had always been a passion of mine, and upon learning this, he encouraged me to practice regularly. Outside of academic life at IIT Kharagpur, the playground became my cherished space. However, my greatest challenge came during my first presentation. Coming from a modest middle-class family background, I struggled with fluency in any language other than my mother tongue. As a result, I could not meet the expectations of the evaluators. That failure shattered my confidence, but Dr. Misra stood by me, offering guidance and encouragement, helping me regain my self-confidence.

In 2009, when he informed me about his appointment as the Pro-Vice Chancellor of SOA University at Bhubaneswar, I was filled with an unspoken fear. But he reassured me and continued to mentor me. As a result, I frequently travelled to Bhubaneswar, where he personally arranged my accommodation and meals. Though those days were exhausting, today they remain with me as fond memories. Spending six years under his mentorship fostered not just an academic relationship but a deep personal bond. His caring nature extended beyond academics—he frequently inquired about my family and invited me to his family events.

One of the most heartwarming moments in my life was when, years after my Ph.D., he and his wife travelled to my village home on the occasion of my wedding. Their presence, spending the entire day with my family, was a priceless gesture that I will cherish forever.

A quote that resonates deeply with me is: "The test of a good teacher is not how many questions he can ask his pupils that they will answer readily, but how many questions he inspires them to ask him, which he finds it hard to answer." Dr. Misra encouraged me to expand my intellectual boundaries rather than confining my knowledge. He taught me how to find joy and fulfillment in unwavering dedication to my work.

Many students like me approach reputed educational institutions and their distinguished professors with a mix of awe and apprehension. However, through my association with Dr. Misra, I realized how humility and greatness can coexist. His values and guidance will continue to shape my journey as an educator. I do not possess the authority to speak about the vastness of his knowledge, but I remain forever grateful for the wisdom he imparted to me.

With deep respect and gratitude, I bow to you, Sir.

CHAPTER 12

A Bright Star in the Sky of Mathematics

Dr. Saktipada Nanda
Associate Professor (Retd.), Department of Mathematics,
Sree Chaitanya College, Habra, North 24 Parganas, West Bengal

While paying tribute to a brilliant mathematician, I am reminded of the words of the world-renowned French philosopher and mathematician René Descartes (1596–1650):

> *"Mathematics is a more powerful instrument of knowledge than any other that has been bequeathed to us by human agency."*

Before delving into any article, readers often try to understand its subject by reading the title. Just as the vast and infinite universe is illuminated by countless brilliant celestial bodies, the realm of mathematics is boundless, comparable to the vast sky, where many bright stars shine. This humble piece is a tribute to one such luminous and creative mathematician.

Dr. Jagadis Chandra Misra was born into a devout family of teachers in Bagmari village, Purba Medinipur district. The eldest son of the late Ganes Chandra Misra and the late Pramila Devi, he was highly intelligent and disciplined from childhood. In June 1969, he became a part of our family through his marriage to my elder sister, Shorasi. As a brother-in-law, we found in him a learned, soft-spoken, humble, polite, and handsome young man. To our late parents, he was the beloved "Babu," while to our neighbors and relatives, he was "Jagadis Da" or "Jagadis Babu."

A brilliant student of Tikrapara High School, Belur Ramakrishna Mission Vidyamandir, and the University of Calcutta (Department of Applied Mathematics), he was, at that time, a popular mathematics professor at Uluberia College, deeply engaged in relentless research. His dedication was recognized when he earned a Ph.D. in science from Jadavpur University. His professional journey saw a remarkable ascent as he joined the faculty of IIT Kharagpur, one of the most prestigious institutions of technology. His scholarship led him to various advanced countries on research fellowships, culminating in the esteemed D.Sc. Degree in Applied Mathematics from the University of Calcutta.

Just as a salt doll cannot measure the depth of the ocean—since it dissolves into the sea—for a humble student like me, comprehending and evaluating Jagadis Da's multidimensional research is nearly impossible. I am fortunate to be one of his many research students, having learned the analysis of research papers and the preparation of new ones entirely under his guidance. Under his mentorship, this modest student was privileged to attain a Ph.D. His research has opened new avenues in solving at least two pressing real-world problems.

With the rapid advancement of technology, human life has become faster, leading to an increase in accidents that cause fatal injuries or disabilities. Globally, brain injuries account for nearly 75% of all deaths resulting from accidents. Moreover, high-speed sports such as football and hockey also witness a concerning number of injuries. Since human activity depends on cognitive function, even a minor brain injury can have severe consequences. Professor Misra's research has successfully identified the precise location and extent of impact-related brain injuries, proving immensely helpful to doctors and surgeons in their treatment.

Another key area of his research is the study of blood circulation in the human body, particularly the obstructions in veins and arteries. Due to poor dietary habits and lack of physical activity, harmful substances like fat accumulate in the blood, disrupting normal circulation. Such blockages can lead to severe conditions like paralysis and stroke. Through mathematical modeling, he has been able to determine the exact location and severity of these obstructions. This groundbreaking research has made significant contributions to diagnosing and treating vascular diseases.

His research is not merely for obtaining degrees but for addressing critical societal issues. His findings have been applied to improve human well-being, offering some relief to modern lifestyles.

After his formal retirement from IIT, he joined Siksha 'O' Anusandhan University in Bhubaneswar as the Pro-Vice Chancellor and served with distinction in academic administration for five and a half years before retiring. However, his research continues to be regularly published in esteemed platforms like *Research Gate* and *Google Scholar*.

CHAPTER 13

Professor Jagadis Chandra Misra in My Eyes

Dr. Mrityunjay Kumar Patra
Associate Professor (Retd.), Pingla Thana Mahavidyalaya, Paschim Medinipur

It was the year 1987. I had completed five years of teaching at Pingla College. According to government regulations, I had to obtain either an M.Phil. or a Ph.D. within the next three years, or else my annual increment would be halted. In this situation, I was frequently traveling to the Science College at Rajabazar, under Calcutta University, to pursue my M.Phil. I was granted admission, but due to some difficulties, I could not avail the opportunity.

The following year, when I tried again, I was told that one could not be given a second chance. Left with no other option, I decided to pursue a Ph.D. Since I had been a student of the Rajabazar Science College of the Calcutta University, I was expecting to find a familiar professor who could guide me. Unfortunately, none of the faculty members agreed to supervise my research. However, Professor B.N. Mandal suggested that I approach Prof. J.C. Misra from the Mathematics Department of IIT Kharagpur, who is known for his dedicated mentorship.

One day, with ample time on hand, I set out for the Mathematics Department at IIT Kharagpur. Upon reaching, I learned that Prof. Misra was at his residence, but I didn't know the location of his house. While walking around, I stopped by a large canteen and inquired about his residence. They pointed out to me a particular direction. Determined to meet him, I kept walking. At that moment, I heard the ring of a bicycle bell behind me. I turned around, and a gentleman asked, "Are you looking for someone?" I replied, "Yes, I need to meet Prof. J.C. Misra." The man smiled and said, "Tell me what you need, I am J.C. Misra."

I was taken aback. His simple attire, ordinary shoes, and modest bicycle made it hard to believe that this was the distinguished Professor I had heard so much about. Initially, I hesitated to believe him, but when he introduced himself again, I had no choice but to accept it.

I immediately said, "Sir, please don't address me in a respectable manner. I wish to be your student." My words puzzled him. I then introduced myself fully and expressed my strong desire to pursue a Ph.D. under his guidance. I pleaded with him not to turn me away. He responded, "Many come with similar enthusiasm, work for sometime, and then leave." I assured him repeatedly that I was committed to completing my doctoral work.

He seemed to believe me to some extent and inquired about my special paper and the different subjects I had taken during my M.Sc. He also mentioned his own research interests. I expressed my willingness to work in Biofluid Mechanics, assuring him that I would study any new subject as per his guidance. That very day, as we walked together, he explained several concepts useful for my proposed research activity and listed some books for me to read.

From the very first day, I realized that I had finally arrived at the right place. I realized that Prof. Misra was very serious about research. He gave me my first lessons in Ph.D. research—how to conduct research studies, search for journals, and approach research problems. He also made necessary arrangements for consulting the Central Library of IIT Kharagpur. I had never seen a library as vast as IIT Kharagpur's. Balancing my college duties and research, I followed a strict routine—returning home to Balichak in the evening, picking up my research materials, studying at the IIT library until 8 PM, and then cycling to Kharagpur station to catch the 9 PM train for returning to my home.

Occasionally, I would meet with Prof. Misra at his department, where he would render necessary guidance for doing further research and would meticulously correct the research manuscripts.

He was highly punctual. Even if he had scheduled a meeting ten days in advance, he would remember it precisely. He expected his students to respect time and to be particular in following his instructions. Understanding this, I would always arrive early and wait outside his office to ensure that he saw me the moment he arrived.

One day, I reached on time but had to stand at the edge of the corridor, as there was no place to sit. I was gazing outside when, at some point, he came to the door, didn't see me, and assumed that I either hadn't come or was disregarding his appointment schedule. That day, he was so displeased that he refused to review my work. Such was his firm personality! However, his displeasure was short-lived, and by the next day, he was back to his usual self.

He often invited me to his home for corrections. I never returned empty-handed from those visits. At his home, I saw his family—his parents, wife, daughter, and sons. He deeply respected his parents and loved his children very dearly. He would bow to his parents after taking a bath as a mark of respect. He was also taking adequate care for the needs of his family, and was extremely conscious of his children's future. His humility and sense of responsibility toward his family were truly inspiring.

Despite holding such a high position, he led a simple and unpretentious life, which greatly influenced me. His intellectual depth, humility, and generosity shaped my outlook and continue to inspire me.

I worked closely with him for three years and six months. Along with his mathematical brilliance, he had a strong command of English literature. My thesis consisted of six chapters, five of which he helped me publish in reputed international journals within that period. By the time the final chapter was published, I had already obtained my Ph.D.

As I mentioned earlier, I badly needed my Ph.D., and it was only possible because of Prof. Misra's support. I take great pride in acknowledging this.

After receiving my degree, my visits to IIT Kharagpur gradually declined as my college responsibilities increased. Prof. Misra wanted me to dedicate the same amount of time for the publication of my final paper, but the immense workload and exhaustion from completing my Ph.D. made it extremely difficult for me to abide by his instruction. However, he took it upon himself to finalize and publish the paper, which was a great relief for me.

In conclusion, I will always cherish the experience of working with such an extraordinary scholar—an erudite, selfless, and down-to-earth individual. The three and a half years I spent under his guidance remain a luminous chapter in my life. I will forever remember him with deep reverence and gratitude. I sincerely pray for his health and long life.

CHAPTER 14

Reminiscences of My Association with Prof. J.C. Misra

Dr. Narayan Chandra Chattopadhyay
Associate Professor (Retd.), Department of Mathematics,
Seva Bharati Mahavidyalaya, Jhargram

First and foremost, I extend my heartfelt respect to my esteemed mentor, Professor Dr. Jagadis Chandra Misra, an internationally renowned mathematician who has received numerous accolades from India and abroad. His research contributions have significantly enriched various branches of Mathematical Sciences, particularly Biomathematics, Physiological Fluid Dynamics, and Continuum Mechanics. Many mathematics professors and research scholars, including myself, have had the privilege of learning under his guidance. His mentorship has led many to achieve remarkable success in their research, earning recognition both nationally and internationally.

I had the opportunity to do my doctoral work under his supervision for a long time, closely observing his dedication and intellect. His extraordinary expertise in mathematics left me in awe, while his relentless work ethics and deep compassion for his students were truly inspiring. He nurtured his students with boundless affection, constantly encouraging them to pursue mathematical research. He remained ever supportive, maintaining personal connections with his students, even after they had completed their work under his guidance—something quite rare in today's academic world.

I vividly recall an incident in the Mathematics Department when I was working in his office. I pointed out a section of a published journal article by one of his former scholars. He gazed at it for a while and then, with a very heavy heart, said, *"He was one of my dearest and most brilliant students. He was from Manipur and completed his Ph.D. under my supervision. But I recently learned that he passed away unexpectedly at a very young age."*

I had never met that student, nor did I even remember his name. Yet, seeing my professor's tearful face that day left me deeply moved. It was then that I truly realized how much he loved and cherished his students as if they were his own children.

During the period of my doctoral studies, I was struggling with numerous personal and professional challenges at my college, making it difficult to concentrate on my research work. As a result, I lost touch with him for an extended period and became increasingly disheartened about my doctoral research. At one point, I felt so overwhelmed by obstacles that I doubted my ability to contribute anything new to the field. I was on the verge of giving up when an unexpected letter from him reignited my hope and gave me a renewed sense of purpose.

Encouraged by his words, I visited him, and he listened attentively to all my concerns. With great patience, he advised me on how to overcome my despair. Ultimately, he suggested that I shift my research discipline and start afresh. This timely and invaluable advice turned out to be a blessing in my life.

With Professor Misra's continued guidance, I ultimately succeeded in completing my doctoral research and being awarded a Ph.D. degree. For this, I remain eternally grateful to him.

Working under Professor Misra significantly enriched my knowledge of various mathematical disciplines. I realized that acquiring degrees through study and conducting research are entirely different pursuits. He was the first to introduce me to the world-class library at IIT Kharagpur, where he encouraged me to study journals and make the best use of the library's resources. The steps he took to ensure my access to the right materials were invaluable, and I will never forget them.

Since I was also engaged in undergraduate teaching in a college, it was not feasible for me to visit IIT Kharagpur every day. However, even on weekends or holidays, whenever I managed to go, he would either come to the department himself to review my progress or invite me to his residence for discussions.

Here, I must also make a mention about the kindness of Mrs. Misra, who always welcomed me with great warmth and ensured that I was well-fed whenever I visited IIT Kharagpur. Their generosity and hospitality remain deeply etched in my memory. I also fondly remember his parents, whose love and blessings I was fortunate to receive. There are countless memories of Professor Misra and his family members.

With deep reverence. I bow to him and pray for his health and long life.

CHAPTER 15

My Esteemed Doctoral Supervisor

Dr. Biswajit Mallick
Assistant Professor, Department of Mathematics,
University of Allahabad, Uttar Pradesh

It was 2015. I had just completed my M.Sc. At Visva-Bharati University, the bond I had formed with Santiniketan over the past five years had come to an end. The question "What next?" weighed heavily on me.

Fortunately, I didn't have to worry for too long. With the onset of monsoon came a new opportunity—I went to appear at an interview for a project fellow position at IIEST Shibpur. That was the first time I met Professor J.C. Misra in person and had the opportunity to speak with him directly. My emotions were a mix of nervous excitement and awe.

Within a few days, the interview results were declared, and I received my selection letter. Transitioning from a student to a researcher overnight was no easy feat. Like a river fish thrown into the ocean—could I survive? I had to. And somehow, I did. But without Sir's expert guidance, I would have either drowned or been swept away by the waves.

Sir first introduced me to his research team—Gopal-da, Aniruddha-da, and Samaresh-da—who soon became like family members. Slowly, I began to learn what research truly meant—the what, the why, and the how. And this learning came with no shortcuts, no compromises. There couldn't be, because Sir's discipline was like a mountain—firm and unwavering. His care was equally immense, and so there was no room for laziness.

And so it went—writing papers, submitting them, getting published—spinning endlessly in that cycle. Somewhere along the way, four or five years flew by, and I didn't even notice. I still search for where they went.

What I consider my greatest fortune is that I didn't remain trapped in that whirlpool of research forever. Sir never let that happen. Thanks to his guidance, I submitted my thesis on time and could finally breathe a little easier.

I vividly remember the final phase of writing and editing my thesis. In early March 2020, Sir called and asked me to meet him at the Ramakrishna Mission in Belgharia, and to bring my thesis draft with me. From the day before Holi, we spent nearly two weeks working on the final touches. Sir had chosen to stay at the Mission during that time to accommodate my schedule.

I was working as an Assistant Professor at Kalyani University from August 2018 to August 2022. Traveling from Kalyani to Belgharia every day during peak spring to edit a dry academic thesis was far from being pleasant. Everything around me was bursting with the colors of spring—and here I was, leaving home before sunrise and catching the last train back just to run after something as "bookish" as a thesis! What luck I had!

Sir's serious expression, his meticulous corrections, and the endless revisions taught me just how intense and meaningful that one word—"thesis"—really was. Without Sir, those stacks of papers would have never amounted to anything more than scattered thoughts.

Over the years, I had the chance to observe Sir up close. I saw firsthand what real patience looks like. Whether I managed to learn it is another matter—but the desire to learn from him will remain with me for life. Despite his packed schedule, Sir always prioritized his research scholars. He guided us with dedication, no matter how far he was—even from abroad, he would respond to emails with precise advice to keep our work on track. Yet beneath the discipline, there was always a layer of affection, an unspoken care.

There's a strange comfort in recalling past scoldings, like gently pressing on an old bruise that now brings relief. I fondly remember every word of his discipline, and I feel immense joy when I do so. I crave that joy, that affection, and that care for the rest of my life.

Today, I am working at one of India's most prestigious academic institutions. At the root of it all is my Ph.D. under Professor Misra, and the many research papers I was able to publish in international journals was only due to his help. That's how I was selected as an Assistant Professor in the Department of Mathematics at the renowned central university—Allahabad University.

We believe that Sir's work will live on through future generations—because even today, just before entering a classroom, I remember him. And I always will.

CHAPTER 16

Prof. J.C. Misra, as I Saw Him

Dr. Bijay Kumar Sahu
Senior Lecturer, Gandhi Mahavidyalaya, Rourkela, Odisha

I had the privilege of being a student of Prof. J.C. Misra at the Department of Mathematics, IIT Kharagpur, during my D.I.I.T. Programme—a post-M.Sc. diploma course offered by the department. He also served as the supervisor for my D.I.I.T. dissertation.

While I was preparing for my dissertation, Prof. Misra had to travel to Germany for some time. However, he was so considerate and supportive that he made all the necessary arrangements to ensure that I faced no difficulties in completing my dissertation on time.

Later, I joined as a Junior Research Fellow (JRF) in a research project titled *"Effect of Wall Deformability on the Dynamical Behaviour of the Cardiovascular System"*, with Prof. Misra as the Principal Investigator. This project was sponsored by the Council of Scientific and Industrial Research (CSIR), New Delhi, and at that time, it was the only research project running in the Department of Mathematics. Alongside me, another JRF, Mr. Bidyut Kanti Kar from West Bengal, also joined the project. I hailed from Odisha.

Prof. Amal Pal from the Materials Science Centre, who was then the Dean of Sponsored Research and Industrial Consultancy (SRIC) at IIT Kharagpur, served as the Chairman of the Selection Committee for the project.

Prof. Misra was not only an honest and dedicated teacher but also highly caring toward his research scholars. His genuine commitment made him extremely popular among students. Every year, many of his B.Tech. students sought his recommendation letters while applying for higher studies abroad. Most of them secured admission with scholarships at prestigious universities abroad, which I believe was particularly due to the high respect overseas institutions had for Prof. Misra's recommendations.

In 1984, he was the sole recipient of the prestigious *IIT Kharagpur Silver Jubilee Research Award*. He was also honored with several "Best Teacher" awards from various academic institutions, recognizing his excellence in teaching. Notably, he was the first recipient of the esteemed *INAE Outstanding Teacher Award* from the Indian National Academy of Engineering, New Delhi.

Prof. Misra was known for his hard work and expected the same from his students. He was a strict taskmaster, and because of his disciplined approach, most of his research scholars completed their Ph.D. within 3 to 4 years. While many other students had to wait long periods to meet their supervisors, Prof. Misra would personally visit the scholars' rooms—even at B.C. Roy Hall of Residence for research scholars—to check on their progress. Whenever we encountered difficulties, he would invite us to his office and patiently resolve our issues through discussion.

Under his close supervision, I completed my coursework, registration seminar, and literature survey within the first year. At the end of that year, he suggested two research problems, both of which I was able to solve with his guidance by the end of the second year. He then encouraged me to write them as research papers and helped me in drafting the introductions and presenting the results and discussions. He personally handled the submission of these papers to reputed international journals, and I still remember the encouragement I felt when the acceptance letters arrived a few months later. That moment greatly boosted my motivation and accelerated my research progress.

By the time I completed three years and six months, Prof. Misra advised me to start preparing my doctoral thesis. By then, four of my research papers had been published or accepted for publication in reputed international journals, and two more were under review. I vividly recall how meticulously he went through every correction in my thesis.

My colleague, Mr. Bidyut Kanti Kar, had to deal with some personal challenges and was not very consistent in his work. Prof. Misra persistently followed up and ensured that he, too, completed his Ph.D. by the end of his fourth year.

I was awarded my Ph.D. in 1989, but even after that, I continued to engage in collaborative research with Prof. Misra.

I sincerely pray to Lord Jagannath to bless Prof. Misra and his family with a long, healthy, and peaceful life.

CHAPTER 17

Some Memories from the Past

Dr. Sukhendu Bikash Kar
Former Headmaster, Tikrapara Ambikamayi Higher Secondary School, Pratapdighi, Purba Medinipur

On July 3rd, 1978, I began my teaching career at Kharagpur Silver Jubilee High School, about 4 km from IIT Kharagpur. Ever since my M.Sc. days, I had a strong desire to pursue a Ph.D. To that end, I explored opportunities at the Mathematics Department of IIT, and eventually, I was fortunate to be accepted by Prof. J.C. Misra as a part-time research scholar.

Around 1980, I officially began my research. As arranged by Prof. Misra, one of his former doctoral students, Dr. S. Samanta helped me in the initial stage, who used to look after my daily progress in research.Gradually, research papers began to take shape. Whenever I got stuck and couldn't find a clear direction, Dr. Samanta and I would visit Professor Misra together at IIT for guidance.

In 1985, I submitted my thesis to Jadavpur University and was awarded the Ph.D. on July 12, 1987. After I could make some progress, I would present my work to Prof. Misra. In spite of his very busy schedule, he would always pay due attention to supervise my research work. He has never told,

"I don't have time." He would often say, "You're not working with full focus. It shouldn't take so long to complete such a small portion."

I used to wonder—I'm working all the time! I even ponder the problems while riding the bus. So, how much faster was I supposed to go? That internal conflict was finally resolved when the thesis was ready for typing. One day, both of them called me to IIT and said, "Sukhendu, you've completed your thesis work very quickly—quicker than even full-time scholars, although you are engaged in teaching full-time at your school."

I was astonished and replied, "But you two used to say the opposite all along!" They laughed and said, "That was just to push you to work even faster."

That moment filled me with a deep sense of joy. How rare is it to find mentors so deeply invested in a student's progress!

If a relevant book wasn't available in the Central Library of IIT, Prof. Misra would buy it himself, so that we could use it for reference. Once, we needed a book belonging to the library, but it was not available in the shelves. He personally met the person who had borrowed it, requested its return, and handed over the book to me.

His compassion for students was extraordinary. During winter visits to his quarters, if I wasn't dressed with warm clothes, he would lend me a sweater from his home.

Professor Misra hails from the village of Bagmari, under Patashpur police station area of the District of Purba Medinipur. His father, late Ganes Chandra Misra, was a teacher at Tikrapara Higher Secondary School.

Jagadis Chandra and his brother were not the only students of his father in their home—5 to 6 other children, both relatives and outsiders, also lived there to pursue education. That level of generosity and sacrifice is not a small thing.

As the saying goes, no good deed goes unrewarded. I firmly believe that his parents' service to students paved the way for their children's success.

After Professor Misra received the Ram Mohan Award, his childhood school, Tikarapara A.M. Higher Secondary School, organized a felicitation for him. At that time, I was serving as the School's headmaster. When I had the honor of placing a ceremonial scarf around his neck and bowing in respect, my heart swelled with pride. How many people are lucky enough to be both a student and then the head of their teacher's alma mater?

He was never particular about his appearance—sometimes his undershirt would show beneath his shirt, or his buttons would be misaligned, or he'd show up wearing old flip-flops and riding an old bicycle. But his students, engrossed in his passion for knowledge, lovingly called him a "Tapasvi of Wisdom."

His research was the most captivating part of his scholarly life. He authored over 250 research papers, all published in international journals. Though he came from a mathematics background, his research in biomechanics and biomedical mathematics has left a lasting impact on medical science and physiology.

In fact, Professor Y.C. Fung, a renowned expert in Biomechanics, who was one of the evaluators of his D.Sc. thesis from the University of California, San

Diego (UCSD) USA, commented that Prof. Misra's work made a permanent contribution to the field of Biomechanics. His work on structural mechanics is also considered highly valuable by researchers in engineering.

A lifelong admirer of the Ramakrishna Mission, it is known that Professor Misra made monetary donations to the Mission—though he never wants to publicize such acts. He also contributed funds to his childhood school, Tikarapara Ambikamayi High School.

Additionally, he helped develop the Nursery school at Pratapdighi (founded by his father) and rendered financial help in establishing a laboratory at the Ramakrishna Sarada Siksha Sadan.

In 2004, he was invited to speak at the All India Students' Conference on Science and Spiritual Quest in Tiruchirappalli. The topic of his lecture was: "Mathematics & Spirituality." It is awe-inspiring to think that he sought and presented the harmony between mathematics and spiritual philosophy.

He was invited as a Visiting Professor at many esteemed universities in Germany, America, London, and Canada. He is respected across the globe and has received many international awards.

Balai Babu, a childhood friend of Professor Misra from Pratapdighi, asked me to share my thoughts for a commemorative publication. But unless one reads his papers, it is difficult to comprehend the depth of his work and recognize his greatness as a researcher.

I spent six years in his presence at IIT—but how much do I truly know about him?

With deep reverence, I offer my salutations to this compassionate, nurturing, and noble soul.

CHAPTER 18

The Guiding Light of Our Lives

Manasi Nanda Raut
Retired Teacher, Belda Prabhati Balika Vidyapith,
Belda, Paschim Medinipur

"Those whose names, when remembered, serve as the perfect prelude to our day's noble pursuits—such individuals are our revered ones."

—Rabindranath Tagore

Today, as I sit down to write a few words about you, I am standing at the twilight of my life—my body at peace, and my enthusiasm restrained. The time for learning has passed. Though I reside in my homeland, I often feel like a stranger, disconnected from all, both known and unknown. And yet, I could not resist the urge to write about you.

I know that I am unworthy of this task—not out of false humility, but as an honest confession. I have spoken enough about myself; now, let me turn to you. You have given us so much over the years, and we have received countless gifts from you. But I lack the words to express my gratitude. Judging your contributions is beyond my capability; it is a task for the truly wise. I do not possess the depth of knowledge and education required for such an endeavour.

But what I do know is that you are one of our own—an inseparable part of our lives. We have witnessed so many moments together, and even today, the touch of those joyous times lingers in my heart. There are memories that still stir my soul.

Do you remember the first time I saw you? You arrived at our home as a groom, adorned in wedding attire.

"O New One, come forth, filling the entire sky with your luminous presence!"

—Rabindranath Tagore

Seeing the two of you together, we were overwhelmed. Such a sight had never before graced our little world. Some said, *"Ah, this is the divine union of*

Shiva and Parvati." Others remarked, *"No, this is none other than Lakshmi and Narayan."* Relatives proclaimed, *"Even calling them Ram and Sita would not be an exaggeration."*

That day's profound joy is a memory I shall never forget. I never imagined that an experience could be preserved so vividly in the canvas of my mind.

You are a scholar, a man of many virtues. I had heard much about you before, but do you know what truly captivated my family that day? It was your honest humility and truthful words.

The morning after the wedding, as you both were about to leave, everyone was in tears. We wept too. My father silently wiped his eyes. My mother, grandmother, and great-aunt (*Dadabhai*) sobbed uncontrollably. My great-aunt held your hands and said, *"Brother, this is my most beloved granddaughter. I entrust her to you—take care of her."*

Just a couple of months later, my great-aunt fell ill and soon embarked on her final journey to the eternal abode. And then, only a few days after that, the two of you returned. The house was filled with boundless joy and celebration. My parents went beyond their means to welcome you back. My mother, under the watchful gaze of the morning star, began preparing an array of dishes. My younger sister assisted her. The responsibility of hosting you fell upon me.

Our grandmother and great-aunt were brimming with happiness. My parents' eyes overflowed with delight. Even my two grandfathers—my mother's father and uncle—joined this joyful reunion. They adored you deeply.

Even now, I sometimes wonder—was there any flaw in my hospitality that day? That joyous memory remains safely locked in the treasure chest of my heart, never to be forgotten. Until that moment, I had never imagined that the heart's emotions could be seen so clearly through the eyes.

Years and seasons have passed since then. Countless sweet memories surround us. Through so many difficult situations, we have continued our journey. But you, like the mighty Himalayas, have remained unwavering in your dedication and duty.

"There is no time to turn back and look."

—Rabindranath Tagore

Just as the endless ocean cannot be measured, just as its depths remain unseen, so too are you—boundless, immeasurable. Our gaze cannot fully grasp you; our understanding cannot reach your depths.

To me, the word *"brother-in-law"* refers only to you—the embodiment of grace, peace, and gentle radiance. Your world is filled with joy, and none but you could bring such light. Even today, your first affectionate call *Khuku* still echoes in my ears, touching every chord of my heart.

Your voice is like sweet nectar, your demeanor filled with warmth. The world around you is bathed in sweetness. May your universe remain ever so blissful—this is my heartfelt prayer to the Almighty.

We have seen you with our own eyes, heard your words with our own ears. It amazes me to think that you are one of us. Some may believe, I am weaving a tale—like a prince from an underground kingdom or a character from a fairy tale. But believe me when I say—this is the truth of my heart, the words of my very soul.

There is one thing I always tell everyone about you—you used to love chewing betel leaves. You used to enjoy sitting by the betel tray, engaging in heartfelt conversations with the villagers. Despite being such a remarkable person, you possess a rare ability to connect with all. That is why our village folk and relatives cherish you so dearly.

Your way of wearing a dhoti is unique—it stands out. I always find it fascinating. Sometimes, I see you in the simplest of attires, and at other times, you radiate an extraordinary brilliance. At moments, you seem like a sophisticated gentleman, and at others, a humble village man. But in every form, you remain remarkable. You are your own comparison—there is none like you.

You have no particular preferences when it comes to food—you enjoy all kinds of dishes. My mother used to find great joy in feeding you.

You chant the Lord's name with unwavering devotion. You offer prayers with sincerity, yet you carry no ornamentation—not even in matters of faith. There are very few people as righteous and devout as you. You are like the hidden stream of the *Falgu River*—flowing quietly beneath the surface.

Your greatness is not immediately visible because, like a vessel, full to the brim, you make no noise. But we, with our limited knowledge, create a loud noise—like empty brass utensils, always making noise to announce our presence. You are our own, and that is our greatest treasure. How many people are fortunate enough to experience such a bond? You and your beloved wife are truly made for each other—divinely matched. Even your names share a beautiful resemblance.

May the Supreme Father continue to bless you both abundantly.

That is why you have given birth to such remarkable children. Speaking of you, one cannot help but mention another—someone who has always been by your side. She is your shadow. You walk ahead, while she remains in the background—your source of inspiration.

Her ever-smiling face, her boundless affection, effortlessly find their way into your writings. She cannot be overlooked. Do you know who she is? None other than our elder sister—your perfect life partner.

> *"May my joy be the joy of all, may my good fortune bring goodness to all, may I share whatever I have with others and enjoy it together."*
>
> ***—Balendranath Tagore***

In the journey of life, conflicts arise. Jealousy, greed, and worldly temptations flow like an undercurrent. People often resort to cunning and deceit. In the pain of unfulfilled desires, we sigh and lament. We rejoice in fleeting moments of happiness, yet deep inside, we carry the burden of neglect and despair. Many of us fade away, unremembered, because we fail to leave behind a path for future generations.

> *"This sorrow lingers in my heart—love did not fulfill my desires, my wishes remained unmet in this short life. Why is life so fleeting in this world?"*
>
> ***—Tarashankar Bandyopadhyay***

Yet, amidst the ordinary, there occasionally emerges an extraordinary soul. You are one of them. You embody the essence of humanity—rich in spirit, noble in heart. Humble, yet possessing invincible strength. You are the guiding light for the generations to come, a symbol of our deepest hopes and aspirations. Your deeds will be remembered through the ages.

I offer my heartfelt reverence to you. May your noble life serve as a guiding force for the youth. May you be our signal of hope, our solace in sorrow. May your wisdom remain ever undiminished.

O guide of a new era! I bow to you again and again.

> *"The pure souls have risen in this world, Bringing the news from the Garden. May they be blessed."*
>
> ***—Rabindranath Tagore***

CHAPTER 19

From the Pages of Memory

Dr. Namita Mahapatra
Former Visiting Professor, Medinipur Homeopathy Medical College and Hospital & Former Medical Officer, B.C. Roy Technology Hospital, IIT Kharagpur

Let me begin with an incident that dates back to 1967, when I was a sixth-grade student at Naipur High School in the Patashpur police station area of Medinipur district.

One day, during our mathematics class, a new teacher entered the classroom. As was customary, all the students greeted him with respect before returning to their seats. He began by asking each of us our names and a little about ourselves. Then, he requested the top three students in the class to stand up. When he called out, three of us stood. After asking the names of the first two students, he instructed them to sit down. Then, looking around with a slight smile, he said, "It seems the top-ranked student is absent today, isn't that right?"

The entire class immediately pointed at me. Surprised, he smiled and said, "Oh! I didn't even see you there."

At that time, I was so young and short that I was barely visible from behind the high bench. Later, I learned that he had initially thought I had simply accompanied an older sibling to school, rather than being a student myself.

That math teacher of mine would later become the world-renowned and distinguished Professor Dr. Jagadis Chandra Misra. However, after teaching at Naipur High School for only two or three months, he left. It was learnt that he had joined a college as a professor.

By a fortunate turn of events, in the month of Jyeshtha (May-June) 1969, he married my eldest sister, Shorasi, the eldest daughter of Pandit Phani Bhushan Nanda of Amarapur village in Patashpur. From that day on, our relationship transformed into a family bond. At the time, he was a lecturer at Uluberia College.

Being both my former teacher and my brother-in-law, I always felt a deep sense of reverence toward him. I was so much younger than him that I would often hesitate and feel shy to speak in his presence. My father had already told me about his extraordinary intellect—how he had excelled in all his school, college, and university examinations.

I first visited his ancestral home in Bagmari during his wedding. Later also, I visited their house many times. The academic environment in his house was unlike most other houses I had ever visited. His father, Sri Ganes Chandra Misra, was a teacher at Tikarapara High School, and his younger son, Parames (affectionately called Kanu), slept in a room with him on the first floor. Whenever we stayed over, we slept in the adjacent room, separated only by a bamboo partition.

Every morning, we would wake up to the sound of his father quizzing Kanu on English translations, word meanings, and Bengali grammar lessons. This was his way of waking him up.

On the balcony upstairs, his father would sit on one side, while several of their cousins and relatives would sit on mats nearby to study. Kanu would bring his books and sit beside his father, who would occasionally call out names, check lessons and ask questions. The aunty (mother of my brother-in-law), would bring puffed rice, milk, bananas, and other food items to ensure they didn't have to go downstairs for breakfast, possibly to prevent any interruption in their studies.

From the very beginning, my brother-in-law was dedicated to fostering a disciplined and scholarly atmosphere at home, which undoubtedly contributed to nurturing such rare academic brilliance. His elder uncle and aunt managed household affairs, while his father, a devoted teacher and education enthusiast, remained immersed in academics. All of the siblings, including my brother-in-law, attended Tikarapara High School.

After retiring from teaching, his parents moved to their son's residence at IIT Kharagpur campus. His youngest brother, Kanu, pursued an M.Tech at IIT Kharagpur, while his other brothers also resided there for their studies. My brother-in-law and my eldest sister wholeheartedly supported and guided them in their higher education.

My eldest sister, after completing her schooling at Naipur High School, pursued a Bengali honors degree at Raja Narendra Lal Khan Women's College in Medinipur. After earning her B.A. degree, she took up a teaching position at Bagmari Girls' School. Later, after her marriage, she completed her B.Ed. at Uluberia College. Though she left her teaching job before marriage, she devoted herself completely to supporting her husband, brothers-in-law, and children in their educational pursuits. She took on the responsibility of household chores, cooking, grocery shopping—everything—so that her husband could remain focused on his academic career without any worries.

My eldest sister is a highly affectionate, devout, and religious woman. She nurtured all of us siblings with immense love and even taught us numerous religious hymns and prayers. While we were in college, she would write down various prayers and mantras and send them to us in envelopes. She herself devoted considerable time to daily worship in the prayer room. She also instilled these values in her children, shaping them into sincere and religious-minded individuals.

During her leisure time, she wrote stories, essays, and poems for various magazines. We have all realized the immense sacrifices she made for my brother-in-law's higher education, long-term research, and eventual establishment as a distinguished scholar. She took full responsibility for the household so that he could dedicate himself to the academic world without distractions.

As I reflect on her life and selfless devotion, a song by Rabindranath Tagore comes to mind:

"You must give everything,
For everything shall be yours..."

After my marriage in July, 1980, I moved into the quarters at IIT Kharagpur. My husband, Prof. Subhash Chandra Mahapatra, was part of the Rural Development Centre at IIT Kharagpur. Since then, we have had the privilege of being very close to my eldest sister and brother-in-law. Our two families have shared joys and sorrows for nearly 35–36 years. My brother-in-law was not just our guardian but also a guide in our pursuit of higher education.

Their three children—Subhas, Sudip, and daughter Sumita—grew up in front of us. We had the joy of nurturing them from a young age. Today, all the three have successfully completed their education through school, college, and university and have excelled in academic profession. They all have inherited virtues like piety, selflessness, humility, and soft-spokenness. Sumita's husband, Dr. Achintya Mukhopadhyay, is a Professor of Mechanical Engineering at Jadavpur University. My brother-in-law's two daughters-in-law, Sulagna and

Satamita, are educated and humble. Both of them have continued the family's legacy, working hard to ensure their children's academic success.

Such extraordinary talent and intellect thrive only in an environment nurtured by dedicated parents like them.

As the rebellious poet Kazi Nazrul Islam once wrote:

> *"Half of all great and noble creations in the world were made by women, the other half by men."*

My brother-in-law's parents were a perfect example of such an ideal couple. We used to call them "Mesomoshai" and "Masima." As mentioned earlier, after retiring from teaching, Mesomoshai along with Masima moved in with their eldest son, my brother-in-law. During that time, they often visited our quarters. Mesomoshai regularly tutored Subhas, Sumita, and Sudip, discussing Sanskrit and English grammar with them. Masima was intelligent, wise, and soft-spoken. We were fortunate to receive their blessings and spend time in their esteemed company.

Our brother-in-law, Professor Jagadis Chandra Misra, is a simple, humble, and modest man who truly embodies the principle of *"plain living and high thinking."* Though a globally respected and distinguished figure, within our family, he remains our dear elder brother-in-law. For many years, he has been an integral part of our family, sharing in our joys and sorrows. From the beginning, I remember how he relished the food my mother lovingly prepared for him. My mother took great pleasure in cooking special dishes for him, and later, we too enjoyed feeding him. Whenever a special dish was made at our home in the IIT Campus, we would feel restless until we sent some over to him or their home.

When it came to family members' medical care, he often sought my advice. As a patient, he was incredibly disciplined. During my nearly thirty years of medical practice at the IIT Kharagpur campus, many professors, scholars, and esteemed individuals sought my medical consultation. Some carried an air of pride due to their knowledge and position, but my brother-in-law was free of any such arrogance. He would visit me three or four times a month to check his blood pressure, always following his morning walk, during which he would recite various Sanskrit hymns and mantras. After returning, he would rest on our sofa for 15–20 minutes before heading home, sometimes after having a light snack.

When I was a medical student, he brought me a stethoscope and a blood pressure monitor from Germany. Despite our vast differences in age, status, and experience, he always respected my knowledge and education. While I was studying medicine, he occasionally invited me to his department to help answer some queries from Anatomy and Physiology, which were useful for the research activities of his research scholars. He never hesitated to discuss important academic topics with us and always listened to our views with great patience.

His knowledge is boundless, and his contributions are immense, though I remain unaware of much of it. We are truly fortunate to have had such a venerable figure so close to us. No matter how great he is in the eyes of the world, to us, he is a member of our extended family—our beloved elder brother-in-law.

Over the years, we have created countless memories together. While I must conclude this writing, I am grateful for the opportunity to share some of these cherished recollections from my personal experiences of the past. This fills me with immense joy and pride, and I consider myself blessed.

"Dhanyo'ham kritakritiyo'ham, safalam jeevitam mama."
(Blessed am I, fulfilled am I—my life has been fruitful.)

CHAPTER 20

My Experience with Professor Jagadis Chandra Misra

Dr. Motahar Reza
Associate Professor & Head, Department of Mathematics,
GITAM University, Hyderabad, Telangana

In 2023, one evening I received a phone call from Mr. Balai Lal Das. Introducing himself as a retired teacher of a Higher Secondary School, and a school mate of my research guide, Professor Jagadis Chandra Misra, Mr. Das suggested that if willing I can contribute an article about my experience of working with Prof. Misra. I felt truly delighted to receive such a suggestion. He also informed that in order to inspire the younger generation of students, he along with some distinguished people of the society have been taking an initiative to publish an edited volume on Prof. J.C. Misra.

Professor Jagadis Chandra Misra was not just my research supervisor; he was a globally renowned scientist, a distinguished educator in India, a philosopher, and, above all, an extraordinary human being. I take immense pride in having had the opportunity to do my doctoral work under his guidance, where I gained not only academic and linguistic knowledge but also valuable lessons in becoming a good human being. He also taught me how an educated society can progress.

In 1997, while pursuing my postgraduate degree at Jadavpur University, I visited IIT Kharagpur for the first time to meet my brother. At that time, I had no prior knowledge about IIT Kharagpur.

However, after visiting its academic environment and vast campus, I felt inclined to pursue my higher studies there.

In 1999, I visited IIT Kharagpur for the second time to appear for an interview for admission as a research scholar. That was my first interaction with Professor Misra, who was then the Head of the Mathematics Department and also the

Chairman of the Ph.D. admission interview panel. His personality left a deep impression on me, filling me with a sense of great respect.

I vividly remember how attentively he examined my academic qualifications and GATE score before beginning to ask questions. His first question was about my specialization in Solid Mechanics during my M.Sc., followed by a detailed inquiry into my knowledge and interest in Fluid Dynamics.

On July 26, 1999, I met him in his office for the second time, carrying my research proposal. The news that he would be my research supervisor brought me immense joy and a sense of pride. Despite his busy schedule, he took the time to listen to me carefully and discuss my research framework. Even though he was a world-class scientist, he patiently explained various aspects of academic life and a scholar's journey. Through personal anecdotes, he taught me how to expand my knowledge, aspire to achieve academic excellence, and dream big.

As the Head of the Department, he was incredibly busy. However, whenever I approached him, he would attentively listen to my research challenges as well as hostel-related issues and guide me toward solutions. His calm and composed personality had a profound impact on me. Since I was new to IIT Kharagpur, I would frequently approach him with minor concerns, yet he never expressed any irritation. Instead, he always helped me resolve both academic and personal challenges.

One thing that stood out about him was that he never imposed his decisions on me. I recall asking him to choose my Ph.D. coursework subjects, to which he responded by asking about my interests. When I expressed my desire to take Computer Science courses, he supported my decision and also encouraged me to learn German. That day, he shared his experiences of working at a German university under the Humboldt Fellowship and described his journey of learning the German language. Inspired by his words, I resolved to apply for a fellowship, so that I could conduct research in Germany someday. With his encouragement, I began preparing both mentally and academically. Eventually, his inspiration led me to secure an opportunity to study in Germany.

He had written a strong recommendation letter for my postdoctoral studies in Germany, which played a crucial role in my selection. I will always remain grateful for his contribution.

During his tenure as the Head of the Mathematics Department, he successfully organized two world-class conferences. Occasionally, he would call me asking for assistance. He had a deep passion for both Bengali and English languages and was highly proficient in them. While typing in English, he would teach me grammar rules and the appropriate language for different contexts. The knowledge I gained from him continues to be invaluable in my professional writing.

As a world-class scientist and professor, he held immense respect for researchers and academicians from across the globe. He introduced me to many distinguished scholars across the globe. Despite his demanding administrative duties, he never neglected my research progress. Thanks to his support, I was able to submit my thesis on time without any delays.

I frequently visited his home for research discussions, and he always treated me like a family member. He never scolded or showed frustration over any mistakes; his patience was boundless. He even visited my hostel multiple times. Although he could have simply called me via an attendant or a phone call, he personally came to check if I was facing any academic or personal difficulties.

Looking back, I realize that working under Professor Misra's guidance was one of the most valuable experiences of my life. His mentorship shaped not only my academic journey but also my personal growth, and for that, I will always be indebted to him. He is truly an ideal mentor. He provided me with immense support—both mentally and physically—when I was submitting my Ph.D. thesis.

Currently, I am working as an Associate Professor and the Head of Mathematics Department at Gandhi Institute of Technology and Management, Hyderabad.

From the very beginning, Professor Misra guided me on how to lead a successful life. He often spoke about three essential qualities of a person, viz. Aspiration, Capability and Perseverence.

He emphasized that only those who possess all three of these qualities can become truly accomplished individuals. Having just two of these traits is not enough to achieve real success.

He taught me how to develop a passion for my work and enhance my skills. I was just an ordinary scholar, but under his guidance, I had the opportunity to see and understand the world. His mentorship helped me establish myself in my career.

For all this, I remain deeply devoted, respectful, and grateful to Professor Misra.

CHAPTER 21

A Distinguished Son of Bengal

Smt. Gita Misra
Wife of Shri Tarapada Misra,
Chand Sarak, Sarat Sarani, Krishnagar-741101

Shri Jagadis Chandra Misra has illuminated the Nation with his brilliance. He is like a radiant star. While the light of celestial bodies may fade, the glow of such scholars' wisdom remains eternal and undiminished.

During his student years at Belur Math, he delved into the teachings of Sri Ramakrishna, Holy Mother Sri Sarada Devi, and Swami Vivekananda. Inspired by the ideals of the Ramakrishna Math and Mission, he received initiation at Belur Math from the then-president of the Ramakrishna Order, Swami Shankarananda Ji. Later, he pursued higher education in Mathematics and, in his quest for knowledge, he travelled extensively to several overseas countries and visited many distinguished universities. Even at an advanced age, he continues to seek new knowledge tirelessly, with no time to look back.

Not only has he enriched the field of Mathematics, but he has also shared his accumulated wisdom generously with his students. His children, too, have been enlightened by his guidance. His research will serve as a beacon for future generations. He is truly a pioneer of knowledge, illuminating the path for Mathematics enthusiasts with his exceptional intellect.

Behind my brother-in-law's remarkable success, my sister has played a crucial role.

"A home shines with a gem-like woman, just as the lotus graces the water."

Though my sister received higher education, she chose to step away from doing any job outside her home to nurture and encourage her husband's intellectual pursuits. Like a lamp that spreads light all around, my brother-in-law has illuminated the world with his wisdom, while my sister has steadfastly supported him like the base of that very lamp. Even today, she shoulders the responsibilities of the family, ensuring their children are well-established in their respective careers.

This humble, unassuming, and simple man, Prof. J.C. Misra happens to be my eldest brother-in-law by relation. But beyond that, my greatest identity is that I am his sister-in-law (his cousin's wife). I feel proud to be a member of the learned joint family—the unique 'Misra family' of Bagmari Village.

One particular incident comes to mind: When my brother-in-law and sister were concerned about the marriage of their elder son, Subhas, fate smiled upon them. A match was arranged with the daughter of a doctor from Nabadwip. Since we live in Krishnanagar (Nadia district), they expressed their desire to conduct the wedding ceremony from our residence. We wholeheartedly agreed, and with our collective efforts, the ceremony was successfully conducted. Afterward, their faces radiated joy and contentment, reflecting the trust they had placed in us. We were witnesses to that heartfelt moment.

My sisters often say that my eldest sister loves me unconditionally. Perhaps I will never be able to reciprocate that love in full measure. I pray at the lotus feet of Sri Ramakrishna and Holy Mother Sarada Devi for my sister and brother-in-law's long, happy, and healthy life.

CHAPTER 22

Remembering with Deep Gratitude

Dr. Sanchita Dandapat (Sikdar)
Nabarun, 110/22C, B.T. Road, Kolkata-700108

Under the esteemed guidance of Professor Jagadis Chandra Misra, I earned my Ph.D. degree in 1982 as part of my postgraduate studies. My research primarily focused on establishing the fundamental principles of biomechanics. To achieve this, I needed a solid foundation in the subject and a critical understanding of its applications.

During those days, Prof. Misra generously devoted his invaluable time to guide me, helping me acquire the necessary knowledge. As a result, the findings of my research continue to be considered significant even today. I remember, with unwavering gratitude, his immense contributions. Had he not provided me with both his mentorship and the keys to unraveling the mysteries of biomechanics, my knowledge would have remained incomplete.

Even after all these years, I can confidently say that his wise counsel, like that of a true guru, has continued to guide me through life's many challenges. It is only fitting that I offer my deepest respect with the following words:

Gururbrahma Gururvishnuh
Gururdevo Maheshwarah,
Gurureva Param Brahma
Tasmai Shri Gurave Namah.

Ajnana timiraandhasya
Jnananjana shalakaya,
Chakshur unmilitam Yena
Tasmai Shri Gurave Namah.

I fondly recall those days of my research career—how, upon returning from abroad, he would immediately convene a meeting with all students of his research group at his office in the IIT Mathematics Department, engaging in long discussions with each research scholar working under his supervision. He meticulously reviewed each student's research progress, inquired about any challenges they faced during his absence, and assessed the work they had accomplished. He would always bring back souvenirs from abroad as tokens of encouragement. Prof. Misra was deeply committed to his students' academic growth. He provided unwavering support, from reviewing drafts of research papers to ensuring their successful publication in scientific journals. His guidance remained steadfast until a paper was finally accepted for publication. Forty years ago, after earning my Ph.D., I returned to Kolkata. Even today, he remains a mentor and well-wisher, whose contributions I can never forget. Remarkably, he has continued to publish my unpublished research papers in leading international scientific journals, aligning them with contemporary research trends.

Om Sahana Vavatu, Sahanau Bhunaktu,
Sahaveeryam Karavavahai,
Tejasvinavadheetamastu Maa Vidvishavahai,
Om Shanti Shanti Shantih.

His unwavering support and encouragement for my success are beyond what any student could ever hope for from their Ph.D. advisor. In gratitude, I offer my heartfelt prayer for his long, healthy, and fulfilling life.

CHAPTER 23

Dr. Jagadis Chandra Misra: Some of My Personal Insights

Ashish Panda
Assistant Labour Commissioner (Retired), Government of West Bengal

Today, the erudition of the eminent mathematician Dr. Jagadis Chandra Misra has earned him a distinguished place among the world's greatest scholars in Mathematics. This humble effort is an attempt to present some of my personal insights about him.

By virtue of family ties, I had the fortune of being in his close proximity since my early childhood. After completing his university education, he began his teaching career at a prestigious college, affiliated to Calcutta University. Coincidentally, I joined the same institution as a first-year undergraduate student and had the invaluable opportunity to spend three years under his mentorship. His perseverance, disciplined lifestyle, and spiritual outlook serve as an inspiration to all.

Over the years, he has dedicated himself to teaching in various educational institutions across India and abroad, guiding numerous talented students who have been greatly benefited from his wisdom. Renowned academic institutions worldwide have honored him with prestigious accolades. A devoted follower of the ideals of Sri Ramakrishna Paramahansa and Swami Vivekananda, Dr. Misra embodies the spirit of scientific pursuit and enlightenment.

He remains a luminous beacon in our lives.

I pray for his good health and long life.

CHAPTER 24

Prof. J.C. Misra—My Research Guide

Dr. Somnath Maiti
Assistant Professor, Department of Mathematics,
Rajendra College, J.P.University, Bihar-841301

It is a great privilege for me to write a few words about my doctoral supervisor, Prof. J.C. Misra. I first saw him in 2003 while pursuing my B.Sc. (Honours) in Mathematics at Uluberia College, Howrah. At that time, Prof. Misra had visited our college to deliver a UGC lecture on *Applicable Mathematics*. His impressive research profile and work on mathematical modelling of biological systems applications deeply inspired me and ultimately led me to seek his guidance for my Ph.D.

In 2006, after securing a CSIR-NET scholarship through the National Eligibility Test, I met Prof. Misra at IIT Kharagpur and requested him to accept me as one of his research scholars. I was overjoyed when he kindly agreed to supervise my doctoral work. This is more particularly because I had heard much about his stature as a renowned mathematician—not only from my teachers at Uluberia College but also from faculty members at the Department of Applied Mathematics, University of Calcutta, where I did my M.Sc.

On our very first meeting, he recommended a number of books and research papers for me to study in the beginning of my research journey. He discussed and explained how I should structure my approach to ensure high-quality research. I am deeply grateful to him for his consistent guidance throughout my Ph.D., for his rigorous supervision, and for the valuable suggestions he offered whenever I faced challenges.

Prof. Misra dedicated long hours to discussing and reviewing the complex aspects of my research work. Without his continuous support, encouragement, and insightful input, it would have been difficult for me to complete my thesis within the stipulated time.

There were also personal challenges during my Ph.D. journey that I would like to mention here. In 2007, my father was involved in an accident, and in 2011, I myself met with an accident. During both these difficult periods, Prof. Misra showed great empathy, allowing me the time needed to care for my father and to recover my own health. Naturally, I couldn't make much progress in my research during those months, but he supported me like a true guardian, offering not only academic guidance but also moral support. His counsel continued to be invaluable during other difficult times in my life as well.

What has always stood out to me is his calm and graceful demeanor. His humility, integrity, inner strength, and compassionate nature have been a constant source of inspiration for me and many others.

In 2009, he joined SOA University, Bhubaneswar, as Pro-Vice-Chancellor, but he continued to supervise my research with the same dedication and sincerity. I visited him in Bhubaneswar several times for research discussions, often staying for extended periods. He even took the trouble to help me find affordable accommodation, reflecting his caring and considerate nature. I fondly remember the warm hospitality of Mrs. Misra, both in Kharagpur and in Bhubaneswar.

Prof. Misra is undoubtedly one of India's most distinguished applied mathematicians. I deeply value the constant encouragement and guidance he has given me over the past twenty years—not only in academic matters but also in navigating personal difficulties. He has always been very friendly, supportive, and genuinely involved in my progress.

It was a joy to interact with him and his family during various social gatherings, including family tours and the weddings of his sons, Prof. Subhas Chandra Misra and Prof. Sudip Misra.

I feel truly proud that my research supervisor, Prof. J.C. Misra, has been recognized among the *Top 2% Scientists in the World for six consecutive years from 2020 to 2025*, according to a global study conducted by a team of researchers at Stanford University, USA.

Section III

Classmates, Colleagues and Educationists

CHAPTER 25

Prof. Jagadis Chandra Misra, A Celebrity Among Contemporary Mathematicians

Dr. Biswanath Das
Head, Department of Statistics (Retd),
Presidency University (formerly, Presidency College), Kolkata

Recently I had an occasion to be elated a great deal when I came across a post in the social media in our academic circle. A group of scientists from the reputed Stanford University of USA have published a list of 2% scientists of the world, based on the quality of their lifelong research, and our classmate and good friend Jagadis figures in their list. This is indeed a coveted international honor and recognition, and we, among his friends and associates, are indeed proud of him, particularly since the name of Jagadish figures in the list published by Stanford researchers for six consecutive years 2020–2025. I could also gather, his two sons—the elder, Subhas teaching in IIT Kanpur, and the younger, Sudip teaching in IIT Kharagpur also appear in the lists.

Jagadis was my classmate at the residential college Ramakrishna Mission Vidyamandira (Belur Math) during 1959–61 when we were students of intermediate course. Thereafter I went to Presidency College to pursue a 2-year Honours course in Statistics, and Jagadis continued at the Vidyamandira in the 3-year honours course in Mathematics. Afterwards, at the post-graduate level, we were united once again at Ramakrishna Mission Calcutta Students Home (Belgharia) for a year during 1964–65. He was at that time a student of Applied Mathematics at Rajabazar Science College, and myself, of Statistics at Ballygunge Science College of Calcutta University. Afterwards, Jagadis started teaching at IIT Kharagpur, while I entered Presidency College, Calcutta for a four-decade long career as a teacher there.

Even after our student days, we had more or less regular connections. Notable developments featuring us would hardly escape each other's notice. He, along with his wife, visited our residence at Belur. I, too, had been at his Kharagpur IIT quarters. On one occasion, at the invitation of Jagadis, I had delivered a seminar feature at the Mathematics Department of IIT Kharagpur. In 2006, when in the annual conference of the Indian Science Congress Association Jagadis was elected as the President of the Mathematical Sciences (including Statistics) Section, our mutual communication got further grounds.

Friends of Jagadis would have frequent occasions to rejoice when news of national and international honors and awards coming to his way reached them every now and then. A few such notable recognitions are: The prestigious Alexander von Humboldt Fellowship Germany; Fellowships of Institute of Engineering and Technology and Institute of Mathematics and its Applications of UK; Fellowships of the National Academy of Sciences India, Indian National Academy of Engineering, New Delhi; Institute of Theoretical Physics, Calcutta. These fellowships from Institutes of international fame apart, Prof. Misra has been honoured with several academic awards from India and abroad. He has also received short-term and long-term invitations from many reputed foreign universities and research organizations as Visiting Fellows, where he has provided inspiring leadership in many large scale research projects. He has adorned many responsible positions in academic bodies. On many such occasions, I had the opportunity to congratulate him on getting the news; on a few others, however, I missed out owing to unforeseen causes. I remember, possibly in 2004, we felicitated Jagadis on behalf of his alma mater, Ramakrishna Mission Vidyamandira and its Alumni Association.

About 30 scholars have received Ph.D. under his able guidance in such areas as Applied Mathematics, Bio-Mathematics, Modelling and Simulation, Mechanics of Fluids and Solids and Physiological Fluid Dynamics. Prof. Misra has authored about 250 research papers in reputed journals, and has edited 14 technical books. These apart, he has written several important chapters in various scholarly compilations. Academic specialisations of Jagadis and myself are by and large non-overlapping, and as such, evaluations of the quality of his research work is not at all my cup of tea. However, he had once presented to me a complimentary copy of 'Mathematics and Mathematicians at IIT Kharagpur', edited by him. I found his commendable editorial ability and proficiency evident all over this informative volume.

I had ample opportunity to watch Jagadis from close quarters as a classmate, a co-resident of two hostels run by Ramakrishna Mission, and a good friend. A true gentleman, polite, always keeping a low profile and very soft spoken.

Self-assertion in any circumstances was always against his nature. Jagadis always used to keep himself hundred cubits away from all sorts of indoor and outdoor games, or events such as music, recitation, acting in theatre, public speaking, debate and the like. He listens a lot, but speaks very little, showing remarkable reverence for Shakespeare's oft-quoted dialogue 'Lend every man thy ears, but few thy voice'. Noticeably spiritually inclined, Jagadis got his initiation from revered Swami Shankarananda, the seventh President of the Ramakrishna Order, as early as in 1960. He was one among the very few lucky inmates like us who got the privilege of performing evening aratrikam at Vidyamandira shrine.

I conclude this sketchy write-up by praying to the Almighty for a long, healthy, peaceful and academically active life for our good friend Jagadis, enabling him to play a significant role in expanding the horizons of different branches of Mathematical Sciences, aimed at all-round development and well-being of mankind at large.

CHAPTER 26

Shaping Lives Touching Lives: The Profound Impact of Prof. J.C. Misra

Dr. Tapas Chatterjee
MBBS, MS, MCh, FRCS (SN)
Consultant Neurosurgeon, Kolkata, India

At the outset it gives me great pleasure and a sense of immense pride to say a few words about this extraordinary gentleman Dr. Jagadis Chandra Misra whom I have the privilege to call uncle (Meshomasai in Bengali). I am immensely fortunate to have known this impeccably perfect gentleman since 2006. He happens to be the father-in-law of my cousin sister. What has struck me from the very beginning about Dr. Misra is his humility. The mark of a true gentleman is his humility and Dr. Misra is a shining example in this regard. A man of Himalayan knowledge and immense fame within and out of the country and yet very simple, humble and down to earth are a combination of virtues found rarely nowadays. Dr. Misra has all these qualities and more. More so he is a lovely human being and a father figure to me. As an academician primarily in the field of Applied Mathematics he is second to none but what is less known to the outside world is that he is a perfect family man and the pillar in his family. I have been very fortunate to get his pearls of wisdom in social and family matters. He is a guiding force to not only his family but to fortunate people like me, always benefitting from his guidance and affection.

Dr. Jagadis Chandra Misra was born in 1943 during Durga Puja, in the small village of Bagmari in what is now East Midnapore. His education started from Tikrapara High School, then on to Ramakrishna Mission Vidyamandira, Belur Math then to Calcutta University, Jadavpur University and then to the Hanover Technical University in Germany. He has been a distinguished Professor and researcher in some of the most premier institutes of India for over 58 years including a distinguished career in the IIT for nearly 38 years. He has been invited to conferences to be a Keynote speaker in Germany, France, UK, USA, Canada, Austria, Japan, Nepal, Malaysia, Singapore and Bangladesh.

He has been appointed as advisor to many National and State Committees. He has also been elected to fellowships to various Indian and Foreign Institutes namely INAE, NASI, IET (UK), The Royal Society of Medicine, The Royal Society of Biology, The Royal Society of Public Health and the Institute of Mathematics and Application. He has also been felicitated by many awards, namely the Silver Jubilee Research award of IIT Kharagpur, *Ram Mohan Puraskar, Bharat Gaurav* Award (Glory of India), INAE Outstanding Teacher Award and the prestigious fellowship from Humboldt Foundation in Germany.

Coming to his research works, Dr. Misra's main research Interest is Physiological Fluid Dynamics and Biomedical Mathematics. Though Dr. Misra is a student of Applied Mathematics, through his genius he has been able to foster a bridge between Mathematics and the Biological sciences, primarily Medical Science. This part of his research, especially the part involving medical science has greatly attracted me as I am a doctor myself.

Dr. Misra has done seminal research in varied medical disciplines namely Cardiovascular Dynamics, Mechanics of Brain injury, Fracture and remodeling dynamics of Bone and mechanics of Fluids and Solids to name a few.

What has particularly mesmerized me is his groundbreaking research in Brain injury. Being a neurosurgeon myself I find his research on the biomechanics of Brain injury sheds new light to us neurosurgeons on the physics behind brain injuries helping us to understand brain injury in an entirely new perspective and help us treat the patients suffering from brain injury better. This way Dr. Misra has had an immense contribution to neuroscience.

To conclude no amount of praise will do justice to this great researcher, teacher and philosopher. Dr. Misra to me is a multifaceted genius. I pray to Almighty God that He grants Dr. Misra a long and healthy life ahead.

CHAPTER 27

Jagadis Chandra Misra: A Friend from the World of Mathematics

Dr. Dhiman Ganguly
MBBS, MD, MRCP (UK), FCCP (USA),
Professor, Department of Medicine,
Vivekananda Institute of Medical Sciences and Hon.Visiting Consultant,
Ramakrishna Mission Seva Pratishthan, Kolkata

It is a pleasure for me to write a few lines about my erstwhile classmate Jagadis. We studied together for a two-year long period in a residential institution, Ramakrishna Mission Vidyamandira, Belur Math. The days and events that I am trying to recollect are memories that are more than sixty years old, and more importantly, Jagadis was one of the thirty or forty odd classmates of mine at the Vidyamandira, who appeared to be from another planet to a very unworthy student like myself at the institution. I looked at them with a great deal of awe and respect. Moreover, Jagadis, in addition to his academic achievements was spiritually inclined, kept a close association with a number of senior monastic members of our faculty including Principal Maharaj Swami Tejasanandaji, and maintained a low profile self-effacing personality. I believe he, in spite of his spectacular success as a teacher, path breaking research worker and mentor for dozens of brilliant mathematicians spread all over the world, is the same quiet polite Jagadis we knew sixty five years ago.

He decided to stay back at the Vidyamandira, even though that meant a loss of one academic year for his graduation. Ordinarily, no student would think of taking such a step. This again goes to show that his thought process worked differently from the rest of us, even in those early days of our lives. What gives me great satisfaction is to see the recognition and adulation he received from our country and abroad, throughout his life. He richly deserved all of them. Moreover, he and his wife succeeded in raising a family with exceptional quality to build up a legacy in his family, just as he did in his capacity as a teacher in world class institutions in India and abroad. This is rarely seen in the lives of people with high academic achievements, as they find it difficult to balance their family and professional lives.

I hope and pray that he remains in good health, for we badly need such examples as a source of inspiration for coming generations.

CHAPTER 28

Our Friend Jagadis

Prof. Nitya Niranjan Kundu
Formerly, Head of the Department of History,
Ramakrishna Mission Vidyamandira, Belur Math, Howrah

I feel very much honored to write something about Jagadis, who was my classmate in the Ramakrishna Mission Vidyamandira, an intermediate College offering some arts and science subjects for two years only. It was 1959, a story from 66 years back.

I was an Arts student while Jagadis belonged to the science stream. There were about 110 students in the first year. The common subjects of the arts and science students were English, Bengali, and religious subjects. So both Jagadis and myself had little opportunity to come closer and hence much intimacy could not develop between us at the initial phase.

It was revered Govinda Maharaj (Swami Gokulananda, after being ordained into Sannyas Diksha) our superintendent who acted as an instrument in developing intimacy between us. In my opinion Govinda Maharaj who was a very good and successful teacher in logic and who could inspire students according to their merit and *Sanskara,* had three groups of students, who were fortunate to come in close contact with him. The first group consisted of prospective position holders in the final examination. The second group included those who were religious minded, god-fearing and sober. The third group belonged to those who were interested in extracurricular activities like debate, drawing, games and sports. Jagadis and myself belonged to the second group. Incidentally Biswanath (Dr. Biswanath Das), my lifelong friend, belonged to both the first and second groups.

Those of us who belonged to the second group had to perform various shrine related activities, like washing utensils, which were used for daily Puja, plucking of flowers, cleaning and sweeping the barricaded area of worship during the time of evening prayer. Jagadis, Biswanath, Nipak (Chaklanavis), Sabyasachi

(Ghosh) and myself used to perform Aratrikam of Sri Sri Thakur, Holy mother and Swamiji in turn. It was a very good team work for months together. It was during this time some intimacy developed between Jagadis and myself.

During our stay at the Vidyamandira, a memorable event took place. The initiative was taken by revered Govinda Maharaj. He took some of us, including Jagadis, to the ancestral house of Swami Vivekananda. It was a dilapidated building. Our mission was to see and offer our pranam to Sri Bhupendra Nath Datta, the youngest brother of Swami Vivekananda. We did not have the opportunity of seeing Swami Vivekananda, but after meeting his ailing youngest brother, who was then about 80 definitely could have a glimpse of what Swamiji was. When we entered his room, he was found lying in his bed, but while talking to us, he slowly became steady, sat on his bed and delivered an intoxicating speech, which was full of spirit and vigour. We are really indebted to our Govinda Maharaj for this.

We passed the I.A./I.Sc. examination in 1961 and left the Vidyamandira for higher studies. Jagadis and two others (Kamlesh Bhowmik and Nimai Datta) stayed back in the Vidyamandira to pursue their studies in the three-year degree course.

Jagadis came to Calcutta Students Home in 1964 for doing his M.Sc. in Applied Mathematics at Calcutta University. So after passing out from the Vidyamandira in 1961 Jagadis and myself had the opportunity to meet each other only on the occasion of reunion of ex-students.

In 2001, I remember, he along with his wife came to our house in Belur one evening and stayed overnight with us.

Jagadis has always been a humble, sober and soft-speaking gentleman, and has a religious bent of mind. When he was a first year student in the Vidyamandira, he used to go to late Ajapananda Maharaj (Purna Maharaj) with whom he was familiar beforehand. Purna Maharaj was then in charge of the store and kitchen at Belur Math. Sometimes I used to accompany Jagadis to Purna Maharaj through whom he came in close contact with other senior monks of Belur Math. One such very senior monk was Swami Shantananda who along with *Jiten Maharaj* (Swami Vishuddhananda—my *Gurudeva*) was initiated by Sri Sri Holy mother Sarada Devi. Jagadis himself was initiated by the President Maharaj Swami Shankarananda Ji in 1960 when he was merely a first year student of intermediate science (I.Sc) in the Vidyamandira.

Years rolled on. Our subjects were different. He did his higher studies in Applied Mathematics, while my subject was History. He spent most of his service life at IIT Kharagpur and I spent the whole of my service life at our Alma-mater Ramakrishna Mission Vidyamandira. Recently, one evening I got a very pleasant information about Jagadis from Shibu (Shibabrata Bagchi, another Vidyamandira friend of mine), that Jagadis figures in the list of top 2% scientists in the world for six consecutive years from 2020 to 2025 according to studies conducted by a team of scientists at Stanford University, USA. The list is based on the assessment of scientists from across the globe for the research carried out during their career span. It was indeed an outstanding achievement of Jagadis.

Apart from this, Jagadis has been accorded various National and International awards, recognitions and fellowships.

Jagadis was a visiting professor at many prestigious universities all over the world. He has to his credit around 250 research papers published in reputed international journals and guided 30 Ph.D. students. The number of books published by him is 14. All this may well suggest forming "J.C. Misra School of Mathematics in the academic world of India".

Glorious achievements of Jagadis have prompted me to know something about his parents. From his autobiography it is known that his father late Ganes Chandra Misra, former teacher of Tikrapara Higher Secondary School and President of Union Board was a noble and kind hearted person, who used to keep poor and meritorious students in his house and help them pursue their studies.

An epitome of truthfulness, late Pramila Devi, mother of Jagadis was a very simple, pious and god-fearing lady. Although she did not have much formal education, I must say she was a learned lady in reality. Quite often she used to recite,

> *"Calling yourself great is not great,*
> *Whom people call great is really great.*
> *................................"*

I believe this encouraging recitation worked well among her children.

She was never sitting idle, but used to always remain busy with different activities.

This reminds me of an important advice of Sri Sri Holy Mother Sarada Devi.

It is good to remain busy all the time. By remaining active, one can stay healthy both physically and mentally. One should not remain idle even for a single moment.

Jagadis is very much fortunate to have an auspicious heritage, which helped him a lot to ride the ladder of fame and fortune step by step.

I shall conclude with a salutation to the district of Midnapore (undivided), which is one of the advanced districts of West Bengal. This district has given birth to many renowned persons, like Ishwar Chandra Vidyasagar—a very bright star of Bengali Renaissance, Khudiram Bose who sacrificed his life to martyrdom, Matangini Hazra (known as Gandhiburi) who sacrificed her life for Indian freedom movement in August 1942 and Deshapran Birendranath Sasmal, another brave freedom fighter. Coming to the recent past, we find Dr. Amalesh Tripathi, a renowned historian of modern India. There are several others, who are still alive and have made a mark in the Society.

To conclude I must admit that our friend Jagadis may well boast of being the most brilliant and bright 'bhumiputra' (son of the soil) of the district of Midnapore.

I pray to the Holy Trio—Sri Sri Thakur, Holy Mother Sarada Devi and Swamiji for granting him a long healthy life, so that he can continue his service to the society in the field of scientific research.

CHAPTER 29

Bow Down in Reverence

Srabani Sengupta
Recipient of President's Award,
Headmistress, Belgharia Mahakali H.S. School (Retd.), Kolkata

Not very long ago, only in the first week of September, 2024 I visited, as I often do, Ramakrishna Mission Calcutta Vidyarthi Ashrama at Belgharia where I had my spiritual initiation into the Ramakrishna Mission cult.

I entered into the Prayer Hall, sat before the deities, prayed and then went to the office room to pay my regards to the Secretary and other monks. Govinda, as usual, served Prasad, tea and snacks and informed that the Secretary Maharaj had just left for some work. I felt a bit depressed at this news and was looking at the photographs of Sri Ramakrishna, Ma Sarada, Swamiji and other Sannyasins of the Mission of the past.

I found one aged gentleman who entered the room with some books and a note book in his hand and had taken his seat. His very calm and tranquil appearance gave me a feeling of fulfillment and I thought to have been blessed by Sri Sri Thakur and Maa. The gentleman had a very tender, satisfying look and I felt that I was in the company of my own elder brother. A simple introduction with Sri Jagadis Chandra Misra and a talk with him gave me an insight into his genius and multi-faceted contribution in the preachings of Sri Ramakrishna and in the sphere of education in general.

He gave me two books written in Bengali—one authored by himself in the form of an autobiography, and the other a collection of articles on him by various authors. I was just glancing over the second book and could understand the depth and magnitude of the person talked about in it. Both the books have been my regular reading companions since then.

I was informed that English versions of the books were proposed to be published. I thought of paying my tribute to him in the English version which had prompted me to write the present article. I was also aware that I was too small to have dared to write about such a colossal personality and could do little justice to measure his magnitude. I pray to be excused for my limitations. Time passed by fast in discussion with Sri Misra and his equally erudite wife, Ms. Shorasi Misra and partner in his successful life. Shorasi was one year junior to me in college, though in different subjects.

Sri Jagadis Chandra Misra had a major breakthrough in 1959 when he entered Ramakrishna Mission Vidyamandira at Belur Math and completed I.Sc. (1961) and B.Sc. (1964). This 5-year period from 1959 to 1964 at the Vidyamandira had a great impact on building the basics of his life. The affection and care in maintaining discipline in life and health build up that were taught and practised by the monks at Vidyamandira made him an ideal human being in later life.

He was initiated by the then seventh President o f Belur Math, Srimat Swami Shankarananda Maharaj in the year 1960. During his M.Sc. at Calcutta University, he was permitted as a special case to stay at the Vidyarthi Ashram at Belgharia (1964–66). He was very much liked by all the monks and co-Ashramite seniors and juniors alike.

His idea about education was built up on the basics of moral teachings and lessons incorporated in the Indian epics, the Bhagavad Gita and the Upanishads. He believed that true education is realization into the inner self that leads to inquisitiveness that delves further into research on the subject. He also thought that the qualities of life, discipline, sincerity, compassion, patience and perseverance, integrity of character, self-confidence, purity, love and affection—all together go into making a cultured mind which is the essence of education. He had practised all these in his life that earned him first ever Outstanding Teacher Award 2013 from the Indian National Academy of Engineering, New Delhi. This had prompted the then President of Belur Math, Swami Atmathasnanda Maharaj to send a personal letter of appreciation and expressed deep satisfaction at the achievement of "our Jagadis".

Despite being a high profile scholastic genius with world wide fame, as an individual he is down-to-earth with affection and compassion for all his students and research scholars. He is soft spoken and always amiable and easily accessible even at home to his students.

He had always encouraged his students to bring out the best from them. He used to make the usually sombre atmosphere in the interview Board of Ph.D. aspirants very congenial to enable the candidates to feel at ease. As a teacher he is like the family guardian of his students. Being aware of the family constraints of his students, he has helped them to find out ways to come out of the same. In this respect he did not think twice to give financial support also. Many of his research scholars who were/are well placed in their own fields later remember with gratitude his support in times of their need.

I had the privilege of some common acquaintance with Sri Jagadis Chandra Misra.

Dr. Subhas Chandra Samanta and Prof. Tarapada Mandal were my teachers at Midnapore College. Dr. Samanta did his Ph.D. under the guidance Sri Misra and Prof. Mandal was his classmate.

Sri Ashok Bhowmick is ex-Headmaster of Sodepur High School. He is like my elder brother and was a class mate of Sri Misra. I could, from time to time, gather stories from them that made me believe how great Sri Jagadis Chandra Misra was as an individual.

In his personal life he seems to be very content, with all his children being highly educated and well placed.He continues to stay at the IIT Campus Kharagpur with his wife, sons and grandchildren.

I wish them all a long life with good health and peace of mind.

I bow my head to Prof. Dr. Jagadis Chandra Misra in great reverence; and I consider myself fortunate enough that I got a chance to pay my tribute to him.

CHAPTER 30

My Elder Brother

Dr. Subhash Chandra Mahapatra
Retired Professor, Department of Rural Development, IIT Kharagpur
Current Residence: Sumangalam, Gonara, Manglamaro, Purba Medinipur

One evening, as I returned home, my father handed me a freshly opened brown envelope marked "On India Government Service." He said,

"This is the appointment letter for the job interview you attended at IIT Kharagpur a few days ago."

I joined IIT Kharagpur as a technical assistant at the Agricultural Engineering Department in 1975.

In March, 1980 my parents sent an urgent message, asking me to visit a prospective bride's family before the Bengali month of Chaitra started. I learned that the bride's family had an esteemed son-in-law who was a professor at IIT Kharagpur. I wondered if this was the same Ganes Babu's son my father had mentioned years ago.

One afternoon, after returning from work at around 4:30 pm, I lay down to rest. As I glanced out the window, I noticed a distinguished-looking man. He had a serene, radiant face, simple attire, curly black hair, thick eyebrows, and large, expressive eyes. He was well-built and rode an old bicycle. He parked it under a banyan tree and looked around as if searching for someone's house.

Since I lived alone, I instinctively got up, opened the small gate, and greeted him. At first sight, I was captivated. *Who was this remarkably striking man?*

Regaining my composure, I asked, *"Are you looking for someone?" "Yes. Is this where Subhash Mahapatra lives?"*

"Yes, that's me. Please, come in!"

Since I was a bachelor, my quarters were sparsely furnished. There was a jute-rope swing, which was hanging on my tiled veranda.

The visitor's eyes fell on it. Without hesitation, he took it down and sat on it comfortably, as if he belonged there.

His warmth struck me. *How could someone become so familiar within minutes?*

Sitting on the swing, he introduced himself:

> *"I am Jagadis Misra."*

Then he said in a gentle, unpretentious tone:

> *"A few days ago, you visited a house in Amarpur to meet a prospective bride. That house belongs to my in-laws, and the girl you met is my wife's younger sister."*

Stunned, I asked, *"Wait, when I first joined IIT, my father mentioned the name, Ganes Babu from Bagmari..."*

He interrupted with a smile, *"Yes, that's my father."*

For nearly five years, this question had lingered in my mind, and now, I finally had the answer. Overcome with gratitude, I bent down to touch his feet, but he quickly stopped me, embracing me warmly instead.

Then, he gestured toward a nearby plastic stool (seat) and invited me to sit beside him.

As our conversation unfolded, he spoke extensively about his in-laws' family in Amarpur and his sister-in-law's virtues. We also discussed many aspects of our own families.

Being accustomed to making my own tea, I offered him some, and he readily accepted. However, I realized that apart from some chanachur (savory mix) and Britannia biscuits, I had nothing to serve.

But Jagadis Misra has always been a man of great humility. He made the entire experience feel effortless, his face radiating kindness, making me feel completely at ease. In those days at IIT, there was always a subtle distinction between faculty, staff, and non-teaching employees. At that time, I was a non-teaching staff member, working as a technical assistant. Naturally, I felt quite hesitant to speak with professors. However, in this particular case, I encountered no such difficulties. He was one of the most humble, down-to-earth, and unpretentious individuals I had ever met. From that moment, I developed great respect for him.

As the evening approached, he warmly invited me to his quarters, providing directions before bidding me farewell. He then rode his bicycle, which had been resting against a banyan tree, and started pedaling away, pushing it forward with both hands. I walked a short distance with him, and as he rode off, he called out to me multiple times with such sincerity that it was indescribable. It felt as though he was a close family member. I watched as his bicycle slowly disappeared beyond my residence onto the long road. Returning home, I felt as if I had been in a trance. It took me quite a while to comprehend how, in just one meeting, I had developed such a deep sense of connection with such a remarkable person.

On May 1st, a holiday, IIT was hosting a May Day event at 7 PM. In the afternoon, following his directions, I searched for and found Quarter No. C1-63. A few days earlier, I had moved from my previous quarters to the main IIT campus, and this house was not far from mine. I opened the gate and stepped in. Seeing me from a distance, he personally opened the door and welcomed me onto the veranda.

It was the beginning of May, an unbearably hot afternoon in Kharagpur. He was dressed in a dhoti, uniquely draped with the front fold wrapped from the waist to the knees. He wore a simple cotton Hawaiian shirt and was barefoot. He looked extraordinary. Inviting me inside, I stepped into a modest living room devoid of any fancy furniture. The furniture reflected his simplicity, with no hint of extravagance—everything was ordinary and natural.

He introduced me to his wife. As the saying goes, "Like god, like goddess." Yes, she was truly a goddess. Fair-skinned, petite, with a well-proportioned figure, and a bright red sindoor dot on her forehead that made her face glow even more. Clad in a plain, everyday sari, she looked absolutely graceful. At first sight, she evoked in me a deep sense of motherly/sisterly warmth. Her face radiated affection and kindness. Later, when I got married, she embraced me as her own brother from the very first day, showering me with boundless love and support—a bond that remains unbroken to this day and will continue forever.

Both of them sat with me and eagerly listened as I spoke about my family—my parents, elder brothers, sisters-in-law, and siblings. They, in turn, shared stories about their family and my future in-laws, including, of course, my future wife. At that time, only three people lived in their house—him, his wife, and their youngest son, Sudip, who was in nursery school. Their elder son, Subhas, and daughter Sumita (Krishna), stayed in their ancestral home in Bagmari with their grandparents. Their grandfather, Ganes Chandra Misra, was known for his expertise in laying a strong foundation of education at the primary level, and this is why the children lived there. A year later, after completing primary school, the children moved permanently to IIT with their grandparents.

After sharing tea along with a plate of sweets and fruits, our first meeting concluded, and I took my leave. I could not stay for dinner, using the May Day event as an excuse.

Within two months, in July, I got married, and from then on, our bond deepened to the extent that our two families became nearly one. Mutual dependence and cooperation grew stronger over time. Professor Jagadis Chandra Misra became simply "Dada" (elder brother) to me—my local guardian. His wife, Shrimati Shorasi Misra, became just "Didi" (elder sister).

Over time, the family expanded. The extended family included revered uncle (Ganes Chandra Misra), aunt (Pramila Devi), beloved younger brother Kanu (Parames), nephews and nieces Subhash (Nupur), Sumita (Krishna), Sudip (Jhumur), my wife Namita, our son Soumyadeep (Suman), and later, many more members. Kanu married Kanika, and they had two daughters. Sumita married Achintya (Runtu), and they had a daughter, Supurna (Tuktuki). Subhas married Sulagna, and they had a daughter Devarati (Tul Tuli), and a son, Devapratim (Govinda). Sudip married Satamita, and they had a son, Devadeep (Gopal), and a daughter, Devadrita (Phul). Though we lived in two separate quarters, there was never any emotional distance between us. We frequently exchanged meals, and within months of my marriage, my grandmother-in-law (Namita's grandmother) moved into our home due to illness. As a result, my uncle, brother, and sister-in-law visited frequently, making it a regular part of our lives.

One of the most remarkable aspects of this family was its unwavering commitment to higher education. No sacrifices were considered too great for the pursuit of knowledge. Compromises were never made. As a result, every son, daughter, brother, and son-in-law became highly educated and secured prestigious positions in academia. Dada (Jagadis Chandra) himself was an institution—a recipient of the highest academic honor, D.Sc., along with numerous national and international awards. His career spanned from school teaching to college professorship and eventually to university-level academia, culminating in his tenure as Pro-Vice-Chancellor. In the field of research, particularly in Mathematics, he was among the top ten mathematicians in the country and ranked among the top 2% of scientists globally (as per the List published by Stanford University, USA). I pray that the Government of India recognizes his contributions by bestowing upon him the prestigious 'Padma' award.

Even after four decades, despite occasional physical distance, there was never any emotional separation. While living on the IIT campus, he would go for morning walks daily, softly reciting verses from the twelfth chapter of the Bhagavad Gita, the Argala Stotra and Stavas (Praising the Goddess) from Sri Sri Chandi, or hymns in praise of Sri Ramakrishna. His walks always ended with a brief visit to our house. He would greet me affectionately, "How are you, Subhash Chandra?" before resting on the sofa for a short while. Then he would call out, "Namita Rani, your sister has instructed that my blood pressure be checked." He would obediently roll up his sleeve and sit quietly while Namita checked his B.P. Despite his slightly heavy build, he remained remarkably healthy throughout his life.

When the two of us were together, I often did most of the talking. He was a man of few words, preferring to listen rather than to speak. His responses were minimal—an occasional "hmm" or a softly spoken remark only when necessary. His composed and wise demeanor was reminiscent of the ideal 'sthita-prajna' described in the Bhagavad Gita—a rare quality. Through all seasons, be it cold, heat, or rain, he remained indifferent to external discomforts. His attire was minimal—one set of simple clothes sufficed, and he rarely used an umbrella. His profound inner vision left little concern for transient worldly matters.

Over four decades, I have observed his humble interactions with people from all walks of life—janitors, clerks, mechanics, officers, professors, and even IIT's highest-ranking officials. His wife, my 'Didi,' played a significant role in this. He treated all students like his own children, embodying the qualities of an ideal teacher.

As an elder son-in-law in our extended family, he took on numerous responsibilities selflessly. My late father-in-law, Pandit Phanibhushan Nanda, once proudly remarked that our family had its own 'Jagadis Chandra' and 'Subhash Chandra,' suggesting we had nothing to worry about. While I may not be worthy of such a mention, my brother-in-law, Jagadis Chandra Misra, certainly lived up to his name—worthy of comparison to the great scientist Acharya Jagadish Chandra Bose. A truly exceptional individual, and I am blessed to have had his guidance for over forty years. I pray to God for his long, healthy, and fulfilling life.

CHAPTER 31

'A Traveller in an Unknown Land' by Prof. J.C. Misra: Some Observations

Prof. G.P. Bhattacharjee
Professor and Head (1995–1998), Mathematics Department,
IIT Kharagpur (Currently in USA)

I am overwhelmed after reading the story of the unknown journey of the familiar Traveller in an Unknown Land, as narrated in his Autobiography with the above-mentioned title (Allied Publishers Pvt. Limited, Noida, 2025).

Undoubtedly it is highly fascinating and enchanting. I felt as if it were a fairy tale.

The traveller's first step was the moment he broke free from the boundaries of his daily life. Leaving behind familiar surroundings, he ventured onto unknown paths in search of new experiences and mysteries. His courage and self-confidence in this moment were truly remarkable.

As he continued his journey, he met various unfamiliar people along the way. Their lives and experiences were entirely different. Gaining new knowledge from them, learning different perspectives on life—all of this enriched him.

At times, the nature of the path through the unknown land was unknown to everybody and full of wonder. On this path, the traveller would lose the sense of time. The allure of discovering something new, the feeling of stepping beyond the known world along the way, deeply influenced his imagination.

Thus emerged a world-renowned mathematician. His creations and theories were revolutionary. Such stories will undoubtedly inspire future generations to venture into unknown paths with great joy.

CHAPTER 32

Prof. J.C. Misra—My Former Colleague

Dr. Sudarsan Nanda
Former Professor and Head, Department of Mathematics, IIT Kharagpur, & Former Vice-Chancellor, North Orissa University, Baripada, Odisha

On August 1, 1980, I joined the Department of Mathematics at IIT Kharagpur as an Assistant Professor. After completing the joining formalities in the Recruitment and Establishment Section, I headed to the Department of Mathematics, where the first person I met was Prof. J.C. Misra, then a senior Assistant Professor. That meeting marked the beginning of a long and rewarding professional relationship. Later, we became neighbors on campus and soon developed a close family friendship.

From the outset, I found Prof. Misra to be an exceptionally brilliant academician—an outstanding researcher, deeply committed, and incredibly hardworking. While his initial research focus was in solid mechanics, he pioneered several new areas in our department, including biomathematics, mathematical modeling and simulation, and physiological fluid dynamics. He was awarded the D.Sc. degree by the University of Calcutta and later served as a Visiting Professor at many prestigious universities across the globe—Germany, in particular, became like a second home to him. He travelled extensively and delivered lectures at leading institutions worldwide. His work has been widely cited by reputed researchers.

Prof. Misra has received numerous awards, fellowships, and recognitions—far too many to list in full. A few noteworthy honors include:

- Recognized among the Top 2% of Scientists in the World, according to a Stanford University study for six consecutive years from 2020 to 2025.
- Fellow of the Royal Society of Public Health, London (2019).
- Fellow of the Royal Society of Biology, London (2020).
- Fellow of the Institution of Engineering and Technology (IET), UK (2019).

- Fellow of the Indian National Academy of Engineering (INAE) (2000).
- Fellow of the National Academy of Sciences, India (1987).
- Fellow of the Institute of Mathematics and its Applications, UK (1988).
- Fellow of the Institute of Theoretical Physics, Kolkata.
- Fellow of the West Bengal Academy of Science and Technology (2025).

Among the many awards he has received are:

- INAE Outstanding Teacher Award, 2013.
- Ram Mohan Puraskar, 2004.
- Silver Jubilee Research Award, IIT Kharagpur, 1984.
- Dr. A.P.J. Abdul Kalam Award, 2017.
- EET CRS Award for Excellence.
- Lifetime Achievement Award, 2015.
- Rashtriya Gaurav Award, 2004.
- Alexander von Humboldt Fellowship, Germany, 1975.
- Platinum Jubilee Lecture, Indian Science Congress, 2005.

He has also been an active member of several prestigious scientific bodies, including:

- New York Academy of Sciences.
- Biomedical Engineering Society, USA.
- International Society of Biorheology, New York.

Prof. Misra has published over 250 research papers in reputed journals, guided 30 Ph.D. scholars, and published 14 books.

He served as the Head of the Department of Mathematics at IIT Kharagpur from 1998 to 2001. During his tenure, he revitalized the department by organizing numerous national and international conferences and seminars, breaking a long dry spell. Many of these events led to high-quality publications of the proceedings through renowned publishers. I had the privilege of succeeding him as Head of the Department from 2001 to 2004.

After my tenure, I took leave from the Institute for three years to serve as the Vice-Chancellor of North Orissa University in Baripada. During my absence, Prof. Misra retired from IIT Kharagpur. Following his retirement, he was appointed Pro-Vice-Chancellor of SOA (Deemed to be) University in Bhubaneswar.

His younger son is currently a Professor in the Department of Computer Science and Engineering at IIT Kharagpur. This allows Prof. Misra and his wife to continue residing on campus. After my own retirement, I moved to Bhubaneswar, and we've had the opportunity to meet on several occasions.

Even after retiring from SOA University, Prof. Misra remains active in academia and continues to stay on the IIT Kharagpur campus with his family. Whether at the department or at home, he has always immersed himself in research and academic activities—often engaged with his Ph.D. students or his children. His unwavering commitment to education and research has clearly inspired both of his sons to become distinguished professors and researchers—one at IIT Kharagpur and the other at IIT Kanpur.

Even at this stage of life, Prof. Misra remains actively associated with many institutions, including IIEST Shibpur, Howrah.

I pray to God for his continued health, happiness, and an active life so that he may keep contributing to the scientific community for many more years to come.

CHAPTER 33

A Conversation with a World-Renowned Mathematician

Dr. Haripada Maity
Former Principal, Mugberia Gangadhar Mahavidyalaya
Mugberia, Purba Medinipur

Around seven years ago, a remarkable event took place at the IIT Kharagpur campus. At the residence of my son-in-law, Dr. Shantanu Dhara, I had the privilege of meeting esteemed Dr. Jagadis Chandra Misra. Shantanu introduced me to him, mentioning that Dr. Misra hailed from the Patashpur police station area in Medinipur.

Dr. Misra is not only a distinguished mathematician at IIT Kharagpur but also associated with the Indian Institute of Engineering Science and Technology at Shibpur and the SOA University at Bhubaneswar, Odisha. Additionally, he has served as a visiting professor, delivering lectures at various institutions in the USA, UK, Germany, Canada, Belgium, Singapore, Nepal, Malaysia, Bangladesh, and some other countries. His significant research contributions include numerous collaborative papers with scientists from around the world.

Recently, I came across a noteworthy piece of information:

> *"Prof. J.C. Misra has been listed among the top 2% scientists in the world for the past six consecutive years (2020, 2021, 2022, 2023, 2024 and 2025), according to a study conducted by a team of scientists at Stanford University, USA, led by Prof. John P.A. Ioannidis. The list evaluates scientists globally based on the impact of their lifetime research."*

Although I am not a student of science—having pursued humanities and written books primarily on history, society, and national issues—I humbly proposed that Dr. Misra write his autobiography.

I then requested a discussion on his life experiences, society, and the era he lived in. He agreed. The following conversation, drawn from my recollections, took place in an informal setting.

On the Importance of Education

"Education is not just the backbone of an individual or a nation but also the foundation for global progress."

At home, parents and relatives, along with teachers at school, help students grasp the knowledge embedded in books. This is the first stage. Next comes deeper contemplation and comprehension, followed by critical thinking and judgment. Ultimately, education finds its true fulfillment when it is expressed through one's character, conduct, and practice.

Proper education sparks a curiosity for the unknown. It fosters independent thinking, creativity, and originality, inspiring innovation and discovery. Those who receive such an education become valuable human resources. Their sense of moral and social responsibility, coupled with integrity, progressive knowledge, and dedication to the welfare of others, contributes to both national and global advancement.

On Culture

"Culture is the essence of true education."

Just as pure milk produces a rich layer of cream, a well-rounded education cultivates cultural awareness. It nurtures an open mind, broad perspectives, and profound human values such as self-restraint, discipline, purity, patience, honesty, generosity, sincerity, self-confidence, self-respect, self-reliance, and inner strength. It fosters good taste, an appreciation of beauty, and, most importantly, a spirit of unity.

A healthy culture acts as a thread that weaves people together, much like a needle stitching fabric. In contrast, an unhealthy or degenerate culture acts like scissors, cutting and dividing. A pair of scissors can tear even the most exquisite cloth into pieces—just as divisiveness, disorder, dishonesty, and intolerance can harm society.

In the 19th century, particularly in Bengal, the fusion of Eastern and Western education and cultural influences led to a great intellectual awakening, ushering in modernity. This movement left a lasting impact on literature, education, music, arts, religion, and philosophy, fostering visionary creativity and progress.

Breaking free from rigid traditionalism, this awakening ignited the pursuit of reason and enlightenment. The 20th-century Indian independence movement against British rule was a direct result of this intellectual and cultural resurgence.

The culmination of this struggle was India's long-awaited independence on August 15, 1947, after nearly two centuries of colonial rule.

Thus, the importance of education rooted in wisdom and culture steeped in creativity cannot be overstated. Their absence leads to moral and societal decline.

On His Early Life in Patashpur

Dr. Misra shared:

> *"I was born in Bagmari village under the police station of Patashpur, on October 7, 1943. My father, Ganes Chandra, was a teacher of Tikrapara Higher Secondary School and my mother, Pramila Devi was a home maker. There was some engagement with Sanskrit literature and scriptures. My grand father, Girish Chandra was a renowned Sanskrit scholar.*

My early education began at Majna Primary School in Pratapdighi, followed by Tikarapara Ambikamoyi High School, and later at the Ramakrishna Mission Vidyamandira at Belur Math. Back then, roads were unpaved, and during the monsoons, they became nearly impassable with mud and waterlogging. Often, people had to roll up their pants or even wear only a towel to wade through the knee-deep mud. If somebody slipped and fell, he had no choice but to return home.

Markets were far apart—unlike today, where shops are at every street corner. There were only two market days a week, and if guests arrived unexpectedly, households often faced difficulties in offering proper hospitality. But this was not just the case in Pataspur or Bhagabanpur; it was the reality across the rural Bengal.

The Legacy of Patashpur

Despite its hardships, Patashpur boasts a rich legacy.

In 1864, Madhusudan Roy, the first graduate from Medinipur district, hailed from Balyagobindpur in Patashpur—a matter of immense pride for its residents.

Moreover, Patashpur was home to culturally rich zamindar families, such as the Das Mahapatra family of Panchetgarh, known for their philanthropy and contributions to education. In 1901, they established the second high school in the Contai subdivision. This family also played a pivotal role in promoting classical music, hosting renowned musicians from Bengal, Bihar, and Odisha.

The Raas festival initiated by this family is not only a cherished tradition of Patashpur but a cultural beacon for the entire region.

Patashpur in the Freedom Movement

Patashpur played an active role in India's fight for independence.

During the Non-Cooperation Movement (1920–22) under the leadership of Deshpran Birendranath Sasmal, the people of Patashpur protested against the Union Board system. Even earlier, during the 1905 anti-Partition movement, the revolutionary Khudiram Bose established a base at Pania Sardabarh of Patashpur P.S., alongside Dhruvanarayan Tripathi of Pratapdighi.

Women also played a vital role in the 1930 Salt Satyagraha, with Saraswati Mishra from Jabda village being a prominent leader. On June 1, 1930, in Pratapdighi, three freedom fighters—Ramkrishna Das, Kartik Chandra Mishra, and Upendranath Mishra—were martyred by British police gunfire.

In 1932, during the second phase of the Civil Disobedience Movement, Sukhada Moyee Roy Choudhury of Balyagobindpur openly defied British orders, holding a public meeting in defiance of Section 144. She was later imprisoned for six months.

Finally, on September 29, 1942, under Kalipada Roy Mahapatra's leadership, the people of Patashpur seized control of the local police station—an extraordinary act of defiance against British rule.

Not only that, but the Patashpur police station was established and operated by the national government for a period of three months—from October 1942 to December—under the leadership of Kalipada Babu.

How did you come to know such historical events about the freedom struggle?

In response, he said—"One must keep their feet firmly on the ground while gazing at the sky. There is joy, peace, contentment, and tranquility in settling elsewhere, while keeping one's birthplace in mind." These informations are available in the following books.

(i) Patashpur in the freedom struggle—Prasanna Kumar Tripathi, Shyamacharan Bera, and Radhanath Das Adhikari, (ii) Patashpur's past and present—Manmathanath Das, and (iii) the freedom struggle in Medinipur—Basanta Kumar Das, Dr. Rasbihari Pal, and Professor Haripada Maity.

Now, a different discussion—personal and familial

The realization of Purushottam Anukulchandra: "As you sow, so shall you reap." You have two sons—affectionate Subhas and Sudip, and one daughter—Sumita. They are accomplished in their studies. They are faculty members at IIT Kanpur, IIT Kharapur and the Indian Institute of Engineering Science and Technology, Shibpur. I congratulate you and Shorasi Devi for the success of your children."

Another question: You could have brought in a highly educated, employed daughters-in-law, but you chose not to.

He replied, "Each daughter-in-law is a master degree holder. But they did not want to do any job outside the home. They opted to be home makers and to take care of the children."

In this context, I notice some character traits of Brahmins, like selflessness.

The real truth is this—being content with little leads to much happiness and peace. Excessive desire, attachment, and greed often lead to turmoil. The Bhagavad Gita warns us about this, especially in verse 16.21:

"Lust (Desire), anger, and greed, are the three gates to hell, leading the soul to destruction. Therefore, one should abandon them, for they are the root causes of downfall."

The current situation in our country and the world is undoubtedly critical. What are your thoughts on this?

He reflected as follows:

Shri Krishna, Buddha, Shri Chaitanya, Shri Ramakrishna, Swami Vivekananda, and Rishi Aurobindo were great spiritual leaders in India. Along with them, there were great political leaders like Mahatma Gandhi, Deshbandhu Chittaranjan, Deshpran Birendranath Shasmal, Sardar Vallabhbhai Patel, Bal Gangadhar Tilak, and Subhas Chandra Bose, and notable humanitarians like Raja Ram Mohan Roy, Ishwar Chandra Vidyasagar, and Rabindranath Tagore.

Did we adopt their ideals of patriotism, sacrifice, moderation, tolerance, generosity, honesty, and selfless service? No, we haven't.

Rabindranath Tagore's view on humanity: "Education without character, science without humanity, and commerce without morality are useless and dangerous. The crown and glory of life is character."

Currently, capitalism has expanded extensively, leading to economic exploitation, oppression, and widespread suffering. This system fosters greed, anger, and violence, as seen in the destructive power of nuclear bombs during World War II, particularly the bombings of Hiroshima and Nagasaki. Along with this, environmental pollution is at an all-time high. Humanity is now at critical crossroads, and if we are not careful, inevitable destruction is on the horizon.

Albert Einstein's famous warning comes to mind:

"Science without religion is lame. Religion without science is blind."

Therefore, the harmonious integration of science and religion, economics and culture, personal interest and societal welfare is essential for a healthy, prosperous world.

Now, coming to India—Do we have any hope for improvement amid the current decline?

He noted the significant influence of the Akhanda Mandaleswar Swami Swarupananda, in the Patashpur region. He said, once he had the fortune of listening to Swami Swarupananda's lecture at a religious gathering in Pratapdighi. According to the Swami,

"India will rise again,
It will awaken again, for sure.
In this brief moment of downfall, My heart is not afraid.
I know that through complete celibacy, India will regain its lost gem.
It will regain its thunderous might, Its deeds, its glorious spirit.
From the current womb of suffering, It will give birth to a future of freedom,
A pure, great, vast world to behold."

I also recall Swami Vivekananda's prophetic words: "The socialist revolution will not happen in England or Germany, but in Russia and China." Regarding India's future, he said, "India will rise again, not with the strength of matter, but with the strength of consciousness (spirituality). It will carry the flag of peace and love, not the flag of destruction and victory."

Furthermore, Swami Vivekananda said, "Now, the center of the world will be India."

India's eternal ideals are: Non-violence, friendship, self-sacrifice, truth, service, tolerance, goodwill, unity in diversity. The right balance between enjoyment and sacrifice will lead to global peace, happiness, and prosperity.

Historically, in the first half of the 20th century, even though most of our ancestors were poor and illiterate, under the leadership of great freedom fighters like Mahatma Gandhi and Subhas Chandra Bose, they fought with courage, valor, self-sacrifice, national pride, and determination, enduring immense hardships for India's independence. Their struggle serves as an undying beacon of hope for a society free from exploitation.

We are the descendants of these great freedom fighters, and future generations will carry the legacy forward. Therefore, in times of crisis, we must not falter. Instead, we must be inspired by strong character, knowledge, humanitarian work, and excellence to build a united, prosperous, and thriving society. The words of great leaders never fail. Light will always pierce the darkness.

CHAPTER 34

Memories are Always Sweet: Recollections of Friendship

Dr. Purnendu Sekhar Das
Professor (Retd.), Vidyasagar University, Medinipur
& Former Professor of Economics, Humanities Department, IIT Kharagpur

Jagadis Chandra Misra is a close friend of mine. We share the same profession—both of us are teachers and researchers. Our ancestral homes are in the same district, barely 7–8 kilometers apart. The high schools we attended were also nearby, just 3–4 kilometers from each other—his being Tikarapara High School, and mine, Chandanpur Anand Institution (High School).

In 1971, Jagadis earned his Ph.D. in Applied Mathematics from Jadavpur University. That same year, he joined IIT Kharagpur as a Lecturer in the Mathematics Department. In 1984, he obtained a D.Sc. from the University of Calcutta. After retiring from IIT Kharagpur in 2009, he continued teaching at various universities in West Bengal and Odisha. He also served as the Pro-Vice-Chancellor of SOA University, Bhubaneswar, for five and a half years. Additionally, he worked as a Visiting Professor in Germany, Canada, Hong Kong, and Malaysia, earning high acclaim. Throughout his long academic career (1967–2025), he has been honoured with numerous awards and recognitions—so many that listing them all would take several pages. Interested readers can refer to his Curriculum Vitae (C.V.) to gain a comprehensive understanding of the vastness and depth of his scholarly contributions. It is truly astonishing.

Our friendship began in 1972, after I joined IIT. However, I had already heard of Jagadis before meeting him, thanks to Prof. Anil Kumar Gayen, then Head of the Mathematics Department at IIT Kharagpur. He was a distinguished mathematician and statistician. Through him, I first came to know of Jagadis—not just by name, but as an esteemed scholar. In a way, Prof. Gayen unknowingly forged a deep bond between us.

After some time, I met Jagadis at his department. Two young men, about 28–29 years old, hailing from neighboring high schools, now found themselves as colleagues at the same prestigious institution. Both of us were deeply engaged in teaching and research. We lived in IIT quarters, just a kilometer apart. Our families grew close—Jagadis and his wife, Shorasi, often visited us, and my wife, Sutapa, and I frequently visited their quarters. Over time, our bond strengthened into a cherished family relationship.

Father of Jagadis was an exceptionally kind and wise man. Whenever he visited IIT Campus from his ancestral home, he would drop by our house as well. If my father was around, the two would immerse themselves in philosophical discussions, primarily on spirituality and the nature of God.

Mother of Jagadis too, would visit and shower us with maternal affection. She addressed my wife as "Bouma" (daughter-in-law), treating her as her own. What began as a friendship between two young men soon extended to our families, creating a lifelong bond.

A few years later, Shorasi's sister Namita and her husband, Subhash Chandra Mahapatra (a faculty of Rural Development Centre), also joined us, further enriching our circle. It felt as if we had recreated our ancestral homeland in this new environment. Our gatherings were filled with conversations—not just about mathematics, economics, or rural development theories, but also about village life, city life, and international affairs. We would chat over tea and snacks, sometimes enjoying spiced puffed rice or crispy potato fritters.

This friendship among the three families remains strong even to this day. Although Namita and Subhash have now moved back to their hometown, we stay connected through phone calls, reminiscing about the golden days. Truly, memories are always sweet. Jagadis and I still reside in Kharagpur—he with his wife, son, and grandchildren within the IIT campus, and I with my wife, son, and daughter-in-law in a house at the Hijli Cooperative Society. Despite our different locations, our bond remains as strong as ever.

The reason behind this unbreakable friendship is the profoundly humble and humane nature of Jagadis.Despite receiving countless awards, honours, and international recognition, he has remained grounded. His humility and deep-rooted connection with his origins set him apart—traits, which are very rare among people of such extraordinary caliber. I feel immensely proud to have him as a friend. His open-hearted nature, warm and sincere way of speaking, and his hearty laughter—these still remind me of the young Jagadis I first met.

Jagadis—the Scientist

A scientist's work is best understood and appreciated by another scientist. While I am not a mathematician, as an economist and researcher, I have attempted to assess his contributions. Below is a brief summary of his academic achievements:

1. Number of research papers published in reputed journals: 250
2. Number of books published: 14
3. Government-funded research projects (as principal investigator): 05
4. Ph.D. students supervised: 30
5. Invited lectures delivered at national and international conferences: 38

Notably, of the 250 published papers, 17 were authored solely by Jagadis, while the rest were co-authored with his students, colleagues, and collaborators. His willingness to share knowledge and mentor others rather than seeking personal glory is a testament to his dedication as a teacher and researcher. Such selfless knowledge-sharing enhances scientific progress and enriches future generations.

If one pauses to reflect on the magnitude of his contributions—particularly his pioneering research in applied mathematics and its impact on neurological/physiological sciences and medical applications—it seems almost unimaginable. The extent of his work and its success in benefiting society worldwide is nothing short of extraordinary. This is what distinguishes a genius from the ordinary. Whether his brilliance is a divine gift or the result of relentless learning is a matter of perspective—but there is no doubt that he is an exceptional talent.

Jagadis is a scientist blessed by the divine, a favored child of the Goddess of Knowledge, Saraswati. And I, too, consider myself fortunate to have such a friend.

I wholeheartedly congratulate him on his remarkable achievements in applied mathematics. I also extend my gratitude to those who have documented his invaluable contributions for the benefit of the academic community. I am confident that future generations will draw inspiration from his work and honor the efforts of those who have preserved it.

Finally, I salute my dear friend Jagadis for his incredible intellect and contributions. I pray to the Almighty for his continued happiness, health, and long life.

CHAPTER 35

The Eminent Personality: Jagadis Babu

Manmatha Nath Das
Former Teacher, Mugberia Gangadhar High School (Higher Secondary), Bhupatinagar, Purba Medinipur-721425

As I sit down to write, I find myself in a dilemma—how well do I actually know the revered Professor Dr. Jagadis Chandra Misra, the very subject of this article? Though our ancestral homes are merely 8–9 kms apart, making us practically neighbors, I never had the fortune of being in his close company. Our educational and professional paths led us in different directions.

In fact, I can count our in-person meetings on my fingers—perhaps four times, as far as I can recall. Our first meeting took place in 2008, though I had known of him for 15 years prior. My acquaintance with him began when I was writing a book titled *Amader Mastermoshai*, which chronicled the lives of several distinguished teachers from the Contai (Kanthi) subdivision. The book, published in 1998, featured a foreword by revered Swami Lokeshwaranandaji.

In my attempt to include the story of the founding headmaster of Tikarapara High School, the esteemed Ganes Chandra Misra, I sought information from his son, Professor Jagadis Babu, through phone calls and letters. He responded graciously and did not disappoint me. Later, after seeing the published book, he expressed his happiness. At that time, my focus was on Ganes Babu, and I saw Jagadis Babu primarily as the accomplished son of a great man, a professor at IIT Kharagpur.

By 2008, however, Professor Jagadis Chandra Misra had already established himself as an eminent scholar, both in India and abroad. My friends from Pratapdighi informed me that his innovative research in mathematics and science had earned him prestigious accolades, including the *Rashtriya Gaurav Award* and the *Rammohan Puraskar*.

It was a matter of great joy for us when he accepted our invitation to be the Chief Guest at the annual district conference of the *Purba Medinipur Pensioners'*

Welfare Association of Retired Teachers and Non-teaching Staff, held at Jhatulal Higher Secondary School in Egra. Even more delightfully, his learned wife, Smt. Shorasi Misra accompanied him. In an extraordinary coincidence, that same year, the association honored a distinguished teacher from Egra Sub-division, Pandit Phani Bhushan Nanda—none other than Shorasi Devi's father and Jagadis Babu's father-in-law. This occasion of pleasant coincidence was a source of immense satisfaction for all of us.

At that time, I was serving as one of the vice presidents of the association. This allowed me the privilege of meeting and conversing with Professor Misra—a moment I consider a personal fortune.

Our second meeting occurred five years later, in 2013. By then, he had retired from IIT and was serving as the Pro-Vice Chancellor of the *Shiksha O Anusandhan University* in Bhubaneswar. Our paths crossed at Tikarapara Ambikamayee Higher Secondary School, and this time, he had come specifically to honor me.

For nearly five years, I had been conducting extensive research and field studies to compile a book titled *Patashpur: Sekal Ekal (Patashpur: The Past and the Present)*, which presented a comprehensive history of the vast area under Patashpur police station. The credit for inviting distinguished guests and organizing the release ceremony of the book at the said venue went to esteemed Baren Da (Patra) of Pratapdighi Rice Mill and the prominent co-operative leader and social activist Golokesh Babu (Nanda Goswami). I will always cherish their generous patronage.

Though he had come at their invitation, the very thought that such an illustrious scholar had travelled from Bhubaneswar to attend the release of a book authored by someone as ordinary as me was overwhelming. The event was graced by eminent personalities like Shri Amalesh Mishra, Professor Jyotimoy Kar, MLA and Principal Dr. Subimalendu Bikash Jana.

During his speech, Professor Misra made a statement that remains etched in my memory. He said, *"Based on this single book, the author could very well claim a Ph.D. degree."* I had never considered such an endeavor, but his affectionate words meant more to me than any academic title. It became one of the most cherished treasures of my memory.

Four years later, we met again—another fortunate encounter for me. The venue was Pratapdighi Rice Mill, where the *Goonijan Sanman Committee (a specially constituted committee)*, under the leadership of Golokesh Babu and other prominent figures, organized a grand felicitation ceremony.

Among those honoured that day were the eminent co-operative leader and revered statesman Barendra Nath Patra, the globally renowned mathematician Professor Dr. Jagadis Chandra Misra, and, in an inexplicable stroke of luck, myself, Manmatha Nath Das.

Once again, the ever-smiling Dr. Misra charmed me with his warm and affectionate conversation, just as Baren Da did.

Three years later, I had another chance to meet him. He had come to attend a prestigious seminar at Mugberia Gangadhar College. He called me, and we met again. I invited him to visit my former workplace, Mugberia Gangadhar Higher Secondary School. My colleague, Mathura Nath Tripathi, and I (both long retired by then) accompanied him to the School.

It was a meaningful visit for him because his revered father, Ganes Chandra Misra, had once been a student there. He had studied at Mugberia while staying at his maternal uncle's house and had received free education under the benevolence of Rai Saheb Gangadhar Nanda. He had always topped his class and had passed his matriculation exam with flying colors in 1933.

In those days, many students from Patashpur came to study at Mugberia. Notable among them were Jatadhari Jana, Sarat Chandra Jana, Surendranath Jana, Upendranath Jana, Lalit Mohan Roy, Gopinath Panda, and Ganes Chandra's classmates Atul Chandra Mal and Atul Krishna Mandal.

As we reminisced about these historical connections, Professor Misra spent some precious moments at the School, seemingly enjoying every bit of it.

With just these four brief meetings, how much could I truly know about him? What could I possibly write? These thoughts left me perplexed. But then, by a stroke of luck, Dr. Misra sent me the final proofs of his autobiography (original version) for review.

And as I went through them, an astonishing realization dawned upon me—Professor Misra, our very own Jagadis Babu, emerged before me as a radiant figure, a man of extraordinary brilliance and unmatched intellectual depth. It felt as though I had been watching him like a neighbor for the past eighty years. Today, countless unknown aspects of his life are gathering in the arena of knowledge. Despite being as ordinary as the rest of us, he remains extraordinarily remarkable—so much so that no matter how much we tilt our heads to grasp the peak of his greatness, it remains elusive. Yet, despite numerous limitations, his relentless pursuit of scientific research, both in India and abroad, seems to touch us with a deep sense of reverence.

Professor Misra—a devoted scientist, started his journey in academia in 1967 at Uluberia College and later continued at IIT Kharagpur, where he has been engaged in scientific pursuits to this day. After earning his M.Sc. in Applied Mathematics, he commenced his research at Jadavpur University, which later expanded globally. He obtained his Ph.D. and D.Sc. degrees and was appointed as a Professor and the Head of the Mathematics Department at IIT Kharagpur.

Over the years, he has been elected as a Fellow of several prestigious institutions, including the Royal Society of Public Health, the Royal Society of Biology, London, the National Academy of Sciences, India and the Indian National Academy of Engineering. Alongside these recognitions, he has received numerous international accolades, such as the Best Scientist Award (2014) and the Lifetime Achievement Award (2015). Recently, he was ranked among the top 2% of scientists worldwide—an honor of immense prestige!

Genius, dedication, and perseverance elevate individuals to great heights, and Dr. Misra has rightfully earned his place on such a distinguished stage. However, had his mathematical and scientific endeavors been solely for his intellectual gratification, they would have remained his personal achievements. Instead, his rigorous research in Applied Mathematics, Biomathematics, Modeling and Simulation, and Physiological Fluid Dynamics has provided groundbreaking support to medical science and various other fields. Moreover, under his guidance, a dedicated group of young researchers has emerged, committed to the advancement of science.

Naturally, through his lifelong dedication to science, he has become a distinguished servant of humanity. His legacy is not confined to his birthplace, Bagmari village, Medinipur district, or even West Bengal. Rather, all of India takes pride in him. He is a national treasure.

Such exceptional individuals often command great respect, and we tend to admire them from a respectful distance. Rabindranath Tagore's lyrics echo this sentiment:

> *"We stand in awe, treating them as deities, yet we do not embrace them as our own. We bow at their feet as fathers, yet we do not hold their hands as friends."*

Indeed, success often builds barriers of ego, creating an invisible distance. But when someone, despite their immense achievements, refuses to be confined by pride and moves seamlessly between the highest academic platforms and the common people, we call them a truly great person. A rare blend of intellectual brilliance and deep compassion—Professor Misra embodies this union.

He is ever-smiling. Every time I have met him, or even spoken to him over the phone, he has radiated joy, warmth, and a genuine sense of connection with all. He is as simple as a child, devoid of arrogance, and speaks with gentle kindness. The great Odia poet Jagannath Das describes such noble individuals:

"Their words are as sweet as nectar, bringing joy to the hearts of others."

Jagadis Babu is, indeed, a great man. Though his academic and administrative responsibilities keep him busy, preventing frequent visits to his village, his heart remains deeply tied to its people. He cherishes his school and college friends, maintaining strong bonds with many of them even today. Despite being a distinguished IIT Professor, he proudly introduces his childhood companions as friends without hesitation.

He has also extended his generosity to his village. He has invited Ramakrishna Sarada Shiksha Sadan, a non-governmental educational institution in Pratapdighi, to perform cultural events at the Netaji Auditorium of IIT Kharagpur. He even welcomes me to his family's celebrations.

Calling him humble would be an understatement—he embodies the true humility of a Vaishnav devotee. He honors even those who receive no recognition from society. Otherwise, why would someone as esteemed as him affectionately call me "Dada" and treat me like an elder brother?

The son of a noble village teacher, he grew up in a large, affectionate joint family. His mother often advised him: *"If you wish to be great, learn to be humble."* From his father, he learned the principle: *"Speak the truth, but speak it sweetly."*

During his higher studies, he was blessed by the Ramakrishna Math and the Ramakrishna Mission. He took initiation from President Maharaj Swami Shankarananda Ji and, as a student, regularly recited prayers that emphasized purity, compassion, and divine love. He used to regularly read a framed writing on the table of the Hostel Superintendent, Swami Gokulananda Maharaj, which emphasized:

"Love is the ultimate path to fulfillment" (Pritih Parama Sadhanam)

His unwavering faith in the Divine Mother gave him a profound sense of security, allowing him to remain fearless and ever joyful.

His brilliance and compassion have always walked hand in hand. That is why, despite his immense global influence, he remains deeply connected to us—one of our own.

To such a great man, Professor Jagadis Babu, I offer my heartfelt respect and admiration.

CHAPTER 36

Dr. J.C. Misra—A Wonder

Prof. Ranajit Kumar Nayek
Ex-Lecturer in English, Mugberia Gangadhar Mahavidyalaya,
Bhupatinagar, Purba Medinipur

Matthew Arnold in his sonnet 'Shakespeare' pays his encomium to Shakespeare by saying 'And thou, who didst the stars and sunbeams know'. The same may be spoken of Dr. Jagadis Chandra Misra who rises from a remote village Bagmari of Patashpur, East Midnapore District, W.B. to a magnificent towering position in his academic research field of Applied Mathematics, Biomathematics, Modelling and Simulation, Physiological Fluid Dynamics, Mechanics of Fluids and Solids, beyond the reach of common scholars of mathematics. His is, indeed, an 'out-topping knowledge' like a loftiest hill around whose ridges we the common educated persons move to vainly gauge his infinite height.

His name has long trailing qualifications which only inspire awe and reverence for him. For his vast erudition and academic excellence, he was invited to deliver lectures in his specialized fields of research in such foreign lands as Germany, France, U.K., U.S.A., Canada, Austria, Japan, Belgium, Nepal, Malay, Singapore, Bangladesh, and he had his close friendship with world-famous scientists as Prof. Oskar Mahrenholtz, Prof. Lothar Gaul, Prof. Horst Irritier, Prof. Y.C. Fung, Prof. Charles Peskin, Prof. Hans Rath, Prof. Joerg Wallaschek, Prof. Heinz Herwig, Prof. Robert Seifried, Prof. Paul Steinmann. He is indeed a world-famous scholar in the field of Applied Mathematics.

Prof. Misra's researches in Cardiovascular Dynamics, Mathematical Modelling of Flow in Atherosclerotic or Stenosed Arteries, Biomechanics of Brain Injury, Bio-Nanofluid Simulation, Biomechanics of Bones, Fracture and Remodelling of Bones have opened up new techniques of treatment in medical science. Applied Mathematics and medical science go hand in hand in Dr. Misra's research. Without being a medical practitioner he has contributed a lot to the service of humanity in medical treatment, by virtue of his mathematical talent and research. He is a scientist par excellence. He figures in the list of Top 2% Scientists in the world for six consecutive years from 2020 to 2025 according to the studies conducted by a team of Scientists at Stanford University, USA.

A popular teacher and research guide, he has to his credit 250 Published Research Papers in International Journals, 14 Published Books on Mathematics, 30 Ph.D. Awarded Research Scholars under him, and 35 invited Lectures in National and International Seminars and Conferences.

Dr. Misra owes much to the spiritual and cultural ambience of Ramkrishna Mission Vidyamandira, Belur Math for his sweet disposition, amiable behaviour, humble nature, energetic and punctual active habits. His modesty and suave manners go safely with his profound erudition and learning. The close relationship with many revered Sannyasins of the Ramkrishna Mission has a solemn and holy influence on his gentle personality.

It is futile to fathom his depth of scholarship. We can best pray to Sri Ramakrishna for his sound health and peaceful long life.

CHAPTER 37

My Schoolmate Jagadis Chandra Misra

Balai Lal Das
Retired Teacher, Panchagram Shiksha Niketan Higher Secondary School, Fazelpur, Patashpur, East Medinipur

In 1957, I passed the eighth grade from Pania Sardabarh Ramakrishna Shikha Sadan and enrolled in the ninth grade at Tikrapara Ambikamayee High School, which was about four miles away from my village. At this school I made many dear friends, some of whom became very close to me. Let me now speak something about my close friend, Jagadis Chandra Misra and focus on my personal thoughts and opinions about him. At my current age, many vivid memories of the past have blurred over time. Life is full of changes, and every moment brings new transformations. This has always been the case from the beginning of time. My bond with Jagadis has also gone through transformations. At Tikrapara School, both of us had deep affection for each other. In the ninth grade, there were three students, whose names began with "Jaga"—Jagdis Chandra Misra, Jagannath Roy, and Jagannath Manna. In terms of appearance, Jagadis was somewhat shorter but had good health and a pleasant face, often smiling. However, when deep in thought, he would become serious, and his face would reflect the gravity of the matter he used to think about.

Jagadis lived with his father, Ganes Chandra Misra, who was a teacher at our school and a prominent social worker, as well as the president of the local Union Board at the time. The School was also attended by other respected teachers such as Lakshmikanta Basu, Lakshmikanta Misra, Ramjivan Misra, Kamalakanta Misra, Sudhir Kumar Ghosh, Manoranjan Roy, Anil Kumar Bera, Gunakar Acharya, and others. The headmaster of the school was Pramatha Nath Basu, who ran the school efficiently and garnered respect far and wide for the school's educational quality.

I would like to mention a few of my classmates, though I cannot recall everyone. Some of them were: Prafulla Mandal, a skilled painter, Shashi Nandi, Ananta

Nandi, Gorachand, Ghanasyam, Bankim Maity, Atul Kamilya, Sirajuddin, etc. In 1959, Jagadis, Tarak, and I sat for the school final exam at the Egra Jhatulal High School Center, and most of us passed. Jagadis and Tarak passed in the first division, which was a rare accomplishment at the time. Most students wrote their exams with ink pens, as ballpoint pens were rare.

Afterward, life moved on in its usual course, and we lost touch. However, I did hear that Tarak enrolled in Contai Prabhat Kumar College, and Jagadis went to the College at Belur Math. At that time, communication was limited to the postal service. Without knowing the address, there was little chance of staying in touch. Mobile phones were not in use yet. After completing my studies at Contai P.K. College, I began my teaching career. Tarak also became a teacher in Contai. A few years later, I was overjoyed to read in the Anandabazar Patrika that Jagadis had received a Doctorate degree.

Life seemed to fly by like a white horse with flowing mane, with moments of dust scattering in the winds of time. Time passed, leaving a trail of memories. In the end, when everyone retired from their careers, I reconnected with some old friends, including Jagadis. I learned a lot about his career and achievements. I encouraged him to write an autobiography, which he eventually agreed to. However, it is not my place to describe his contributions to society and the research he has done. Those will be better understood through his own words. His work has been praised and acknowledged by the scientific community and the respected circles of the world.

As we notice in the case of mango trees, many flowers bloom, but only a few turn into fruit. There are many people, but how many individuals are able to make discoveries for the betterment of human society? Education is a means by which society passes down its thoughts, traditions, and acquired experiences to future generations and prepares the youth with the necessary knowledge to guide future societies towards the desired goals. The autobiography of my dear friend, Jagadis, will definitely be a source of inspiration for future students. I also say of my friend—"The glow of simple truths, rare restrained calm words... May this wish never fail." I further say—"Even those who are yet to be born and haven't seen you in their land, you have given enough to them too. In the characteristics of my dear friend Jagadis—"The gentle, modest smile, that pure, fresh simplicity, the glow of simple truths, rare restrained calm words... May this wish never fail." Finally, I say—"People come in groups, singing your praises in different languages, in various voices. Though I wish to adorn you with a garland, you neither need it nor is it necessary for you."

CHAPTER 38

In the Company of Jagadis at the Vidyamandira for Five Years

Dr. Kamalesh Bhowmik
Professor (Retired), Saha Institute of Nuclear Physics, Kolkata-700064, and Former Registrar, West Bengal State University, Barasat, Kolkata-700126

In 1959 I was admitted to Ramakrishna Mission Vidyamandira, Belur Math. Even today, the Vidyamandira is a prestigious college, but at that time, its reputation was even more extensive. It was almost a tradition for three or four of the top ten students from the secondary exams to enroll there. Unlike today, when bright students primarily choose science to become doctors or engineers, back then, many talented students were keen on studying literature (now referred to as the Humanities). As a result, most bright students with a passion for literature attended the Vidyamandira.

During my initial days at the college, I felt quite overwhelmed by the presence of so many brilliant peers around me. However, I eventually grew comfortable as friendships blossomed. One of the friendly students I met during that uncertain phase was Jagadis, and knowing him brought me a great sense of relief. I found out that like me, he came from a village, and our socio-economic backgrounds were quite similar. This common ground quickly cemented our friendship, which remained unbroken until our last day at Vidyamandira.

Jagadis and I lived in the same hostel for five years, in adjacent rooms. We shared an exceptional camaraderie. He was a quiet and well-mannered young man. During our B.Sc. Programme, we pursued different honors subjects—he chose Mathematics, while I took Physics—so our academic focus was a bit different. However, outside of the study hours, we spent most of our time together.

After completing our B.Sc., we moved to Kolkata for our M.Sc., but since we were on separate campuses, our interactions became infrequent. Gradually, our friendship loosened, though I kept hearing about his outstanding academic performance and dedicated research. Later, I learned that he had made remarkable contributions to his fields of research. Eventually, his brilliance became widely recognized, and he was appointed the Head of the Mathematics Department at the Indian Institute of Technology, Kharagpur.

Looking back, I sometimes marvel at how this calm, soft-spoken village boy achieved such acclaim in the academic world. But I have realized that it was not magic—it was the foundation laid in his childhood and his inherent qualities that led him to success. This article is an attempt to reflect on those qualities.

What stood out to me the most about Jagadis was his unwavering loyalty to his friends. From the day we met, he never wavered in his friendship. He was always ready to help me in case of any difficulty. Since our hostel rooms were next to each other, we often spent our free time chatting. Over time, our group expanded to include close friends like Suprakash, Debashish, Subhash, Debiprasad, Sarojbandhu, and many others. We moved around together as a close-knit group. I noticed that Jagadis was equally kind and generous to all his friends. Childhood friendships often come with misunderstandings or conflicts, but no one ever quarrelled with Jagadis. Even if minor misunderstandings arose, he took the initiative to resolve them.

Jagadis was incredibly disciplined. He woke up on time, maintained personal hygiene, attended prayer sessions, went to meals punctually, attended every class, and studied systematically to stay ahead. He also encouraged his friends to follow a disciplined routine.

One significant change we experienced upon joining the hostel was the transition to wearing dhotis. In school, we mostly wore half-pants, but at the Vidyamandira, dhotis were preferred. Initially, wearing a dhoti was challenging for me, but Jagadis adapted effortlessly and even helped us learn how to wear it properly.

Hostel life also required us to maintain our utensils—washing them before and after meals. The hostel food was decent—dal, rice, vegetables, and fish curry during lunch/ dinner, with meat served on Sundays and Wednesday nights. Some wealthier students from Kolkata often complained about the food, but Jagadis never did so. In his company, I too never felt the need to complain. Now, I realize that given the fees we paid, providing such quality meals was a significant effort on the part of the hostel.

Jagadis was not one to protest for trivial issues. While some students would frequently complain to the warden about minor inconveniences, such as dim lights or inadequate fan cooling, Jagadis preferred to find solutions himself and discouraged unnecessary complaints. He was an idealist who never strayed from his principles and tried to inspire others to follow them.

The leisure time was spent playing football, cricket in winter, or table tennis in the hostel. Jagadis and I were not particularly skilled in sports, so we often strolled along the banks of the Ganges. In the evenings, after prayer, our warden, Swami Gokulananda (Govinda Maharaj), would sometimes gather us in the common room to share stories. One day, he read out Swami Vivekananda's Chicago speech, which deeply influenced Jagadis. Over time, he developed profound interest in Vivekananda's writings and encouraged me to do the same. Govinda Maharaj always supported this interest. At that young age, we were drawn to an ideal but did not fully grasp its significance. Later, after a long discussion with the college principal, Swami Tejasananda, we understood Swami Vivekananda's philosophy—that merely sitting in a temple and praying is not true devotion; rather, leading an honest life and helping others, irrespective of caste or religion, is the real practice of faith.

Jagadis was not reclusive—he loved socializing and traveling. Whenever we had a couple of days off, we would go on short trips. If Jagadis went, I would go too. Together, we visited places like Khardaha, Panihati, and various parts of Kolkata. Once, along with some close friends and Govinda Maharaj, we took an extended trip to Jayrambati, Kamarpukur, and Bishnupur—places that had not yet become popular tourist destinations.

These memories of my time with Jagadis at the Vidyamandira remain dear to me, as they shaped my journey and friendships in ways that still resonate today.

It was Govinda Maharaj who arranged for our stay in Jayrambati and Kamarpukur. While staying in Jayrambati, we would often go to bathe in the nearby Amodar River. At that time, the river had a strong current, and the water was quite deep. There were also some large trees along the river bank. We all climbed up onto the branches and sat there. Suddenly, Govinda Maharaj told us to jump into the river from the trees. I was sitting on a branch alongside Debiprasad. Without hesitation, Debiprasad pinched his nose with one hand and jumped in immediately. But no matter how hard I tried, I got scared every time.

On our way back, we visited Bishnupur. I had no idea that the place was so rich in heritage and had so much to see. Govinda Maharaj told us about Raja Hambir—how he encountered Vaishnavism throughout his life as a bandit and later embraced the faith. We listened in awe to these fascinating stories.

Once, we took the Martin Rail from Howrah Maidan to visit Antpur, the birthplace of Swami Premananda. The intricate wooden craftsmanship in the houses there left us amazed. I don't know whether those works of art still exist or have been lost to time.

During all these trips, Jagadis and I were always inseparable, sharing endless laughter and fun. We spent hours chatting with friends, especially in the evenings, sitting by the Ganges with our feet dangling over the edge.

Jagadis was straightforward and honest, so we all respected his opinions. We never attempted anything new without first seeking his advice.

The five years of our stay in the Vidyamandira hostel were simply incredible. We made the most of that time, balancing our studies with various college festivals and celebrations. Whenever there was a festival at Belur Math, we volunteered to help. One year, instead of going home during the *Durga Puja* holidays, a few of us, under the leadership of Jagadis, actively participated in the celebrations there.

Back then, our study methods were quite different from today. Private tutors and coaching centers were not common. Instead, we learned from each other. We had already studied calculus before, but we had to revisit it again. Though physics heavily relied on calculus, we realized that our understanding of the subject and its definitions was still unclear. We had mechanically mastered differentiation and integration, but we lacked a logical grasp of the concepts.

We wanted to understand the very foundation of the subject. Jagadis, being exceptionally skilled in mathematics, became our guide. It was through him that we first learned that this area of higher mathematics was called "Analysis." He worked tirelessly to explain the logical foundations of the definitions in a clear and precise manner. For days, we struggled with delta and epsilon, trying to grasp their meaning. I don't know how much we truly understood, but we realized that in mathematics, nothing could be taken lightly—everything required strict rigor.

As time went on, Jagadis became increasingly immersed in his studies, and we, too, became more absorbed in our respective fields. Before we knew it, the years had flown by in a whirlwind of activity.

Eventually, after our final exams, we had to leave the college. This was the moment when we truly began to drift apart. We had always found great comfort in the presence of Jagadis, and suddenly, we felt the void of his absence.

In course of time, we all graduated and set out on our respective paths in life. Suprakash, Jagadis, and I chose the path of scientific research. Though I no longer saw Jagadis in person, I constantly heard from others about how he was steadily establishing himself as a distinguished mathematician.

As we embarked on entirely new lives, time passed. Now, standing at the twilight of life, I look back and realize that the journey of Jagadis serves as an inspiration for future generations. Even in childhood, his gentle nature, innocent laughter, and pleasant demeanor drew us toward him. Back then, we never imagined that within this child lay the roots of a towering tree.

Today, as this grand banyan tree spreads its branches, offering shelter to countless seekers of knowledge, I am reminded of a verse from the *Bhagavad Gita*:

> *"Whatever a great person does, others follow. Whatever standards they set, the world adopts."*

CHAPTER 39

In Search of Old Memories

Ashok Bhowmik
Recipient of President's Award,
Former Principal, Sodepur Higher Secondary School, Kolkata

As I look back in my retired life, memories of old friends resurface, along with recollections of my school, college, and university classmates. One day, as I was reminiscing, the name of Jagadis Chandra Misra came to mind.

In late July 1964, I enrolled in the M.Sc. program in Applied Mathematics at Rajabazar Science College of Calcutta University. Classes started in the first week of August, and after three periods on the first day, a formal freshers' welcome event was organized. It was an occasion for introductions, concluding with a cultural program. However, it wasn't possible to learn everyone's names and addresses that day.

At that time, I lived in Rahara, Khardaha. My daily commute involved taking a train from Khardaha station to Sealdah, followed by a 10–12 minute walk to Rajabazar Science College. One day, while walking from Sealdah, I noticed a fellow classmate heading toward the college, just like me. As we walked together, we exchanged names and addresses. That classmate was Jagadis. He stayed at the Ramakrishna Mission Students' Home in Belgharia and travelled from Belgharia station to Sealdah by train.

Over time, our daily commutes led to a deep friendship. We discussed various topics during our walks, including personal matters. Another close friend I made during this time was Bhavesh Ranjan Pal. Though I was not very close to everyone, I had a fondness for some of our other classmates, such as Ashes Ray Choudhury, Birendra Nath Mandal, and Charugopal Chakraborty.

Another name that comes to mind is Pradosh Dasgupta.

Jagadis and I even shared a similar sense of dressing. Among our classmates, only two or three others wore dhoti and shirts like us. During the monsoons, water would often accumulate on the roads from Sealdah to Science College.

On such days, we would lift our dhotis above our knees and wade through the water, enjoying the adventure but also wary of open manholes—something that particularly worried me.

Jagadis had completed his college years at Belur Ramakrishna Mission Vidyamandira, where he pursued his I.Sc. and B.Sc. (Honours) before joining the M.Sc. programme while staying at the Belgharia Ramakrishna Mission Vidyarthi Ashrama. Being deeply influenced by the Mission's values and principles, he was soft-spoken, polite, and of a calm disposition. We shared a strong intellectual connection. Whenever I faced difficulties in my studies, I would visit Jagadis at his hostel for discussions, as my home lacked enough space to host him. Through these discussions, we would resolve our academic challenges together.

For our M.Sc. programme, we both had the same special paper—"Theory of Elasticity and Plasticity." That year, a dissertation was introduced as part of the final-year curriculum. As a result, I frequently visited Jagadis at his hostel to work on it. After thorough discussions, we prepared our dissertation. The next challenge was typing it—about 100 pages filled with number of mathematical formulae and equations.

Jagadis and I searched around Belgharia for a suitable typist. Since we couldn't afford the high fees charged by most typists, many refused the task. Finally, one typist agreed, and the work was completed within five days. Next, we had to get it bound, which we managed at a bookstore near Belgharia Railway station. These shared experiences strengthened our friendship even further.

Our M.Sc. exams were originally scheduled for November 1966, but were postponed and eventually held in late February 1967, concluding in mid-March. After the examinations, Jagadis left the hostel, and we lost touch. We briefly reconnected when our M.Sc. Examination results were published.

Jagadis secured a first-class M.Sc. degree and started teaching at Uluberia College. Simultaneously, he pursued research in Mathematics for four years, earning a Ph.D. He later joined IIT Kharagpur as a lecturer in Mathematics. That was the extent of my knowledge about his career, and after that, we completely lost contact.

Years later, one of my dear students, Dr. Indranil Ghosh, who is currently a professor in the Cryogenics Engineering Department at IIT Kharagpur, came to visit me. During our conversation, the name of Jagadis came up. Indranil mentioned that he had heard of him, so I asked him to find out more and, if possible, get his phone number.

Indranil could collect the contact details of Jagadis from IIT and share them with me. After 58 years, I was able to talk to Jagadis over the phone. I was wondering—would he be able to recognize me after such a long period of time? Does he still remember me? These thoughts raced through my mind. But to my delight, he recognized my voice instantly! We had a hearty conversation for 15 minutes, reviving our old memories.

The lines from Rabindra Nath Tagore's song echoed in my mind:

"How could you forget those old days?
The glimpses of those eyes, the words of the heart—Can they ever be forgotten?"

Indeed, the memories of the student life are unforgettable.

Curious about his academic journey, I requested Jagadis to send me his CV. When I received his 25-page CV, I was awestruck. In 1981, he was awarded a D.Sc. from the University of Calcutta—a truly remarkable achievement. Over the years, he had delivered 150 guest lectures worldwide and published 250 research papers in prestigious international journals. Under his supervision, 30 scholars earned their Ph.D. degrees. Additionally, he published 14 books on advanced mathematics.

Most impressively, Stanford University recognized him as one of the top 2% of scientists in the world, an extraordinary achievement. He is currently serving as an Adjunct Professor at IIEST while also being a proud and devoted father. I sincerely wish Jagadis continues to have the best of health, happiness, and achieve even greater success. My heartfelt best wishes are always with him.

CHAPTER 40

My Friend Sri Jagadis Chandra Misra—A Classmate of My Early College Days

Sibabrata Bagchi
Retired General Manager, India Government Mint, Kolkata

After my School Final Examination in 1959, I took admission in the Ramkrishna Mission Vidyamandira, Belur Math for studying a two-year Intermediate Science (I.Sc.) course there. Belur Vidyamandira is a reputed residential College. At that time, this Institution was offering two-year courses on Intermediate Arts (I.A.) and Intermediate Science (I.Sc). Successful students from different parts of West Bengal used to come here to enrol in these courses. The students usually had to clear a preliminary test and personal talk before admission to the college. I met Sri Jagadis Chandra Misra as my classmate in this Vidyamandira only. Jagadis also had been admitted to I.Sc. Course at Vidyamandira. He came from a village located under Midnapore District in West Bengal.

I remember, Jagadis was very polite and disciplined as a student. These qualities made him very dear to all his friends and classmates in Vidyamandira. Monks who were in charge of student Hostels of Vidyamandira liked him very much.

Jagadis was one of the most affectionate students of the then Respected Principal, Swami Tejasanandaji Maharaj. Jagadis was one of the few selected students who used to perform evening Arati at the prayer Hall of Vidyamandira in the evening.

Reverend Swami Shankaranandaji Maharaj was the then President of The Ramakrishna Mission. Respected President Maharaj agreed to bless a few Vidyamandira students with spiritual initiation (Dikhsha) during the first half of April 1960. Amongst those few students of Vidyamandira, Jagadis was also initiated that time by the Reverend President Maharaj.

At this time, we have noticed Jagadis to be involved in spiritual activities along with his studies at the College. He used to visit Belur Math frequently and join spiritual discussions with monks of the Ramakrishna Math.

After completion of two years of our studies of I.Sc course in 1961, I went to meet our Reverend Principal Maharaj in his office. Jagadis was also present there. At that time, we all were thinking of joining a proper institution for further higher studies. Respected Principal Maharaj expressed his wish that Jagadis and myself may continue our higher education in Vidyamandira in the 3-year degree course which was started at Belur Vidyamandira a year back in 1960. Principal Maharaj wished Jagadis to continue his studies there with Honours in Mathematics and advised me to take Honours in Chemistry. Principal Maharaj also explained about several opportunities for continuing studies in the 3-year degree course at the Vidyamandira.

Due to several other reasons, I could not avail the opportunities explained by the respected Principal Maharaj to continue further studies at the Vidyamandira. I had taken admission elsewhere.

However, as per the wish of Principal Maharaj, Jagadis continued his studies at Vidyamandira by taking admission there in a 3-year degree course with Honours in Mathematics.

Jagadis was an ideal student and very good at his studies. After continuing studies in Vidyamandira, he had done extremely well and performed excellent research work thereafter. I am quite sure that affection and blessings of the then Principal Maharaj of the Vidyamandira had inspired Jagadis to achieve such excellent performance in his studies and research work. He later joined Indian Institute of Technology (I.I.T.), Kharagpur in teaching faculty of Mathematics Department and succeeded himself as Departmental Head in this highly reputed Institution. Jagadis has published innumerable research papers which are of the highest standard, which have been appreciated nationally and worldwide. He is also holding several prestigious national and international awards and recognitions in Mathematics.

I personally feel proud of being a classmate of a person like Jagadis in my early days of college.

CHAPTER 41

Jagadis Da, as I Saw Him at the Vidyamandira

Debiprasad Dutta
Assistant Teacher (Retd.), Bolpur Vivekananda Vidyapith,
Birbhum, West Bengal

In 1961, I was admitted to the first year of the three-year degree course at Ramakrishna Mission Vidyamandira, Belur Math. Since it was a residential college, all of us stayed in the hostel. At the sound of the bell in the morning and evening, every student had to go to the prayer hall. In the morning, we sang devotional hymns in unison, and in the evening, we sang the Sandhya Arati.

Inside the *puja mandap*, there were images of Bhagavan Sri Ramakrishna, Sri Sri Maa Sarada Devi, and Swami Vivekananda. Just below the *mandap*, in the seat of the pujari, sat our revered Jagadis Da, draped in white garments and an *uttariya*, his eyes gently closed in deep devotion. At the designated time, as he rose with the *panchapradip* (five-lamp aarti) in his right hand and the bell in his left, the entire hall resonated with the collective chanting of the evening arati:

"Khandana-bhava-bandhana, Jaga-bandana, Bandi tomay..."

After dinner at night, under the guidance of our hostel superintendent and professor, Brahmachari Murari Chaitanya (later known as Swami Gokulanandaji), a few of us, including Jagadis Da, participated in the Vivekananda Study Circle. Jagadis Da was an initiated disciple of Swami Shankaranandaji Maharaj, the then-president of the Ramakrishna Math and Mission. I have also seen a rare photograph of Jagadis Da with Swami Shantanandaji Maharaj, a senior monk and a direct disciple of Sri Sri Maa Sarada Devi.

Jagadis Da's personality radiated purity and spiritual depth. His facial expression always carried a gentle, serene smile, reflecting his inner peace. I held him in the highest regard.

In April 1964, after completing our B.Sc. Final Examinations, our daily life at the Vidyamandira came to an end. In his later years, Jagadis Da pursued higher studies with remarkable brilliance, excelling in academics and research. His extraordinary contributions to education and research earned him numerous prestigious awards and recognition, both in India and abroad.

Knowing about his achievements, I feel immense pride in having been his fellow student at the Vidyamandira. I sincerely pray to Sri Ramakrishna, Sri Maa, and Swamiji that our beloved Jagadis Da continues to scale the highest peaks of honor in India and receive a long and healthy life.

CHAPTER 42

Jagadis Da

Shyamal Chowdhury
Retired Manager, United Bank of India, Kolkata

Swami Vivekananda proudly declared that his life's goal was to shape individuals of character. He placed immense emphasis on education, believing that purity, patience, and perseverance were essential to overcoming all obstacles. To uphold these ideals, the revered monk Swami Nirvedananda established *Kolkata Vidyarthi Ashrama* over a century ago. This institution, possibly the first of its kind under the Ramakrishna Mission, was dedicated to providing higher education to meritorious yet underprivileged students.

Over the past hundred years, many brilliant and talented students have emerged from this Ashrama, reaching the pinnacle of success in their respective fields. Among them, Shri Jagadis Chandra Misra stands as a shining star.

During my time at Vidyarthi Ashrama, I had the privilege of being in Jagadis Da's company, a memory that remains fresh in my heart even today. His gentle and ever-smiling demeanor immediately drew everyone's attention. His polite nature, unwavering dedication, and strict discipline were integral to his character. He also possessed an extraordinary ability to remain calm and composed in all situations.

At the Ashrama, we students would often engage in debates and discussions. Even when present, Jagadis Da would listen more than he spoke. And whenever he did speak, he was always careful never to hurt anyone's feelings. He never sought to impose his opinions or showcase himself.

I once read in a book that nature has given us one mouth and two ears so that we listen more and speak less. Jagadis Da had mastered this art effortlessly. Even today, after nearly sixty years, when we former students gather at various Ashrama events, we engage in lively discussions. And if Jagadis Da is present, he joins in with a quiet smile—listening more, speaking less.

Deeply inspired by the ideals of Sri Ramakrishna, Holy Mother Sarada Devi and Swami Vivekananda, Jagadis Da embraced Ashrama life wholeheartedly. The proof of this lies in the fact that he spent his entire period of higher education, residing in hostels run by the Ramakrishna Mission. During his years at the Vidyarthi Ashrama, Belgharia I never saw him express frustration or dissatisfaction.

At the Ashrama, we had the rare opportunity to observe ideal monks up close—individuals worthy of deep reverence. Many of the virtues we admired in them were also evident in Jagadis Da. Some of us even speculated that he might renounce the world and become a monk himself. That did not happen, but I am convinced that had he chosen that path, he would have been an exemplary monk.

Instead, Jagadis Da scaled the heights of success in the world of research, driven by his single-minded dedication and relentless perseverance—qualities that many brilliant students lack, preventing them from reaching their full potential. Achieving excellence in any field requires overcoming numerous obstacles, which demands immense courage and mental strength.

I once asked Jagadis Da if he had faced any challenges on his path to success. With a gentle smile, his first response was, "Oh my goodness!" He then went on to recount a few incidents.

His contributions to the field of research are vast and awe-inspiring. His numerous awards and honors, both in India and abroad, are a testament to his brilliance. For every student of the Vidyarthi Ashrama, Belgharia, his achievements are a source of immense pride—for me, even more so.

I was particularly overjoyed when he received the Rammohan Puraskar—the kind of happiness one feels when a close family member achieves something great.

Even today, Jagadis Da continues his work with unwavering dedication. Like many others, I too pray for his good health, well-being, and a long life.

CHAPTER 43

Jagadis Da, Our Revered Elder Brother

Swapan Bhadra
Retired Manager, Central Bank of India, Kolkata

Balai Babu called me and informed me that a book is being published about Professor Jagadis Chandra Misra, and suggested that I write something about him. The request made me feel important, but soon after, I was filled with apprehension. How could I possibly do justice in writing about such a knowledgeable and accomplished person? I feel unworthy of capturing even a fraction of his wisdom. Here, I will share my experiences of seeing Jagadis Da up close as an elder brother. I first met Jagadis Da in 1964. I had completed my Higher Secondary a year earlier, while he had just enrolled in the M.Sc. Applied Mathematics programme at the University of Calcutta. At that time, he resided at the Ramakrishna Mission Kolkata Vidyarthi Ashram in Belgharia. It was at this Vidyarthi Ashram that I first met him. He had completed his undergraduate studies at the Ramakrishna Mission Vidyamandira in Belur and had come to the Vidyarthi Ashram for his postgraduate studies. During his five years at Vidyamandira, he was deeply immersed in the philosophy of Ramakrishna.

The word *Snaatak* (graduate) is fittingly linked to *Snaat* (immersed), as he had imbibed its essence profoundly. In fact, he even took formal initiation there.

At the Vidyarthi Ashrama, Jagadis Da stayed in a two-seated room on the first floor of Yogananda Dham. I stayed in a nearby four-seated room. Our proximity allowed for frequent and meaningful interactions. He was incredibly disciplined, especially in attending prayers and fulfilling his duties at the Vidyarthi Ashrama. In those days, the path leading to the Ashrama was not paved with stones or gravel; it had open drains covered with water hyacinths. I remember working with him to clear them. He also guided me in my studies.

How can I ever forget such brotherly affection?

He joined the Mathematics Department, IIT Kharagpur as a faculty member. Among the distinguished professors of the time, he carved out a space for himself. His career flourished, extending beyond IIT Kharagpur to various universities and higher education institutions across India and abroad. Numerous accolades and recognitions followed, both nationally and internationally.

During the 50th anniversary of IIT Kharagpur, he served as the Head of the Mathematics Department. His efforts in compiling and publishing the department's commemorative volume were truly commendable. That labour-intensive initiative will serve as an invaluable reference for the department for the next fifty years.

Now, let me talk about something beyond these external accomplishments—*Para Vidya* (spiritual knowledge). While Jagadis Da has achieved immense success in material knowledge (*Apara Vidya*), I believe he holds spiritual wisdom (*Para Vidya*) in high regard. He does not openly express this side of him, but I have always sensed it. Even within his family—his wife and children, all of whom are well-established—he seems to have prioritized spiritual growth above all else.

When I saw the news that both Jagadis Da and Dr. Jayant Vishnu Narlikar received the *Rammohan* Award in the same year, I felt immense joy. Interestingly, I believe both of these scientists hold deep reverence for *Para Vidya* (spiritual wisdom). Perhaps I have gone a bit overboard in expressing this thought, but it is one of the things I admire most about Jagadis Da and his family—their spiritual atmosphere.

CHAPTER 44

Looking Back

Swapan Bhattacharya
Retired Acting Principal, Government College, Kailashahar, Tripura

At a certain age, looking back on life brings a sense of joy. Whenever I think of Jagadis Da, the image of Ramakrishna Mission Vidyamandira at Belur Math comes alive—a dream institution envisioned by Swami Vivekananda himself. It was Swamiji who named it *Vidyamandira*, and under his blessings, it has flourished and continues to shine brighter.

When I joined Vidyamandir in 1964 and stayed at East Hostel, the person who left the strongest impression on me was none other than Dr. Jagadis Chandra Misra, a man who is now internationally recognized and a former professor of IIT Kharagpur.

I have met very few people in my life as honest and soft-spoken as Jagadis Da. Even today, in my retired years, his radiant, cheerful face vividly appears in my memories. To us, the students of the Vidyamandira during that time, he was an inspiring and respected elder brother.

Many years later, when I visited IIT Kharagpur in connection with a training programme for my daughter, I happened to come across Jagadis Da, who was then the Head of the Mathematics Department. Seeing him, I was amazed—he was still the same, always smiling, exuding the same luminous personality.

For some reason, Jagadis Da was also deeply cherished among the monks of Belur Math. During our time at the Vidyamandira, revered Swami Shantanandaji Maharaj lived at Belur Math. He was a mantra-disciple of Holy Mother Sri Sri Sarada Devi and was regarded by the monks as a spiritually enlightened soul. Jagadis Da was especially dear to Swami Shantanandaji, who showered him with immense affection.

I remember how, during various Vidyamandira events, our then-principal and East Hostel's Warden, revered Swami Gokulanandaji, would send Jagadis Da and me to distribute invitation letters to the monks in the Monks' Quarters of Belur Math. Even after sixty long years, those memories remain crystal clear in my mind.

On the occasion of Holy Mother Sri Sarada Devi's birth anniversary, it was often our responsibility, under Jagadis Da's leadership, to decorate the temple with flowers.

Author Pratibha Basu once wrote in *Desh* magazine, *"Memories are always sweet."* Today, as I reminisce about Jagadis Da, I deeply understand the truth in those words.

Memories of Jagadis Da are forever joyful.

CHAPTER 45

My Intimate Friend Jagadis

Paresh Manna
Retired Inspector, Food and Supply, Government of West Bengal

Some memories of our close companionship of student life, with my childhood friend Jagadis, often peeps in my mind. Sitting side by side during the Saraswati Puja celebrations, and the day of the Mathematics exam in the School Final—those moments are unforgettable. Egra Jhatulal High School was our examination center. On our way to the center, Jagadis suddenly felt the urge to have some rasgullas before the exam. The three of us—Jagadis, Tarak, and I—went to a sweet shop, enjoyed rasgullas, and it was Jagadis, who paid for all of us. Thankfully, none of us "scored a zero" in the exam.

Another time, Jagadis along with Boudi (his wife) was going to his house by rickshaw. I was walking toward Kharai on my way to Medinipur. Boudi seemed to enjoy the journey quite a lot. Then Jagadis took out a betel leaf from a container and handed it to me, saying, "Take one and have a chew." The taste of that betel leaf and the flavor of our friendship linger with me to this day, bringing me joy during my leisure hours.

"The hand that rocks the cradle rules the world."

What could better capture the immense influence of a mother on shaping her child's character? The life of Ishwar Chandra Vidyasagar, shaped by his mother Bhagavati Devi, is a bright example in this context.

I am reminded of an incident related to this. Once, I had some particular piece of work at IIT Kharagpur, where I suddenly met Jagadis. He took me to his office room in his department and introduced me to his colleagues as his childhood friend without slightest hesitation. Later that evening, he insisted on taking me to his residence at IIT. His mother and his wife were so delighted to see me, as if I was a long-lost acquaintance.

To my surprise, during dinner, I learned that at his mother's request, non-vegetarian dishes had been specially prepared that day, only because of me.

Since his father passed away, his family had adopted a strictly vegetarian lifestyle. When I thought about his mother's willingness to break that rule for me, I felt deeper respect for her. Reflecting on the fact that Jagadis has inherited the noble qualities from her fills me with pride.

Jagadis married to his wife at a tender age. After marriage, she did not take up any job to dedicate herself to making their life more comfortable.

Jagadis became a distinguished teacher of Applied Mathematics, and I consider myself enriched by having a friend like him.

Having crossed eighty springs and now in my eighty-third year, while reminiscing about my intimate friend, Jagadis I feel highly delighted. *"Past memories are always a source of happiness."*

CHAPTER 46

Our Beloved Jagadis Da

Prof. Pranabesh Jana
Former Head of Mathematics Department,
Kalyani Government Engineering College, Kalyani, Nadia

The first successful embodiment of Swami Vivekananda's concept of "Man-Making Education," as envisioned by Swami Nirvedananda, was brought to life at the Belgharia Ramkrishna Mission Calcutta Students' Home. It was here, in the middle of 1964, that I first met Jagadis Da. At the time, I was a second-year B.Sc. student, and Jagadis Da had joined the Mission as a first-year M.Sc. (Applied Mathematics) student at the University of Calcutta.

Before this, Jagadis Da had graduated from Belur Ramakrishna Mission Vidyamandira. Many of us at the Mission, including myself, regarded him with great respect. His dignified demeanor, ever-smiling face, and genuine warmth made him everyone's favorite in no time. I often felt that he had a special fondness for me, which was immensely encouraging for me.

In 1966, after leaving the Mission, about 8–9 of our classmates established our first shared mess in Belgharia. Jagadis Da would visit us there occasionally, and his presence always filled us with enthusiasm.

The Belgharia Vidyarthi Ashram became a medium for maintaining our connections. Later, as I progressed in life's journey, I learned that Jagadis Da had joined IIT Kharagpur as a faculty. At that time, I had moved from Shibpur B.E. College to join Chandannagar Government College. Though I received UGC approval for doing Ph.D. under Jagadis Da, my plans were thwarted when the West Bengal government did not grant me the necessary leave. This was a significant setback for me.

However, Jagadis Da was kind enough to write me a glowing recommendation, stating: *"Pranabesh Jana's Optional Mathematics books for classes IX and X are very helpful to the students. They are particularly useful for bright students to develop their mathematical skills."*

Encouraged by Jagadis Da, I became the first to write a *Joint Entrance Mathematics* book specifically for students of West Bengal. Jagadis Da has always been a source of inspiration to me.

The establishment of "Medinipur Bhavan" (7B Balaram Ghosh Street, Shyampukur, Kolkata) by the Medinipur Coordination Association is a proud achievement for the people of Medinipur. Jagadis Da appreciated our collective efforts, which brings me great joy.

I sincerely wish for Jagadis Da's continued good health and happiness and hope that his contributions and influence grow even more expansive.

CHAPTER 47

Prof. J.C. Misra in My Eyes

Saroj Narayan Misra
Assistant Headmaster (Retd.), Tikrapara Higher Secondary School, Pariharpur, Pratapdighi, East Midnapore-721440

A rare soul, born in auspicious time, whose simplicity and divine growth could be observed from the very childhood. The innocence in his eyes, the smile on his lips, the words from his mouth, his writing style, and his thoughts all reflected purity. His attire has always been simple, and his manners, speech, and behavior ever graceful and restrained. This simple-hearted person is my dear uncle, the esteemed Dr. Jagadis Chandra Misra. He is a distantly brother of my mother, which is why I lovingly call him 'Mamu' (maternal uncle).

This remarkable soul was born in a remote village. From his childhood, he became beloved not only to the influential people of our area but also among the general public, due to his multiple virtues. I too am one of his great admirers. I keep track of all information about him, collecting them diligently. His childhood was shaped in a simple manner under the sincere care of his father, Ganes Chandra Misra, and his mother, *Ratnagarbha* Pramila Devi, in Bagmari village.

In the humble, unpretentious rural environment, a rare personality was nurtured into a life full of generosity and discipline. The joint family setup helped him grow into a well-behaved, disciplined, and rational individual. With the kindness of his father, Ganes Chandra, many poor and orphaned students found shelter in his home and had their education. Among them, the competition between Jagadis and Tarak Pahari of Bhairabadari village was particularly exciting. Though his father wanted him to become a doctor, fate had a different plan, and Jagadis became a renowned professor and devoted researcher.

After completing his primary education, Jagadis pursued his education at Tikrapara Ambikamoyee High School, where the sincere support of the teachers left a lasting impression on him, especially the English lessons by the Headmaster, Shri Pramatha Nath Basu, the Mathematics lessons by Shri Anil Kumar Bera, and the Sanskrit teachings of Panditmashai Jayanarayan Acharya (Gunakarbabu). Their influences enriched his educational journey considerably.

A crucial phase of his life began at the Belur Math residential Ramakrishna Mission Vidyamandira. Here, he dedicated his heart, mind, and intellect to the divine teachings of Sri Ramakrishna and Ma Sarada, strengthening the foundation of his character and personality. According to the scriptures: "Santoshah paramo labhah, satsango paramagati"—it is in good company that our mental transformation takes place, making our minds pure and our inner vision awakened. Jagadis himself says, "This is where my life's most valuable chapter began."

Though briefly, Dr. Misra started his career as a school teacher at Naipur Shanti Shudha Institution. Within two and a half months, in 1967, he joined the teaching faculty of Uluberia College. In 1971, he was awarded a Ph.D. in Applied Mathematics from Jadavpur University for his valuable research work In Applied Mathematics. In the same year, he joined IIT Kharagpur as a Lecturer. He became an Assistant Professor in 1978, a Professor in 1985, and the Department Head in 1998. In these administrative roles, he exhibited exceptional leadership.

Dr. Misra continued his research in addition to teaching and administrative duties. His research in applied mathematics, in different areas, like biomathematics, modeling and simulation, and physiological fluid dynamics, earned him international recognition.

Dr. Misra's research achievements and innovative teaching methods earned him the "Outstanding Teacher Award" from the Indian National Academy of Engineering (INAE) in 2013. He also received the *Ram Mohan Puraskar* for his distinguished contributions to the field of Mathematics in 2004, and several other accolades such as the Silver Jubilee Research Award from IIT Kharagpur (1984).

Dr. Misra served as the Pro-Vice Chancellor of SOA University in Bhubaneswar during 2009–2014 and later he joined the Centre for Health Care Science & Technology at IIEST Shibpur as an Adjunct Professor in January, 2015. He has worked as a Visiting Professor in renowned universities across Germany, Canada, Hong Kong, Malaysia, and several other countries. His research papers have been widely respected, and he has been an examiner and judge for numerous scientific works.

As a dedicated researcher, Dr. Misra's work spans a wide array of fields. His contributions to public health, biomedical engineering, and applied mathematics have earned global recognition. His relentless efforts and innate talent have transformed him from a boy from a remote village into a renowned scientist.

As a proud member of his community, we hold a deep sense of pride in his success. Moreover, as a native son of the area, he has repeatedly returned to support social welfare efforts and serve as a key patron of several institutions of our area.His father once wrote in a letter, "Jagadis has earned Ph.D. and D.Sc. Degrees at a young age. Some day, he will be a great scientist like Jagadis Chandra Bose."

His worthy wife, Shorasi Devi has been his constant source of encouragement since 1969. His children, Subhas and Sudip, have followed his footsteps. After pursuing higher education, they are occupying responsible positions at IIT Kanpur and IIT Kharagpur in the field of engineering, while his daughter, Sumita, is a faculty at IIEST Shibpur.

Dr. Misra's family continues his legacy. I offer my heartfelt prayers to Sri Sri Ramakrishna Dev and Sri Sri Ma Sarada Devi, that Dr. Misra's remaining years be filled with peace and fulfillment, bringing his life to complete success in every aspect."

CHAPTER 48

As I See Prof. Jagadis Chandra Misra

Saktipada Giri
Head Teacher, Ramakrishna-Sarada Shiksha Sadan,
Pratapdighi, Purba Medinipur-721440, West Bengal

The first time I saw Jagadis Babu was from a distance during my student years. At that time, I was in the ninth grade at Tikrapara Ambikamoyee High School. He was introduced on stage by our revered headmaster, Pramatha Nath Basu, as a distinguished alumnus of our school. Though I didn't fully understand the significance back then, I could guess that he must be an extraordinary person.

Despite being born in a humble school teacher's home in a remote village of Bengal, his father, Ganes Chandra Misra, through unwavering dedication, nurtured him into a scientist who earned recognition on the global stage. By a stroke of fate, when I came to establish the Ramakrishna-Sarada Shiksha Sadan at Pratapdidighi, I had the privilege of meeting Jagadis Babu face-to-face in 1987 at his residence in Kharagpur IIT campus. I was taken aback by his simple and modest lifestyle. Despite his immense knowledge and scholarly achievements, he remained deeply rooted in the values of rural Bengal. Over time, I developed a close bonding with his family, and I came to realize that such individuals could only be shaped by an extraordinary household and a truly meaningful education.

I attended several social gatherings at his home, where many esteemed scholars were present, but what touched me most was how he warmly welcomed us, his fellow villagers. His hospitality remains etched in my memory. Though an eminent scientist, his passion for Bengal's cultural heritage has been profound. In 2000, he proposed hosting a cultural event by the children of Pratapdighi Ramakrishna-Sarada Shiksha Sadan at IIT. We enthusiastically embraced the idea and staged a memorable bilingual (Bengali and English) program at IIT's Netaji Auditorium. News spread like a wildfire in and around Pratapdighi region that, under Jagadis Babu's guidance, we had performed at a globally renowned institution. Many prominent figures from our hometown attended, and not a single detail of the event's organization was overlooked. We were accommodated in fifteen rooms—all arranged by none other than this remarkable son of rural Bengal, Jagadis Babu!

In 2004, he was honored with the prestigious 'Rammohan Puraskar' for his outstanding research contributions in the field of Mathematics. Instead of keeping this accomplishment to himself, he brought the Puraskar to his birthplace, offering portions of the prize money to Pratapdighi Ramakrishna-Sarada Siksha Sadan and *Amarpur Shri Guru Ashrama*. To commemorate this, we arranged a small felicitation ceremony. Dressed simply in a traditional *dhoti-panjabi*, he humbly introduced himself as just another son of the village. Though only a few people were formally invited, a large number of local dignitaries turned up unannounced just to meet him. It was then that I truly realized—Jagadis Babu was not just a scientist; he was a revered figure of the Patashpur Police station area.

Often, society underestimates the contribution of women, but it would be improper to overlook the role of his wife, Srimati Shorasi Boudi, in the life of Jagadis Chandra. She has been a pillar of love and support, standing steadfastly beside him throughout his life. Despite being the parents of two sons and a daughter, Jagadis Babu and his wife cared for his aging parents, Ganes Chandra and Pramila Devi, with the devotion one would show to deities. His attachment to his homeland remains as strong as ever. He regularly attends local events and frequently inquires about the well-being of our village. We will remain grateful to him forever.

In my lifetime, I have never encountered another person who, despite being so far away, maintains such deep connections with his roots. A few years ago, the Pratapdighi Vidyasagar Mela Committee honoured him as one of Patashpur's most distinguished intellectuals and scientists.

CHAPTER 49

A Few Words about Dr. Jagadis Chandra Misra

Dharanidhar Gayen
Former Teacher, Dashagram M.B.K.B. Girls' School,
Dashagram, Sabang, Paschim Medinipur

Dr. Jagadis Chandra Misra is the son of Ganes Chandra Misra, a renowned teacher of Tikarapara High School and Pramila Devi in Bagmari village of undivided Medinipur district. The name 'Jagadis Chandra' was given by his father with the hope that he would grow up to be a scientist like Sir Jagadis Chandra Bose. That wish has been fulfilled, as Jagadis has become a globally renowned scientist, receiving numerous honors and awards from India and abroad.

The school where he studied, later gained fame as Tikarapara Higher Secondary School. Jagadis Chandra, a meritorious student of the School, earned an M.Sc. in Applied Mathematics from the University of Calcutta in 1966, followed by a Ph.D. from Jadavpur University in 1971, and a D.Sc. from the University of Calcutta in 1984. During the past six decades, he has been involved in teaching and research in India, Germany, and North America.

In 1971, he joined IIT Kharagpur as a lecturer, was promoted to the position of Assistant Professor in 1979, and became a full professor in 1987. He also served as the department head from 1998 to 2001 at IIT Kharagpur. He has been invited as a Visiting Professor to Universities in Japan, England, the U.S., Canada, and other countries. With over 250 research papers published in prestigious journals, his contributions to *mathematical modelling in physiology and medicine* are noteworthy.

Dr. Misra received the IIT Kharagpur Silver Jubilee Award in 1984 and was elected a Fellow of the National Academy of Sciences in 1987. He has been a member of several high-level policy-making committees in India, focusing on science education. After his retirement from IIT Kharagpur, he served as the Pro Vice-Chancellor of SOA University in Bhubaneswar and then as Adjunct Professor at IIEST Shibpur.

He has been honoured with numerous awards, including "Bharat Gaurav" and "Rammohan Award," and continues to dedicate himself to education, cultural advancement, and scientific research.

To honour his father's memory, he donated funds to establish the *Revered Ganes Chandra Misra Children's Science Laboratory* at Ramakrishna Sarada Shiksha Sadan, a beloved institution in the Pratapdighi area.

A Tribute Through Poetry "The Glory of Jagadis"

Time and again, Bengal's homes give rise
To intellectuals whose knowledge fills the skies.
With their contributions, the world's knowledge grows,
Leaving behind legacies everyone knows.

Such is Jagadis, a worthy heir,
Whose brilliance the world cannot compare.
We often overlook greatness in our midst,
Only to hear the world sing their praise in earnest.

World-class institutions call him with care,
Welcoming his wisdom with love to share.
From his efforts, humanity gains,
While our nation's honour he sustains.

With "Bharat Gaurav" and other awards in hand,
His research continues to expand.
Two hundred fifty papers, a tidal wave of thought,
Have brought him the highest honours sought.

In journals worldwide, his works appear,
Praised by scientists both far and near.
Jagadis, once our own, is now the world's pride,
Illuminating science, a beacon and guide.

Through his dedication, new branches sprout,
Enlightening the world with profound discoveries.
With united voices, we sing his glory,
Celebrating his legacy, an inspiring story.

(This is a tribute to Dr. Jagadis Chandra Misra, a scientist of global repute, honoured with "Bharat Gaurav," "Rammohan Prize," and many other accolades. He is a great pride of our region and an inspiration to us all.)

CHAPTER 50

The Song of Jagadis Chandra
(Rhythm: Dadra | Scale: Ma-Ga)

Binod Bihari Jana
Headmaster, Majna Primary School (Retd), Pratapdighi,
Purba Medinipur-721440

Jagadis Misra's contributions to mathematics
Have elevated the honour of Bengal and India's inhabitants.

We know of many Indian mathematicians,
Aryabhatta and Srinivasa Ramanujan among them.

Radhanath Sikdar, no less significant,
Is famed for calculating Everest's height with brilliance.

Jagadis Misra joins their esteemed ranks,
Unveiling new discoveries in mathematics.

In Purba Medinipur's Patashpur police station area,
Lies Bagmari village, known to all familiar.

Born to Ganes Chandra and Pramila Devi, their cherished son,
He solved complex problems with ease and precision.

His father aptly named him Jagadis,
Hoping he'd become a scientist like Jagadis Bose, a wish fulfilled.

Education began at Majna Primary in Pratapdighi,
Then on to Tikarapara High School from there swiftly.

His father was a teacher at the same school,
Jagadis excelled, unmatched in intellect and rule.

From there, he moved to Belur Ramakrishna Mission,
At Calcutta University, he achieved stellar distinction.

Teaching at Naipur High and Uluberia College,
Students adored him, a jewel of knowledge.

He earned a Ph.D. from Jadavpur University,
And built relationships with mathematicians across the country.

Joining IIT Kharagpur as a professor,
He spent decades there, a mentor and researcher.

Even in retirement, he finds no rest,
Travelling tirelessly for work, east and west.

Japan, Germany, Great Britain, and Rome,
Invited as a professor, he carried wisdom from home.

Applying mathematics to medical science,
adding a novel dimension to its alliance.

With over 250 research papers to his name,
His studies in math have garnered great acclaim.

Honoured by the various awards of India,
Prestigious awards like "Bharat Gaurav" and "Rammohan."

Elected to the National Academy of Sciences,
And adorned with the Outstanding Teachers Award for his brilliance.

He received IIT's Silver Jubilee Award,
And delved further into research as his reward.

Excelling in teaching new facets of math,
Honoured and celebrated across the globe, his unique path.

His two sons, Subhas and Sudip, excel too,
Both IIT Professors, carrying forward his view.

His daughter Sumita shines no less,
Teaching at IIEST Shibpur with finesse.

Soft-spoken and humble, Jagadis leads a simple life,
Has earned admiration from all, far and wide.

A mathematician, an educator, a rare genius,
The world recognizes his extraordinary brilliance.

May this global mathematician stay in everyone's heart,
wishing him a healthy and fulfilling life to chart.

Jagadis Misra's legacy is like nectar divine,
Binod Bihari says, "Hearing this, you are blessed in kind."

CHAPTER 51

Mathematician from Patashpur Renowned in Europe and America*

Debmalya Bagchi
Journalist, Anandabazar Patrika, Kolkata

Born in a remote village, he was inspired by his father to devote himself to mathematics from an early age. That very passion for mathematics took him to the pinnacle of research. His professorial work at IIT Kharagpur has been recognized by many prestigious institutions. The story of mathematician Jagadis Chandra Misra, as told to **Debmalya Bagchi.**

Q1. You were born in a rural area. Are you from a farming family?

A: Not exactly. Many of my ancestors were Sanskrit scholars of distinction. Some practiced Ayurvedic medicine and even prepared medicines themselves. My father, Ganes Chandra, was a teacher at Tikarapara Higher Secondary School in East Midnapore. He was proficient in Mathematics, Sanskrit, and English. He also served as the President of the Union Board. He was a social worker too. My mother, Pramila Devi, was a homemaker. We lived in a joint family and owned some land. My uncle managed the household and ran a charitable homeopathy dispensary. I was born in Bagmari village under Patashpur Police Station in the undivided Midnapore district on October 7, 1943 on the day of *Maha Ashtami* during *Durga Puja*. My childhood was spent there.

Q2. Were you a student of Belur Ramakrishna Mission Vidyamandira?

A: My primary education was at Pratapdighi Primary School in a nearby village. I passed my school final examination from my father's school in 1959. Only

* Original Bengali version published in the District News Supplement (under **'Kriti Katha'** – Story of Accomplished Persons) Anandabazar Patrika, Kolkata, 31 October 2025 is included at the end of this book.

two of us received first division marks—one was me, the other was an orphan whom my father had brought home and admitted to Tikarapara High School. As per my father's wish, I joined Belur Ramakrishna Mission Vidyamandira because the institution emphasized not only academics but also character building, physical fitness and self-reliance. I passed my I.Sc. (Intermediate in Science) from there.

Q3. Did you pursue higher studies there as well?

A: When I was in my second year of I.Sc., Belur College started a three-year degree course. After passing I.Sc., I got an opportunity to study at Presidency College, where I could have completed my degree in two years. But I chose to stay at Belur College for its enriching academic environment. I earned my B.Sc. (Honours) in Mathematics there and later enrolled at Calcutta University for M.Sc. in Applied Mathematics. I lived at the Belgharia Ramakrishna Mission Calcutta Students' Home and completed my M.Sc. in 1966.

Q4. Have you always been drawn to mathematics?

A: Yes, since childhood. My father was the main reason. He used to make me solve many problems from various books. I had completed the eighth-grade mathematics book while in seventh grade. I received letter marks in Mathematics both in my school finals and ISc.

Q5. Did your career begin at IIT?

A: No. After completing my master's degree, in March 1967, I joined Naipur Shanti Sudha Institution in East Midnapore as a mathematics teacher. After teaching there till June, I joined Uluberia College as a lecturer on July 23. I began research under Prof. Bibhuti Bhusan Sen of Jadavpur University, a renowned scholar. I earned my Ph.D. in 1971, and that same year, on August 9, I joined IIT Kharagpur as a faculty in the mathematics department. I earned my D.Sc. from Calcutta University in 1984.

Q6. What was the main area of your research?

A: My work mainly focused on mathematical modelling based on applied mathematics. That means I worked on creating mathematical models to aid theoretical research in various fields. For example, in the study of blood flow in arteries, the analysis of fluid movement within tubular structures can be modelled mathematically. Most of my research was based on similar principles.

Q7. That's quite a broad field of research?

A: Yes, I have worked in Applied Mathematics, Biomathematics, Physiological Fluid Dynamics, and Mechanics of Fluids and Solids. But my primary focus has been Biomechanics — studying cardiovascular dynamics, fracture and remodeling dynamics of bones, and more. My research has contributed to identifying the location and extent of brain injuries when head is subject to an impact load, analyzing different patterns of blood flow, and other biomedical problems. I have published over 250 research papers in international journals.

Q8. Was your first trip abroad related to research?

A: Yes, in 1975. I received a Humboldt Fellowship from Germany — my first trip abroad. I was awarded for my work on estimating the thermal reactions of solid materials when heat is applied to the body in an uneven manner. I spent two years doing research in biomechanics at Hannover Technical University, jointly with the Biomedical Engineering Division of Hannover Medical University. In 1981, I went to Japan, and later to Europe, the USA, and Canada, before returning to India. I delivered lectures and participated in international conferences at prestigious institutions such as Courant Institute of Mathematical Sciences and Cornell Medical Center in New York, University of Calgary, Canada, Tokyo Medical University, and Kobe University.

Q9. You've received numerous awards for research and teaching, both in India and abroad?

A: Yes. The Rammohan Award (2004) for outstanding contributions to mathematics moved me deeply. Earlier, in 1984, I received the Silver Jubilee Research Award from IIT Kharagpur, which remains unforgettable. The INAE Outstanding Teacher Award (2013) from the Indian National Academy of Engineering, Delhi, was also a great encouragement. Moreover, many institutions across countries have elected me as a Fellow, their highest academic honour.

Q10. Did you continue teaching or research after retirement?

A: I retired from IIT Kharagpur on April 30, 2009. The very next day, on May 1,

I joined SOA University, Bhubaneswar as Pro Vice-Chancellor. My main objective there was to promote research activities. In 2015, I joined Indian Institute of Engineering Science and Technology, Shibpur, continuing my research until 2019. Since then, I have spent time doing limited research and writing books. Encouraged by scholars and well-wishers, I have been writing my autobiography. My Bengali book *"Achinpurer Ak Pathik"* (A Traveller from an Unknown Land) has already been published, and its English translation, "A Traveller in an Unknown Land," is nearing completion.

Several literary figures, historians, and former college principals and professors have published a collection about me titled "Nana Chokhe Ak Borenya Ganit Sadhak" (A Revered Mathematician in Many Eyes). Its English version, "A Mathematics Wizard in Different Eyes," has also been completed. Both books are being published (now in Press) by Allied Publishers, a reputed publishing house based in Noida.

Q11. In one English publication, you were described as 'A Mathematics Magician (Wizard).' Another article referred to you as "An Extraordinary Person." How do you feel about such titles?

A: It's hard for me to say why they described me that way. I believe they did so in recognition of my successful application of mathematical research in various fields, including physiology and medicine.

Q12. Are you still living on the IIT campus?

A: Yes. I have three children. The elder son, Subhas Chandra, is a professor in the Department of Management Sciences at IIT Kanpur. Daughter, Sumita Mukhopadhyay (Misra), is a faculty member at the Indian Institute of Engineering Science and Technology, Shibpur. Son-in-law, Achintya Mukhopadhyay, is a professor in the Mechanical Engineering Department at Jadavpur University. Younger son, Sudip, is a professor in the Department of Computer Science and Engineering at IIT Kharagpur. That's why, after retirement, I didn't have to leave IIT. I live here with my wife in the midst of my sons, daughters-in-law, and grandchildren—occasionally spending time in Kolkata and Kanpur.

CHAPTER 52

Encourager of Children's Mathematical Pursuits*

A Staff Correspondent
Anandabazar Patrika

Renowned internationally for his dedication to mathematics, Professor Jagadis Chandra Misra continues to inspire young learners in the field—a passion he inherited from his father. Today, his efforts to promote mathematical interest among students have earned well-deserved recognition.

During his tenure as Head of the Department of Mathematics at IIT Kharagpur (1998–2001), Prof. Misra began organizing initiatives to encourage students' enthusiasm for mathematics. He hosted several national and international conferences at IIT Kharagpur, and for three consecutive years, he conducted special workshop and mathematics quizzes and geometric model competition for school students from across the state.

Reflecting on his life, Prof. Misra believes that three key phases shaped his journey. The first was his education at Belur Ramakrishna Mission Vidyamandira, where he developed both academic depth and moral character as well as self-reliance and physical fitness.

The second was his teaching career at IIT Kharagpur, which expanded his intellectual horizons.

The third was his experience in Germany, where he received the "Humboldt Fellowship" and spent two years researching in biomechanics. That work, he says, brought him international recognition in research circles.

"Opportunities alone are not enough—you must know how to use them," he says. "I've worked very hard. If today's youth possess honesty, perseverance, and patience, nothing can hold them back. Success is inevitable."

* The Original Bengali version (at the end of this book) was published in the District News Supplement of the **Anandabazar Patrika,** Kolkata on 31st October, 2025.

He adds, "It's important to have the mindset to work for your country. Just as I returned home despite opportunities abroad, my children too have chosen to stay and work in India, ignoring many attractive offers from overseas."

Prof. Misra places great value on family bonds. He credits both his father's encouragement and the selfless support of his wife, Mrs. Shorasi Misra.

They married in 1969; Shorasi, daughter of Amarapur village under Patashpur Police Station, was an honours graduate with a B.Ed degree, teaching at a high school in Bagmari village. After marriage, she left her job to take care of their household.

"I've travelled abroad many times," Prof. Misra recalls. "But she always stayed here to care for my mother. She never complained. After my mother's death, when I went to Germany again in 2019 for research, she accompanied me."

Prof. Misra's life is a blend of academic excellence, dedication to teaching, and deep personal values—an inspiring example for generations of students and scholars alike.

CHAPTER 53

Banyan Trees of the Society*

Mrs. Sonali Ghosh
Director, Nikkon Dance Academy, IIT Campus, Kharagpur–721302

This morning, I read the articles based on Debmalya Bagchi's interview with Prof. Jagadis Chandra Misra, a former Professor of Mathematics at IIT Kharagpur. The articles bearing the headlines "Mathematician from Patashpur Renowned in Europe and America" and "Encourager of Children's Mathematical Pursuits" have appeared on 31 October 2025 in the Anandabazar Patrika, the most popular Bangla Daily published from Kolkata.

I felt very good—especially for his philosophy of life, dedication, and honesty towards work. It gave me fresh inspiration and energy to live and work anew. I convey my respect to him. People like him are like banyan trees of the society. Reading such writings makes one realize how much peace, courage, and understanding of life awaken in their shade.

* Private communication (English version) with a campus resident, IIT Kharagpur, dated 31 October 2025.

CHAPTER 54

A Scientist Who Thinks for the Nation*

Nikunja Bihari Ghorai
Former Teacher, Panskura Bradley Birt Higher Secondary School,
Panskura, Purba Medinipur

Attracted by better research prospects and facilities, many of the finest scientists and technologists of our country, after completing their education in India, have long continued to go abroad. In many cases, they even accept foreign citizenship and settle there permanently—virtually forgetting their own country. Sometimes their names even appear on the list of Nobel laureates as foreign nationals.

However, scientists like Acharya Jagadish Chandra Bose, Prafulla Chandra Ray, and C.V. Raman were exceptions. Despite immense hardship, they pursued scientific research in India and served their nation.

Thanks to the District Edition of the Anandabazar Patrika's district edition for publishing, on October 31, 2025, the article titled "Encourager of Children's Mathematical Pursuits" featuring the inspiring life of Professor Jagadis Chandra Misra, former Head of the Department of Mathematics at IIT Kharagpur.

He is not only an encourager of children's interest in mathematics but also a promoter of moral and character building through education. Ignoring lucrative research opportunities abroad, he has devoted his entire life to the pursuit of mathematics in India—a practice he continues even after retirement. Despite receiving chances abroad, he returned home.

To truly embody the saying "Preach by practicing", his children too have stayed back in India, resisting the lure of foreign offers, and are continuing to work in their homeland—a rarity today.

* Original Bengali version appeared under the "Letters to the Editor" section in Anandabazar Patrika on 3rd November 2025.

He organized seminars, geometric model competitions, Mathematical puzzles and quizzes to inspire school students in mathematics. As an alumnus of the Ramakrishna Mission educational institutions, he is also one of those who instill the importance of character building.

In his own words: *"It's not just about getting opportunities—one must know how to use them. If today's generation possesses honesty, perseverance, and patience, nothing can stop them. One must also have the mindset to work for the nation."*

At a time when tragic incidents like repeated student suicides are occurring in higher educational institutions such as IITs, the presence of dedicated motivators and character-builders like him—a mathematician and a true mentor—is profoundly necessary.

CHAPTER 55

Inspiring the Young to Love Mathematics*

Correspondent
Teerbhumi Daily, Contai, Purba Medinipur

Internationally acclaimed for his devotion to mathematics, Prof. Jagadis Chandra Misra traces his inspiration back to his father. The same passion for encouraging mathematical learning in others continue to define his life. His contributions to fostering enthusiasm for mathematics among students are now widely recognised.

While serving as the Head of the Department of Mathematics at IIT Kharagpur, Prof. Misra organised several national and international conferences at IIT, creating a vibrant academic environment. Among these were annual workshops and math quizzes for school students held for three consecutive years attracting participants from across the state of West Bengal.

Prof. Misra reflects on three distinct phases of life that shaped his journey. The first was his time at Ramakrishna Mission Vidyamandir, Belur Math where he believes he advanced not only in academics but also in the building of character. The second was his tenure at IIT Kharagpur where teaching and research expanded his horizon. The final turning point came with the "Humboldt Fellowship" in Germany, where he spent two consecutive years from 1975 to 1977, working in biomechanics—a field of research that brought him global recognition.

The mathematician remarks, "Opportunity alone is not enough—one must know how to use it properly. I have worked very hard. If today's young people possess the same honesty, perseverance and patience nothing can stop them. Success will definitely come to them".

He adds another note of wisdom: "One must have the mindset to work for one's country. Even though I had opportunities abroad, I chose to return to

* English version of the report published in Teerbhumi Daily, Contai, East Midnapore, 2nd November 2025.

India. My children, too, despite many lucrative offers overseas, have continued their work here at home."

A life marked by discipline, humility and devotion—Professor Jagadis Chandra Misra stands as a living example of how true passion for mathematics can inspire generation.

Section IV

Relations

CHAPTER 56

My Brother, My Inspiration: The Story of Dada

Parames Misra
Section Manager, Ontario Power Generation, Canada

How do you describe someone who is both a loved and respected elder brother in your personal life and a distant figure in your professional realm? This is the challenge I face when speaking of my esteemed elder brother, Prof. Dr. Jagadis Chandra Misra, who is a globally renowned expert in the field of mathematics, with a particular focus on biomechanics. His groundbreaking contributions to biomechanics and biomedical mathematics have earned him international acclaim. Through his pioneering research, he has advanced the understanding of complex medical issues and garnered prestigious accolades worldwide. His expertise has taken him across the globe, where he shares his knowledge through lectures at renowned universities, inspiring countless students and researchers. Despite his global success, he remains deeply rooted in his faith, leading a humble life dedicated to both his work and spiritual values. This unique blend of academic excellence, global recognition, and simple living makes him a role model for many.

As I begin to write about Dada, I must admit that, despite being his younger brother, I was unaware of many aspects of his life until recently, when I received the two books published not long ago. One book, "Achinpurer ek Pathik" (A Traveller in an Unknown Land), is written by him and details his life from early childhood to the present, sharing his vast knowledge in a simple, readable style that reflects his own simplicity. The other book, "Nana Chokhe Ek Barenya Ganit Sadhak" (An Admirable Devotee of Mathematics Through Many Eyes), is a compilation of writings by various people who have known him, beautifully edited by Prof. Dr. Haripada Maiti, Sri Manmatha Nath Das, and Sri Balailal Das. These books have revealed many information and facets of his life to me and have become my treasured possessions. I extend my sincere gratitude to all the publishers, editors, writers, and contributors who made these publications possible. As I analyze Dada's life for this article, much of the information is based on my personal experiences, but some are drawn from these newly acquired facts.

In this article, I will not attempt to describe Dada's academic achievements, as I am neither competent nor capable of doing so. Instead, I will try to describe other aspects of his life outside his academic realm, based on my observations and thoughts. Examining his life, we observe his upbringing in a rural environment until high school, followed by his college and university years immersed in the spiritual ambiance of the Ramakrishna Mission at Belur Math and Belgharia. He then embarked on a long and distinguished academic career fetching him national and international recognition and fame. Now in his post-retirement days, he remains highly active and engaged in various pursuits, while enjoying his time with his family, especially the grandchildren. Each phase of life leads to the next, beginning with birth and early childhood, which form the foundation of a longer life. Dada was born on the auspicious day of Durgashtami (the eighth day of Durga Puja or Navratri) in October, 1943 at Bagmari in the Midnapur district of West Bengal in India. He grew up in a joint family in a rural setting, devoid of luxuries and even many necessities we take for granted today. This minimal lifestyle helped him develop valuable qualities early in life. I have always known him to be simple and modest.

To give readers a glimpse into the rural setting where Dada grew up, especially after spending the rest of his life in the bustling towns and cities or traveling around the world, the famous Dwijendrageeti by the renowned poet Dwijendralal Ray, "Dhana dhanya pushpa bhara, amader ei basundhara" (Lavished with a wealth of grains and flowers is our Mother Earth), comes to mind. Our two-storied mud house in the village of Bagmari was vibrant with life, filled with lively interactions among people of all ages, from toddlers to the elderly. It was surrounded by ponds and gardens brimming with fragrant flowers and delicious fruits. I remember the long stretches of paddy fields swaying rhythmically in the breeze during the growing season and the empty fields after the rice was harvested. The melodious sounds of birds would awaken us at dawn and doze us to sleep at night. Without electricity, our evenings were illuminated by kerosene lanterns to do the evening activities, e.g. to study, have dinner. In this rural setting, Dada completed his primary education alongside Didi at Majna Primary School, located next to the Pratapdighi marketplace. After finishing primary school education, Dada went on to complete his secondary education at Tikrapara High School, where our father was a teacher, teaching English and Mathematics.

Our father had a keen interest towards gardening and cultivated a variety of flowers, vegetables, and fruits. We also had pets, including cows, bulls, cats, hens, and ducks. Some of our necessities were met by our own resources: rice from our fields plowed by our bulls, milk from our cows, vegetables and fruits from our gardens, fish from our ponds, and eggs from our hens and ducks. Thus, Dada developed a sense of necessity for fresh and pure food that he consumes. So, on a humorous note, he rebelled when he was given a glass of milk mixed with water during his childhood. Dada's love for gardening was evident when he brought a Nagalingam plant from Belur Math and planted it at our village home. It grew into a magnificent tree with beautiful, fragrant flowers. Later, Dada, Boudi, their son Sudip, and daughter-in-law Satamita cultivated beautiful gardens at their quarters in IIT Kharagpur, with the help of gardeners as needed. The fresh flowers from these gardens are offered to the deities daily, maintaining a spiritual atmosphere at home.

Rural and urban lives each have their pros and cons. Let's explore the qualities Dada may have developed from his rural upbringing. Rural life often means spending more time in nature, fostering an appreciation for the environment, mindfulness, and tranquility. Activities like walking, farming, or simply being outdoors become part of daily life. Dada experienced this through regular walks to school (about 2 km) or to catch a bus (about 8 km) to go to distant places. Rural communities are often tight knit, with people depending on each other for borrowing items, helping with tasks, or providing support during tough times, fostering a strong sense of community and cooperation.

Rural living offers more opportunities for solitude and reflection, supporting mindfulness and mental well-being. The absence of constant noise, crowds, and stimuli promotes inner peace and mental clarity, blending well with the spiritual atmosphere at Belur Math and Vidyarthi Ashrama, Belgharia where Dada spent time later in life. In rural areas, people are often more attuned to using resources carefully, fostering a minimalist or conservationist mindset. This is important in a world where extravagant spending coexists with widespread poverty. Limited entertainment options in rural settings encourage simpler pleasures like stargazing, outdoor activities, or community gatherings, embedding simplicity in Dada's daily life.

Now, let's delve a bit into his spiritual journey. Our parents were deeply pious and spiritually minded. We would wake up in our childhood to the sound of our father chanting mantras, and we have seen our mother doing japam even amidst her busy schedules. Dada inherited this spiritual mindset from his childhood. Our parents were initiated by Sitaram Das Omkarnath Thakur, a renowned spiritual saint in West Bengal, and followed spiritual practices in this tradition rooted in Bhakti Yoga (devotional love) and Vaishnavism (worship of Lord Krishna).

His spiritual foundation from childhood seamlessly integrated with his later life when he was admitted to Ramakrishna Mission Vidyamandira at Belur Math for post-secondary education. Here, he nurtured his spiritual mindset and aspirations. Adolescence, a crucial period in everyone's life, saw him studying in the pure, sublime atmosphere of the Ramakrishna Mission—first at Belur Vidyamandira, and later at the Ramakrishna Mission Calcutta Students' Home in Belgharia while pursuing his Master's degree from Science College (University of Calcutta) in Kolkata. Regular interactions with the spiritual Swamis at Belur Math further strengthened his foundation. In his book, he describes his admission to RK Mission Vidyamandira at Belur Math as the first turning point in his life. This opportunity granted him access to a spiritual powerhouse, where he was initiated by Swami Shankarananda, then President of Ramakrishna Math & Mission and a disciple of Swami Brahmananda, the first President of RK Math & Mission and "spiritual son" of Thakur Sri Ramakrishna. He also had the privilege of interacting with and receiving blessings from other esteemed Swamis of the Ramakrishna Sangha, including Swami Shantananda, a direct disciple of Ma Sarada Devi.

As I was reading the third chapter of his book, where he describes his time at Belur Vidyamandira, I could clearly envision his personal development during this period. This phase laid the foundation for a life marked by numerous achievements and accolades. His daily routine was highly structured and disciplined: rising early before sunrise, participating in morning and evening prayers in the prayer hall, and adhering to regular study times both in the mornings and evenings under strict supervision. I also learned that he had the opportunity to perform the evening Arati in the prayer halls for extended periods at both Belur and Belgharia. With Vidyamandira being adjacent to Belur Math, he took advantage of making regular visits to the temples of Thakur, Ma Sarada Devi, Swami Vivekananda, and Swami Brahmananda. Additionally, I discovered his involvement in volunteering for various special events at the Math and writing articles for the monthly wall magazines in their hostels, which helped develop his multi-faceted skills. The relevant chapters in his book offer valuable information and tips for anyone with spiritual aspirations.

I have seen him regularly practicing japa (repetition of God's name) and meditation following the instructions from his initiation at the RK Math & Mission. These practices have had a profoundly positive impact on his body, mind, and spirit, keeping him fit and agile even at this age. According to him, admission to RK Mission Vidyamandir and the introduction to its values and ideals transformed his life immensely, and I firmly believe this too. His spiritual practices radiate through him, reflecting in his daily activities. When our parents were with him, he always began his day by offering pranams to them. After his marriage, I remember him and Boudi reading together from "Swami Vivekanander Bani o Rachana," the original Bengali version of the "Complete Works of Swami Vivekananda." They would take turns reading and listening to each other. In more recent times, I had the opportunity to stay with Dada when our mother passed away. During this period, I felt fortunate to be with Dada for about a month, from our mother's last days until the completion of the rituals. I watched him chant mantras, which I would then follow. Boudi, with her spiritual upbringing, also played a significant role in helping us to perform those rituals.

Spirituality fosters resilience and patience. While it might seem that his life, marked by success, was free of difficulties, this is not true. He also faced many challenges and obstacles along his journey. However, I believe his spirituality helped him overcome those hurdles and stay on his path to success. Spiritual living nurtures humility, and this is evident in Dada's life. He is simple and can socialize with anyone without any trace of ego or the countless successes he has achieved.

Dada and I have an age difference of about 16 years, so I did not experience my childhood alongside him. The year I was born, he was already attending Ramakrishna Mission Vidyamandira in Belur Math and received his initiation. During my childhood, which overlapped with his late teenage years, I have fond memories of him bringing home delicious chocolates. All the neighborhood children and I would eagerly rush to him, each of us receiving a chocolate one by one. I have heard many stories, some funny, about his childhood from our parents, Didi, and others, as well as from the books I mentioned earlier. My deeper memories of him began in his adulthood when he was a professor at Uluberia College and got married. I was the groomsman at his wedding, and I remember the warm reception in the house of Dada's in-laws at Amarpur, followed by a long, religious ceremony typical of a devout Brahmin family. Though I was too young to witness the entire ceremony, I recall the pleasant memories and the return to our home in Bagmari the next morning with Boudi and her sister Namitadi, the bridesmaid, amidst tearful farewells from Dada's in-laws.

I also fondly remember staying with Dada and Boudi at Uluberia on my way to appear for an examination in Kolkata. During this period of his initial teaching career as a professor of Uluberia College, they were blessed with their first son, Subhas. Life events soon led Dada to join IIT Kharagpur as a professor, and I went to Purulia RK Mission for my schooling in 1971. He accompanied me to Purulia, and I remember the evening we arrived at the railway station. It was late, so we stayed in a hotel overnight and went to school the next morning. It was heartbreaking for me when he left me in Purulia and returned to Kharagpur, but it shaped my life. I am grateful to Jamaibabu for noticing the newspaper posting and bringing me the forms, to Dada for accompanying me to the examination center and selecting the school after I was accepted, and to my parents for their vision and for giving me the opportunity to pursue a better education away from the comfort of home at such a young age.

In the early days of my childhood, his presence was a rare gift. Yet, as I was growing older, his love, care, and guidance became evident in my life. When the opportunity arose for me to attend the residential school at Purulia Ramakrishna Mission, it was he who took me there for admission. During my final school years, he embarked on a significant journey to Germany in 1975, having been awarded a Humboldt fellowship. This was a milestone in his life, a momentous event for our family and his academic peers. For me, he was a beacon of inspiration. During those years when he was in Germany for the first time, we would eagerly wait for his letters, as there were no phone connections to our home back then. His letters and picture postcards brought us news of West Germany, his academic endeavors, and his daily life. When he returned in 1977, I already completed my school and joined Jadavpur University as a student. I remember accompanying our Jamaibabu to the Kolkata airport to receive him back. He brought with him a treasure trove of gifts from Germany for all of us that included shirts and pants for me which I wore throughout my university days, a Grundig tape recorder with numerous audio cassettes of famous Bengali and Hindi songs, and a slideshow projector with slides from his trip. He appointed me as the projector operator during his gatherings, while he narrated the stories behind the slides to the guests. Times have changed, and technology has advanced, rendering those slides obsolete. Yet, back then, they were precious windows through which we could peek into a developed European country.

During my time at Jadavpur University, I remember the time when he visited me at my hostel within his busy schedule. When I moved to IIT Kharagpur for my Master's degree, he embarked on a "Round The World" (RTW) trip, in 1981 visiting universities in Japan, USA, Canada and various European countries. I recall the year I stayed at their quarters and another year at JCB Hall of Residence while studying at IIT, Kharagpur. After my studies, as I began my career and subsequently got married, my wife Kanika and I were glad when our parents and Dada, Boudi, visited us with my nephews and niece in Kumardhubi and Mumbai.

Dada has a vast circle of family, friends, colleagues, and students who deeply respect and admire him. His regular contact with them and frequent invitations to social events and community gatherings demonstrate just how much he is loved and adored. When I think about his students. especially his research students. I see them as family. He formed deep personal and professional connections, creating an ideal learning environment. I've seen students visit his quarters at all hours to discuss research and other matters. He would invite them for meals, and they would gladly join. The profound sadness he felt upon hearing about the untimely death of one of his research students from Manipur, Dr. S.I. Singh, reflects the strong bond he shared with his students. I knew Dr. Singh personally when he was pursuing his Ph.D. under Dada's supervision. Dr. Singh was truly a pure soul and his untimely death is a shocking loss for everyone who knew him. Each and every person has infinite potential, and our goal should be to manifest that potential. Dada's life can inspire many to pursue their aspirations and achieve success. Watching Indian TV programs like "Indian Idol," "Dance India Dance." and "Kaun Banega Crorepati," I am amazed to see how children, youth and adults from deprived backgrounds also are given platforms to showcase their talents and excel in their fields, whether in music, dance, or knowledge. These successes, which were once unthinkable, prove that every person has infinite potential that can be manifested. On September 14, 2024, I attended an annual seminar at the Vedanta Society of Toronto on the theme of "Your Infinite Potential." One of the panel speakers, Prof. Donna Kostopoulos, shared her inspiring life story. Despite being homeless and a school dropout, her determination and willpower led her to complete her higher education and achieve great heights. Her story also demonstrates that each of us has infinite potential that can be manifested through hard work and resolve. Prof. Kostopoulos, now a Dean of Education at the University of Western Ontario, has received several awards for her service, research, and teaching, and serves on the Board of the

Fields Institute for Research in Mathematical Sciences. Both of them with their backgrounds in Mathematics, have climbed the administrative ladder, embodying the idea that "Education is the manifestation of the perfection already in (hu)man."

Not long ago, I was watching an episode of "Kaun Banega Crorepati", an Indian TV serial, on October 11, 2024, hosted by a Bollywood icon who turned 82 that day. His energy and grace at this age were astonishing. It was Durgashtami, and I couldn't help but think of Dada, who also turned 81 in October 2024. In addition to the many awards and accolades that he has received earlier, he was recently elected as a fellow of the West Bengal Academy of Science & Technology (WAST). I get amazed and inspired by his ability to skillfully manage so many tasks even at this age, including adjunct professor at IIEST, fellow of many academies and societies, and writing books. His legacy is one we can all follow.

As a "Bhai," I conclude this tribute to my illustrious Dada with a quote from a famous Nazrulgeeti by Kazi Nazrul Islam: "*Tumi sundor tai cheye thaki*" (You are beautiful, so I keep on staring at you). To my Dada: you are such an accomplished person with your higher education, research in complex fields, and spiritual living, yet you always maintain simplicity and humility. I keep gazing at you mentally, even when separated by a long physical distance. "*Jane surjere pabe na, tobu abujh suryamukhi cheye cheye dekhe tar debotare, dekhiyai se je sukhi*" (The sunflower knows it cannot reach the sun, yet it keeps looking at the sun, its deity, and becomes happy just by looking at it). I know I can't reach your accomplishments and achievements that are so high, but I will keep on looking at you as my distinguished elder brother and be happy by doing so. I pray for your continued good health, mind, and spirit, inspiring many in the present and future generations.

CHAPTER 57

My Younger Brother Jagadis

Durgarani Bhattacharya
Ward No. 1, Vivekananda Sarani, Digha More,
Egra, Purba Medinipur-721429

"Boundless fields where the sky kisses your sacred feet—
Shady, tranquil nests of peace, little villages all around."

This lyrical description by the great poet Rabindranath Tagore fits perfectly with our beloved birthplace, the village of Bagmari. We are two brothers and a sister—my elder brother Jagadis (junior to me), younger brother Parames, and I, the only sister. We all lived together with our uncle, aunt, and cousins in a joint family. I was born in August 1941, and Jagadis in October 1943. Our youngest brother Parames is eighteen years younger than me.

During childhood, Jagadis and I spent a lot of time together. Reflecting on those treasured memories now fills me with emotion and joy. At that time, our father had just started working at Ambikamoyee High School in Tikrapara with a monthly salary of 20 rupees. With his first month's salary, he bought a cow.

I may share a story of childhood mischief of Jagadis. He was very particular for drinking pure milk. Sometimes, out of necessity, our mother would mix a little water in the milk. Jagadis would refuse to drink it and, in protest, would roll on the floor crying. A helpless mother would hide in a corner of the house. Jagadis loved mother very dearly, and when he couldn't find her, he'd be distraught. On finding her, he would calm down and say, "If you give me milk, give me pure milk, or don't give it at all."

Mother never scolded or hit us. Since there weren't many children in the neighbourhood, everyone doted on us. We played with cloth balls, and traditional games like kadi-dang, kula, dhapa, and ludo.

Life in our joint family was bustling. Our mother and aunt had to work a lot—boiling paddy, puffing rice, preparing meals for farmhands, and taking care of us. Mother, following medical advice due to a stomach ailment, drank only water from a hand pump. Since there were only very few hand pumps in the village back then, Jagadis and I fetched water in small pots from quite a distance. Everyone else drank pond water.

After a day of play and small chores, we would go to the prayer room in the evening, bow in devotion, and then sit down to study. Jagadis was my constant companion.

Our father played an invaluable role in shaping our lives, though we didn't get to spend much time with him. A schoolteacher and President of the Union Board, he was often engaged in social work. As a child, Jagadis used to sleep beside him at night, while I slept with our mother. Until he fell asleep and again from 4 AM as he woke up—father would ask Jagadis math tables, mental arithmetic, translations, and other questions. This might have been the seed of the banyan tree that later grew into my brother Jagadis with deep love for learning and unwavering dedication.

Both Jagadis and I passed the fourth grade from Pratapdighi Majna Primary School. In those days, co-education was not allowed and there was no girls' school nearby, so I couldn't continue my studies further. Jagadis always stood first in class. Our father, a noble and generous man, was a source of constant inspiration for all of us. Jagadis passed the School Final Exam in 1959 with First Division and letter marks in Mathematics. I was married in 1958, at the age of 16, My in-laws' house was in another village named Jabda.

Jagadis later studied at the Ramakrishna Mission Vidyamandira, Belur Math and earned his M.Sc. degree in Mathematics from Calcutta University in 1966. He was deeply loved by the monks there. At one point, he even developed an inclination toward renunciation. Our parents felt very worried about this. A monk reassured them, saying, "One cannot become a monk without having the virtues of past lives. Besides, his studies are not being affected. So you needn't worry."

Even after my marriage, Jagadis won the hearts of my in-laws with his charming behaviour. My in-laws and husband were very fond of him. He visited us every year during *Durga Puja* and *Bhai Duj*. Sometimes, our parents and younger brothers would accompany him. Jagadis used to like simple meals like rice with mashed potatoes, tamarind fish curry, and green chilies.

Above all, his passion for learning through hard work was unparalleled. The day after completing his M.Sc., he didn't rest. That very night he returned from Kolkata, and the next morning started teaching at Naipur High School. In 1967, after results were announced, he was appointed a lecturer in Mathematics at Uluberia College and simultaneously began his Ph.D. at Jadavpur University.

In 1969, Jagadis got married. His wife Shorasi brightened our home in Bagmari. We all celebrated the wedding with great joy. This marked the beginning of a new chapter. In 1971, he joined IIT Kharagpur as a faculty member and in 1975, went to Germany for two years for advanced research. His thirst for knowledge and visionary thinking took him far ahead. When he returned in 1977, he brought sarees and many other gifts for all of us from Germany.

As a family man, Jagadis has always been responsible and devoted. After joining IIT Kharagpur, he brought our parents and middle brother Dines to live in the quarters. Jagadis has two sons, Subhas and Sudip, and a daughter, Sumita. He used to take enough care for their education, and our father also guided them in Math and English. My son Debashish too had the opportunity to study under his grandfather while staying with them for two years.

Our mother showered her grandchildren with love and affection. Today, Subhas is a faculty at IIT Kanpur, Sudip at IIT Kharagpur, and Sumita at IIEST Shibpur. Our son-in-law (Sumita's husband) is a professor at Jadavpur University. I still feel thrilled when they fondly call me "Pisimoni."

They used to visit us during festivals, and when our parents stayed at IIT, we had many reunions—those joyful memories remain vivid. It was hard to refuse Shorasi's heartfelt invitations, and her warmth and hospitality made partings sorrowful. Her siblings also joined every celebration, making the atmosphere lively.

Jagadis rendered timely advice regarding the education and marriages of my three daughters—Namita, Kabita, and Sumita—and son Debashis. He even helped manage the wedding ceremonies. After my husband's passing in 1993, Jagadis stood by me. Parames arranged all the paperwork to start my pension.

The academic contributions of Jagadis—teaching, research, and lectures across the globe—along with honors like the Rammohan Award (2004) and Outstanding Teacher's Award (2013), brought him national acclaim. He is humble, gentle, modest, and bears an ever smiling face. His ability to connect with common people in a down-to-earth way makes him truly extraordinary.

CHAPTER 58

Prof. Jagadis Chandra Misra: Glimpses from a Different Perspective

Achintya Mukhopadhyay
Professor of Mechanical Engineering (Son-in-law of Prof. J.C. Misra), Jadavpur University, Kolkata-700032

It was late 1996. I had just returned from a trip to Puri with my parents. It was also the time when my parents and my uncle (my father's elder brother) were seriously discussing plans for my marriage. At this stage, one day my father informed me that one Professor of Mathematics from I.I.T., Kharagpur would visit us for some preliminary matrimonial discussions. Although mathematics was my favourite subject in school, my confidence in the subject had ebbed quite a lot, possibly due to what I thought was somewhat superficial use of it in my engineering career. So, on the night before his scheduled day of visit, strange apparitions like Riemann invariants, Gram-Schmidt Orthogonalization, Sturm-Liouville problems crowded my dreams, or what I should probably call night mare.

Anyway, on the scheduled day, he came. To my surprise, he did not have the sombre and awe-inspiring looks of a mathematics professor. He came and touched the feet of my father and my uncle as they were both considerably older than him. He tried to do the same with my mother too but she desisted him. Instead, they greeted each other with folded hands. They maintained this form of exchanging greetings every time they met till my mother passed away. Very soon, my initial stiffness disappeared, mainly due to his gentle manners and polite way of talking. He enquired a few things about my teaching at Jadavpur or my studies at Indian Institute of Science at Bengaluru. He also enquired about some of the professors in the mathematics department at Jadavpur University. Our conversations touched upon my ongoing doctoral research also. By that time, I had realized that this mathematician was not one to be afraid of. In fact, to show off my knowledge, I started bringing up what I thought were mathematical intricacies of my Ph.D. work. He kept on listening to it indulgently, occasionally punctuating my monologue with some small but appreciative comments. At the end, he said, treat your doctoral research with utmost priority and complete it at the earliest.

A few months after this first meeting, I acquired the credential to call him "Baba". During this intervening period, he visited us a few times. I think I should mention one such visit in particular. That day, he arrived very early in the morning, much earlier than he normally reached from Kharagpur. We came to know that the previous evening, he was returning from somewhere but due to some reasons, the flight got cancelled and he was left stranded at the airport. To make things worse, due to a heavy rush of stranded passengers, he did not get a place to sit inside the terminal building. So he had spent the whole night on a concrete slab outside and took the early morning flight to Kolkata. As we would be waiting for him, he headed straight to our house from the airport. I was dumbstruck to see such a humble down to earth approach from a scholar of international renown like him. Now I realize that at that time, he was a few years older than what I am now. I wonder at his physical and mental stamina to fulfil all his commitments after a tiring ordeal like that.

My next significant memory of him is a bit amusing. Just a few days after our marriage, my wife and I were going to Khargapur for the first time as a couple. Following family tradition, he was accompanying us on the journey. Those who have travelled by local train from Howrah to Kharagpur know of the rich diversity of food that hawkers on the train offer. Every time a vendor appeared with a new commodity, he would be telling me that this stuff is quite famous (*Mechedar chop bikhyato, khabe naki? Or Ei line e jhalmuri khub bhalo kore* etc). I have a little reputation among my acquaintances that I never say no to food. So, I also kept acceding to his proposals all along. But this childlike simplicity of him turned out to be a true ice-breaker in our relationship.

Within a very short time after our marriage, a crisis developed in our family. My father suddenly became critically ill and was soon confined to bed. The sight of an ever-active man, who had been my father, friend and the guding star in my life, becoming dependent on others for even the most basic needs of life, completely shattered me mentally. The support I received from my wife, Sumita in that phase will remain ever fresh in my memory. But from that time, the soothing and guiding presence of my second father has remained a constant feature in my life. At that time, I was also doing my Ph.D. Apart from giving me wise counsel in that matter, he guarded me from all hazards.

We shall always remember his Gita recital during the *Shraddha* ceremony of my father.

Sometime later, he was seriously ill with typhoid and had to stay with us in Kolkata for treatment for some time. Even when he was seriously ill, I would find him having long discussions with his students or contacting others to resolve different problems faced by his students. Being a teacher myself, I could appreciate his deep affection and strong commitments towards his students. I saw this same commitment from him years later. He was recuperating from a knee surgery. Yet, within days of release from the hospital, he became busy making a trip to NIT Warangal (Andhra Pradesh) to fulfil his commitment for being an External Member of an Expert Committee for the selection of faculty members of the Mathematics Department. Even though he was still having considerable pain due to the surgery, he was ready to ignore it in the interest of the Institute.

I am a professor of mechanical engineering and the person whom I am writing about is one of the pioneers in the field of biomechanics research in India. So it is but natural that a large part of my tribute to him would encompass the breadth and depth of his biomechanics research. However, the main reason for this writing not taking that expected course is the man himself. He is always so restrained about his achievements that I can hardly claim to know anything more than what most others already know of him. The other reason is that his scholarly achievements are all very well-known. So, I felt the urge to portray the man from other perspectives and try to bring out the other aspects of this scholarly person. But still I find it difficult to completely restrain myself. His work on biomechanics started with bio-solid mechanics but later on, his works mostly were on bio-fluid mechanics. Since I also work in fluid mechanics, it surprises me to see him making high quality contributions to emerging topics in the fields like electroosmotic flow, entropy generation and microfluidics. So, it is hardly a surprise to me that his name consistently features in the list of top 2% of the worldwide most cited scientists published each year by Stanford University. Although I never had the opportunity to be a student in his class, I could understand the quality of his classroom teaching when I saw many of his former students, who are now luminaries in their fields in their own right, getting overwhelmed at the very mention of his name.

I would not prolong this tribute further. I would end it with a prayer to the Almighty that he may lead a long, healthy, happy and active life.

CHAPTER 59

Honourable Shri Jagadis Chandra Misra

Sukdeb Chakraborty
Superintending Engineer (Retired),
Eastern Coalfields Limited, Parbelia, Purulia

We did not have much knowledge about the early professional life of our esteemed relative. This is because our acquaintance with him began only towards the later part of his career.

Let me briefly recount how we came to know each other. Prof. J.C. Misra had placed a matrimonial advertisement in the newspaper for his younger son's marriage. Seeing the ad, I sent my younger daughter's bio-data and photograph to his residential address at IIT Kharagpur.

After some time, I received an unexpected phone call one evening. A voice on the other end asked, "Are you Mr. Shukdeb Chakraborty?" I replied, "Yes, speaking." He then asked, "Did you send a bio-data for your daughter to my IIT Kharagpur address?" I confirmed that I had.

He then inquired about my daughter and our family background. I provided him with some details over the phone. Then he asked me to proceed with discussions regarding the probable marriage between his younger son and my younger daughter. Thus began our initial acquaintance over the phone.

At the same time, I gathered excellent feedback about him from a close colleague, who was a former student of his at IIT. My colleague described him as a highly respected, responsible mathematics professor with an extraordinary bond with his students, treating them as his own children. I would later describe my own experience about him as an extraordinary student-loving professor.

My friend also mentioned that Jagadis Chandra was a distinguished scholar, who had been invited to lecture at various prestigious universities in India and abroad. He had received a number of accolades for his contributions to the field of mathematics. Hearing all this filled us with immense pride and reassured us that our daughter was about to become a part of a truly educated and esteemed family.

In November 2006, my younger daughter, Satamita, married his younger son, Sudip, thus establishing our familial bond.

After our daughter's wedding, we visited his residence in Kharagpur and saw several of his awards and recognitions, including the Rammohan Puraskar, which he received in 2004. A portion of the cash Prize money was donated to various religious and educational institutions, reflecting his deep sense of generosity and philanthropy.

Let me share an incident that illustrates his dedication to his students. One night, around 11 PM, while we were seated at the dinner table, his phone rang. He answered the call, and a student on the other end asked, "Sir, have you gone to sleep?" He replied, "No, I'm just about to have dinner. Do you need something?" The student explained a problem he was struggling with, and without hesitation, Jagadis Babu said, "Bring it to me, and let's see what we can do."

He then told me to continue my dinner while he worked on solving the student's problem. It was nearly midnight when he finally sat down to eat. He casually remarked, "These students have heavier workloads at night." What amazed me most was that he showed no signs of irritation or fatigue—his dedication to his students was absolute.

Despite his remarkable success, he remains humble, free from arrogance or self-importance. He leads a simple, honest life and treats everyone with kindness and warmth. Never have I heard him utter a harsh or hurtful word to anyone.

Even now, he devoutly recites the *Bhagavad Gita* and performs *Chandi Path* every day without fail.

Behind every great man, there is often a supportive woman. Jagadis Chandra' wife too, has played a significant role in his success. He himself has acknowledged this many times. We have personally witnessed her pious, compassionate, and benevolent nature. She is deeply moved by others' suffering and always tries to help in any way she can.

We do not know much about his father, as he passed away much before our families became connected. However, from what we learned from his mother, it seems that his father was an ideal teacher and social worker. Despite not being financially well-off, he helped the poor and the needy in his village and neighbouring villages and took active interest in the education of local children.

After our daughter's wedding, we were fortunate to spend several years in the company of Jagadis Chandra's mother. She was an incredibly wise, kind, and religious woman, always cheerful and welcoming. Whenever we visited their home, she was overjoyed. And when we had to leave, she found it hard to part with us, often urging us to visit again soon.

Jagadis Chandra, is a devoted disciple of Belur Math and the Holy Trio. He supports religious and charitable causes—financially, emotionally, and physically—and actively participates in spiritual events. Inspired by his devotion, we, too, sought spiritual initiation at the Ramakrishna Mission.

It is impossible to fully capture the essence of such a wise, virtuous, and spiritually devoted individual in mere words. To us, he is a person of immense respect and admiration.

We sincerely pray to the Almighty to bless him with good health and many more years of active life. We also pray to Sri Ramakrishna and Ma Sarada to grant him the strength to continue his noble work, for that would bring us great happiness and fulfillment.

CHAPTER 60

Arya Acharya Jagadis

Dr. Bishnupada Nanda
Professor and Head, Department of Education, Jadavpur University, Kolkata

In the sun kissed mid-day skies of fiery Baishakh
Behold the sun dance in 'drimi drimi' rhythm of a resonant
 Pakhowaj with the Dipak ragini.
Fireballs rush forth in every step,
Setting the horizons on fire.
O Arya Acharya Jagadis,
With the resonating melody of a fiery Veena,
You shatter the mid-day silence.
With fiery frenzied flames.
While we all are busy losing ourselves
In cowardice and blatant imitation of words,
 Attire and postures not ours –
From where did you get your sagacious self and
A mind controlled in meditative silence?
The blazing mid-day Sun of Mid-Baishakh is
 All set to sacrifice all lust,
Conflict and selfish interest of the by-gone days,
And you sit composed as a brighter sun.
O you priest of the great sacrificial fire.
You sit composed, serene in profound meditative Silence
Like an ancient Rishi –
Like Shulopani Shiva atop
 The snowclad Kailash With his throat
 Glorified blue with the poison Devoured
 To salvage mankind.
Destroy the profound dark night once again today.
O Acharya, issue the clarion call to all mathematicians.
May they assemble at the pulpit of Truth,
Beauty and Goodness

CHAPTER 61

Dr. Jagadis Chandra Misra: A Multifaceted Personality

Dr. Soumyadeep Mahapatra
Associate Professor, ESI-PGIMSR, Joka, Kolkata

"A rising sun dispelling all darkness."
"An immense vessel of infinite knowledge, cloaked in disarming simplicity."
"The tallest tree in the forest of wisdom."

It is truly difficult to find an apt metaphor to describe a personality as profound and towering as Dr. Jagadis Chandra Misra. In fact, to offer any commentary on such a remarkable soul feels like an act of boldness on my part.

Since childhood, I've had the rare privilege of knowing him personally, being one of his close relatives. I often visited his residence, and what struck me each time was the extraordinary simplicity with which he and his family lived. Despite his eminence, there was no grandeur or pomp and pride in his lifestyle—only quiet dignity and grace.

However, beneath that modest exterior lies a firm commitment to his principles and values. While unassuming in demeanor, he stands firm in his ideological convictions.

Over time, I came to learn more about his immense achievements—not just from my parents and relatives, but also from academic circles and publications. A silent and tireless academician, he steadily rose to become a pioneer in one of the most intellectually demanding disciplines of our time—Mathematics. His contributions have earned recognition and acclaim across the world.

According to a recent study conducted by Stanford University of the United States, he has consistently ranked among the top 2% of scientists globally for six consecutive years—from 2020 to 2025. This recognition, though significant, only partially captures the depth and impact of his life's work.

In short, Dr. J.C. Misra is a legendary scientist of international renown—a true *teacher of teachers*. Throughout his illustrious career, he has been honored with numerous prestigious awards, fellowships, and distinctions from institutions around the globe.

Yet, what makes him truly extraordinary in the eyes of his students is not just his brilliance, but his gift for clarity. He possesses a rare ability to make the most complex and intimidating topics not only comprehensible but genuinely enjoyable.

As a child, I occasionally had the fortune of learning directly from him. Despite his position as a renowned mathematician at one of India's most elite institutions—the Indian Institute of Technology, Kharagpur—he remained approachable, kind, and incredibly patient. His humility, combined with his dedication to teaching, left a lasting impression on me.

Indeed, his unbounded patience was something I experienced firsthand during those early lessons. Even then, he taught with the same care and dedication that he extended to his doctoral students.

Dr. Misra is not just a mathematician, scientist, or teacher. He is an inspiration, a symbol of how great intellect can reside in the simplest of lives, and how true greatness is always accompanied by humility, compassion, and unwavering dedication.

CHAPTER 62

My First Interaction with a Bright Star

Dyutiprava Bhattacharya Mahapatra
Sumangalam, Gonara, Manglamaro, Purba Medinipur-721434

It was a special day in my life—one that marked the beginning of a new chapter, a journey into a future with someone new. It was my *bride-looking* ceremony, and the bride-to-be was none other than myself.

At our ancestral home, a few people had assembled—highly educated and dignified men and women from my would-be in-laws' family. Among them was a gentleman, possibly in his mid-seventies, sitting quietly on a chair in our home. Dressed very simply, his presence was humble and unassuming.

During the initial phase of our introduction, he was the first person to ask me a question. It was not a typical inquiry, but something unexpected:

"What is the true ornament of a human being?"

I was taken aback, surprised by the profundity of the question. After a moment of reflection, I answered, "Character."

Later, I was requested to sing a song. My father gently nudged me to perform the one I had been rehearsing before the guests arrived. However, my in-laws suggested a different song. I sang the one they requested, and that seemed to conclude the session.

Some time afterward, as I sat alone downstairs, the same elderly gentleman approached me once again. To my surprise, he quietly requested me to sing the song I had prepared earlier—the very one I hadn't sung before the others. I was amazed—how did he know what was on my mind?

Nonetheless, I sang the song for him. He smiled warmly throughout the performance. Afterward, he asked, half playfully, whether I ever raised my voice at home. His demeanor was so lighthearted and innocent that, for a moment, I wondered if he was truly there for the bride-looking ceremony or simply enjoying a casual visit.

It wasn't until after their departure that we learned the true identity of this unassuming man. He was none other than Professor Jagadis Chandra Misra, my would-be elder uncle-in-law—an internationally acclaimed scientist, known not only in Bengal or India, but across the globe.

Coming from a modest background in a small village in the East Medinipur district of West Bengal—my father a schoolteacher, and my mother a homemaker—I could never have imagined that such a distinguished figure would one day visit our home. Both my father and I were completely overwhelmed by the entire experience.

Here was a man of towering intellect and global recognition, yet he carried no airs. What stood out to me more than his achievements was his gentle, childlike nature and humility. From the very first day, he encouraged me in every way possible. He would often say, "No matter how many degrees or how much fame you hold, it is your moral character that truly defines who you are."

When I first met him, I knew nothing of his qualifications, professional stature, or international acclaim. All I saw was a kind, loving, and simple human being—someone whose warmth and childlike charm shone through. And even today, I always see the same calm, fulfilling smile on his face. I sincerely pray to God that this beautiful soul, so full of wisdom and grace, continues to enjoy good health and a long, prosperous life. It is my pride and privilege to call someone like him my relative.

CHAPTER 63

A Few Words about My Father

Subhas Chandra Misra
Professor, Department of Industrial and Management Engineering, Indian Institute of Technology, Kanpur, Uttar Pradesh

It was summer. After attending an event at Bagmari School, I was returning home with my aunt Geeta Rani and some neighboring aunts. Before I could enter the house, my older grandmother (father's aunt) said, "Your father has arrived!" As I stepped inside, I saw a fair and well-built gentleman descending the stairs. Holding a lantern, I observed him closely and remarked, "You are quite chubby." Immediately, my father lifted me in his arms and, while showering me with affection, asked, "Do you recognize me? Can you tell me who I am?" Later, I learned that my father had gained weight during his stay in Germany, but after returning home, he gradually regained his usual physique.

At that time, my sister Sumita and I both were in second grade. My sister, a year younger than me, was admitted to school a year early by our grandfather so that we could study together. When we were very young, our father went to Germany for two years on a Humboldt Fellowship, and we stayed at our ancestral home in the village. After returning from Germany, he brought our mother and younger brother to IIT Kharagpur. Meanwhile, my sister and I stayed with our grandparents and continued our education there until the fifth grade. Later, our father enrolled both of us in Hijli High School at IIT Kharagpur—my sister in the Bengali medium and me in the English medium. When she reached the eleventh grade, she switched to the English-medium at the Central School on the IIT campus, where I also joined in the eleventh grade. Our younger brother studied at St. Agnes School up to the fifth grade before being transferred to the Central School, where he completed his twelfth grade.

One of the main reasons for our extended stay at our ancestral home was that our grandparents enjoyed having us there, and they wanted us to grow up under their guidance. Although we studied in the English medium, we had to learn Bengali up to the tenth grade.

Our parents visited us frequently. Occasionally, my father would bring Hilsa fish from IIT Kharagpur Market or Prembazar, which we all relished in different preparations. At home, he would sit on the swing on the first floor and teach us multiplication tables and different problems from Arithmetic. My grandfather was a retired teacher of a higher secondary school, and shortly after his retirement, both he and my grandmother moved to IIT Kharagpur to live with us. My uncle was pursuing his M.Tech at IIT at the time and would sometimes stay in the hostel and sometimes with us. We all lived together, creating cherished memories that I still hold.

Our home was always filled with relatives, friends, and visitors. My grandfather's former students and people from our native village often came to see him at our IIT residence, and my mother and grandmother warmly hosted them. One of our paternal uncles stayed at our IIT quarters while studying at Medinipur College. My father made arrangements for him to learn shorthand and typing and later helped him secure a job. He also assisted other uncles in various ways, including their education and career guidance.

Our mother was extremely hardworking. She used to walk to drop my younger brother at his school every morning and, upon returning home, would perform her daily prayers. I remember watching her take her morning bath and quickly completing her puja before preparing meals for everyone. Our grandmother assisted her in cooking. When my father's colleagues and friends visited IIT, he often invited them home. Even his former teachers visited us, enjoying my mother's delicious cooking.

On one occasion, my father invited the entire first-year batch of students from the School of Medical Science and Technology at IIT. My mother and sister prepared all the food, with help from our grandmother. Additionally, my father would often invite his research students to our residence for home-made meals.

One of my mother's remarkable qualities was her ability to make the best use of her time. She was also passionate about literature and spent her spare moments writing poetry, stories, and essays, many of which were published in local magazines.

My father led a disciplined life. Every morning, he would go for a walk, reciting Durga and Chandi mantras. Sometimes, he visited temples in the morning, where he read from the Chandi and the Srimad Bhagavad-Gita.

Upon returning home, he performed his daily puja, with my mother arranging everything in the prayer room. As a professor, he was dedicated to his work, never shirking responsibilities. Whether in his department office or at home, he would often be found mentoring his Ph.D. students while also taking time to teach us.

My mother managed household shopping and handled both indoor and outdoor responsibilities, which allowed my father to focus on his career. He lived a simple and contented life, eating whatever was available without complaint. My maternal grandparents loved my father dearly, and he, in turn, respected them as his own parents. He often recalls their kindness and expresses gratitude for having such wonderful parents-in-law.

My father deeply loves his siblings and cousins. He frequently calls my paternal uncle and aunt, maintaining close bonds with them. Before the COVID-19 pandemic, he used to visit his cousins occasionally, and they also visited us. His cousins also share great affection for him. He remains emotionally attached to our ancestral home and the people of Bagmari and neighboring villages. My parents visit my uncles and aunts from time to time, and they, along with their children and daughters-in-law, take great care of my parents. Our extended family, including Bhanu Kaku, Naresh Kaku, and my maternal aunt Geeta Mashimoni, all have immense respect and love for my parents.

My father is extremely resilient. If he couldn't get a reserved seat on a train, he would simply lay down on a newspaper on the floor and sleep without complaint. In our home, former students of the Ramakrishna Mission would gather for reading sessions, discussing religious texts like 'Kathamrita,' 'Leelaprasanga,' 'Sri Sri Mayer Katha,' and 'Swamiji's Life and Teachings.' Devotees, sometimes with their families, would attend, and there would be arrangements for prasad and refreshments. My parents also visited other devotees' homes for such gatherings, and when time permitted, we accompanied them.

When my brother and I moved abroad, my parents accepted it with courage despite the lack of internet and mobile phones back then, which made communication difficult. Upon returning, both of us joined different IITs as faculty members. Our parents frequently visit us in Kanpur, staying for a few months at a time, enriching our lives with their wisdom and experiences. My father often says, "One must complete one task before moving on to the next."

Above all, my father is not just a parent but also a mentor and a guiding light in our lives. With deep reverence, I conclude by offering my heartfelt respects to both of my parents.

CHAPTER 64

My Father in My Eyes

Dr. (Mrs.) Sumita Mukhopadhyay
Assistant Professor, School of Advanced Materials, Green Energy and Sensor Systems, Indian Institute Engineering Science and Technology (IIEST), Shibpur

I was about 3 years old when my father went to Germany on Humboldt Fellowship. Before that, my elder brother and I used to stay with our parents in the IIT Campus at Kharagpur. However, before my father went to Germany, my mother, my elder brother and I along with our grandparents shifted to our native village house. When his letters used to come in aerogrammes or occasionally on picture postcards addressed to us individually, it used to be a matter of great excitement. My grandfather used to open the letter and read it out to everyone. I cannot describe the excitement that used to accompany the arrival of his letters. I have faint memories of the serious illness of my uncle (*mejokaka*), my father's middle brother. He was suffering from an ailment for which good medicines were not available in India at that time. So my father used to send the medicine from Germany. One such parcel took a longer time to reach us. When it finally arrived, my uncle had left us forever. My father had to endure this colossal grief all alone, staying in Germany.

The day my father returned from Germany, we had gone to attend a function in the school where one of my aunts was studying. On our way back, we came to know that he had returned even before we reached our home. What an excitement it was for us! After reaching our home, we saw a fair-complexioned well-built person. I still remember my elder brother climbing up the stairs with a lamp in his hand to meet my father, while my grandmother and I were following him. My elder brother excitedly asked my grandmother, "Grandma, is this stocky, fair-complexioned man our father?" Everyone broke into laughter. My father took him in his arms.

As our grandparents had lost their middle son (our *mejokaka*) not too long ago, my father decided that my elder brother and I would stay back with our grandparents to make them feel a little better while my mother and my younger brother would go back to IIT, Kharagpur campus with my father. My father used to visit us almost every weekend. Sometimes my mother and my younger brother would come and stay with us for a few weeks. Every winter, after the Annual Examinations, my elder brother and I used to go and stay in my father's quarters at Kharagpur. My father's residence in Kharagpur had a large kitchen garden, where my father used to grow various seasonal flowers and vegetables like cauliflower, tomato, cabbage, potato and onions. He used to do the gardening himself. I still cherish the memories of my father bringing new dresses before the Durga Puja not only for us but many of my distant uncles and aunts, many of whom were our playmates.

My grandfather used to teach in a higher secondary school. When we were in Standard 5, he retired from his service. After that, we, along with our grandparents moved to my father's quarters in IIT Campus. My elder brother and I got admitted to Hijli High School on campus. My elder brother stood first in the admission test. He took admission in the English medium section of the school while I took admission in the Bengali medium section. My father was very eager to get me admitted to St. Agnes High School, run by Christian missionaries. But I was a bit inattentive towards my studies right in my childhood. Consequently, my results used to be somewhat mediocre while my elder brother always used to excel in the examinations. But my father never made any distinction in his attitude towards the two of us, on the day of publication of results or afterwards. Before the Annual Examination, my father used to pay more attention to my studies. But how strangely I used to behave! I would lie in bed at ease. My elder brother used to suggest important topics to my father, like trade winds and convective rain. My father used to read out those topics and I used to listen to it lying in my bed. As far as I remember, even after studying in this mode, I secured the second highest marks in Geography in the Annual Examination of Standard 9.

I gave my father so much trouble, but he never let his attention towards me drop. After every examination in school, I used to come home and say, "it is impossible for me to pass this exam, even God is helpless". But my father never even scolded us, and corporal punishment was out of question. His only punishment was that he used to stop interactions and maintain complete silence, when he was displeased. I remember that my father used to stuff our school tiffin box with a boiled egg, a cucumber, a carrot and a tomato. I marvel at his attention to providing us healthy nutritious food all along. When we were young, my father used to give us sprouts and peanuts in the morning. Along with studies, my father got me into singing, dancing, drawing and yoga classes. When I used to practice singing, my father used to sit next to me. He likes to listen to Tagore songs (*Rabindrasangeet*). Once, while arranging things in his room, I found an exercise book containing his collections of favourite songs from his student days. The first song in that book was: *Aguner Paroshmoni*.......

Now I realize how far-sighted he always has been. Even when I was in Standard 7 or 8, my father asked me to help my mother with her household chores, whenever our domestic help did not turn up. He used to say that a little household work in between studies actually helps in concentrating on studies. Unfortunately, when I am a mother today, I cannot even think of engaging my daughter in household work. My husband often tells my daughter, "Your grandfather has trained your mother into a smart person in the truest sense. The real smartness lies in not getting puzzled in an adverse situation and handling all odds."

My father took special care in inculcating a sense of responsibility in me. There were regular streams of visitors in our residence at IIT round the year. The custom in our house was that no visitor would return without having lunch or dinner in the house. My father used to give us money to go to the market and buy necessary vegetables and other ingredients for cooking.

I remember another thing from my childhood. Every year, after the Annual Examination was over, my father used to assign all the three of us to arrange things properly in the 3 rooms in our house and based on the quality of the work, awarded us first, second and third prizes. If I did not win the first prize, it used to turn out to be quite an earth-shaking event in the house. It is father again who had to put things back to order.

From my childhood, I have seen my father do some Puja after taking a bath and then he used to touch the feet of my grandparents. I used to like another action of my father. Whenever he used to return from an overseas trip, he used to bring some souvenirs and gifts for all of my uncles and aunts. Even to this day, whenever he returns from a trip, his bag is full of gifts for everyone.

I cannot but mention one incident in my life. In our year, the school-leaving secondary level board examination (*Madhyamik Pariksha*) got deferred by three months due to leakage of question papers. These extra three months gave more time for my fear of examination to strike its root deeper in my mind. I was determined to skip the examination while my father, naturally, was equally firm that I must appear in it. Our examination centre was Silver Jubilee High School in Kharagpur town. It was a usual practice that after we reached our school, we would be taken by 5–6 buses arranged by the School to the examination centre. Three to four teachers from our school used to escort us. A few guardians also used to take turns in joining the group. My elder brother used to go to the school on his own bicycle. But because of my fear of examinations, my father did not let me go alone; he used to drop me at the school. On the day we had examinations for the second paper of Bengali, my father was taking me to our school on his cycle. Suddenly, he felt the cycle light. Turning around, he saw that I had jumped from the cycle and was running towards home. My father convinced me with great difficulty to go for the examination. Since both I and my brother were examinees, my father got more opportunities to accompany us to the Silver Jubilee High School. In this way, eventually the examinations ended. As usual, I had told everyone in the house that I would fail in the examination. Finally, when the results came out, I found that I had secured First Division. That year, the overall results for the examination were very poor. Only 1% of all examinees secured First Division. My father was happy that his *Mamani* (as he calls me) has been within the top 1% of the students.

In this way, he stood by me during several incidents of my college and university days. Then, when I was doing my M.Tech. in IIT Kharagpur, I got married. I remember before my marriage, during study breaks, he used to advise me that I was going to live in a new environment and that I should adapt myself to that new environment. But so nice was his way of speaking, it never appeared that he was giving me lectures. My father's words still ring in my ears. He always says, do not muddy the water in which you will take a dip. He also says very often that this world is like a magic mirror, it will show your face in whatever way you want to see it. My father has always been deeply attached to me but he did not talk with me over phone or visit me very often after my marriage. He used to say that his frequent visits or phone calls may make it difficult for me to integrate myself with my new family. It may sound funny but when I was coming to my in-laws after my marriage and was being seen off by my parents, I did not shed a single drop of tear as most girls do. Instead, I bid them a smiling farewell. It may be noted that our marriage was arranged by the two families by the help of advertisement in newspapers. Although the marriage was finalized six months before it actually took place, I did not have any contact with my husband or my in-laws as I was busy with my M.Tech studies.

In this way, I completed my M.Tech. The very next day, I came to Kolkata and joined the Indian Association for the Cultivation of Science as a Senior Research Fellow. I remember, when I was very young, two ladies, Kasturi and Minati (whom I used to call *Kasturi Masi* and *Minati Masi*) were doing their Ph.D. under the supervision of my father. When they used to go to conferences, my father used to tell my grandmother that he wished that one day I would also go to conferences like them to present my research. It is very gratifying to me that I have been able to fulfil my father's wishes. I have got the opportunity to go to various conferences both in India and abroad. Now I am engaged in teaching and research at the Indian Institute of Engineering, Science and Technology, Shibpur. Five students have already completed their Ph.D. under my supervision. When my first two research students got their degree, I sent my photograph with them in their convocation robes to my father. He was overjoyed like a child.

I wish to mention here another facet of my father. Alongside my academics, he has always emphasized family values. Towards the end of my M.Tech. programme, after I had got married, I got a job at the R&D Centre of Indian Telephone Industries at Bengaluru through campus placements. It was considered a dream job in those days. To get a break from academics, I felt inclined to take up the job. Seeing my keenness for the job, my mother, who has always been very affectionate and supportive towards her children, must have got swayed. Worried about how I would manage to stay there alone, she had even proposed to go and stay with me. But my father told her that now I was a part of a new family and the decision about taking up the job should be left open for them only. I did not face any opposition from my in-laws. Rather they left the whole thing to my decision. I think by that time, the initial excitement of getting the job had ebbed a little and I had started enjoying my new life with my new family. Today, after all these years, I am convinced that my decision to stay back in Kolkata was the correct one. Even now I feel grateful to my father for showing me the right approach at that critical juncture of my life.

CHAPTER 65

Our Father

Dr. Sudip Misra
Professor, Department of Computer Science and Engineering
& Associate Dean, Indian Institute of Technology,
Kharagpur-721302, West Bengal

As I sit down to write about our father, I find myself at a loss for words. To us, our father is a great man, possessing numerous admirable qualities. His sense of duty, integrity, generosity, devotion to God, love for humanity, respect for his parents, humility, and kindness have all earned him a special place in our hearts.

Let me begin by recalling my early childhood. When I was just three and a half years old, my father enrolled me in St. Agnes School, the best English-medium Christian missionary primary school on the IIT Kharagpur campus, to ensure I received a quality education. Although my mother played a significant role in overseeing my studies, my father always ensured that my academic foundation was strong. He wished for me to pursue my secondary and higher secondary education at Kendriya Vidyalaya, one of the best schools in Kharagpur at the time. However, gaining admission there was quite challenging. At St. Agnes school, my second language was Bengali, whereas Kendriya Vidyalaya's admission test included Hindi, not Bengali. Recognizing this challenge, my father took the initiative to learn Hindi himself so that he could teach me. Additionally, one Hindi teacher at Hijli Primary School, Dubey Ji, helped strengthen my Hindi skills, for which we remain grateful.

To facilitate my holistic development, my father encouraged me to participate in activities such as yoga, table tennis, and tabla lessons. My mother diligently managed all these activities. This enabled my parents to raise their three children well. We were fortunate to grow up under the care and affection of our grandparents. Our daily routine was highly disciplined. My grandfather, a retired teacher of a higher secondary school, was a scholar in multiple subjects, including Bengali, English, Mathematics, and Sanskrit. He was a man of integrity, kindness, and forthrightness. My grandmother, on the other hand, was extremely caring and loving. Sadly, I lost my grandfather when I was in my first year at IIT.

My mother, who was deeply devoted to our grandparents, took care of them to the best of her abilities. She is a pious, calm, and dutiful woman. I always saw her emerge from the prayer room and bow to my grandfather, grandmother, and father daily.

My father made significant efforts to ensure I received a quality higher education. With the support and encouragement of my parents, brother, and sister, I was able to pursue my higher studies at the University of New Brunswick, Canada. I am especially grateful to my mother, who whole-heartedly permitted me to go abroad. Without her approval, my father would not have sent me. Fortunately, my paternal uncle and aunt were in Toronto, Canada. I benefited from their guidance from time to time, particularly during my initial days in a foreign land.

My father, as well as my elder brother, always wanted me to pursue an academic career. Though I initially worked in the industry for a short period, I eventually pursued a Ph.D. at Carleton University. Thanks to the encouragement of my parents, brother, and sister. After completing a postdoctoral fellowship in the U.S., I returned to India to teach at IIT Kharagpur. With the blessings of Sri Sri Thakur Sri Ramakrishna, I have had the opportunity to raise my children with Indian values while staying in my homeland.

My father, a distinguished scientist, received the prestigious Alexander von Humboldt Fellowship from Germany. Inspired by him, I also applied for the fellowship and was fortunate to receive it on my first attempt. I traveled to Hamburg, Germany, with my family. A few months later, my father received a three-month offer from Hamburg Technical University. Although I was conducting research at Hamburg University at the time, we were able to live together in Hamburg. My son, Devadeep (Gopal), was about two years and a half then. Over the years, my father and I received the Humboldt Fellowship three more times, allowing us to spend two to three months together in Germany. In 2019, my father, mother, wife, children, and I traveled to Friedrich-Alexander University in Germany. That time, both my father and I received three-month Humboldt Fellowships, and we stayed in Nuremberg. Having my mother with us made the experience even more enjoyable.

Additionally, living in Germany provided us with an opportunity to witness European civilization and culture firsthand.

Our father, a dedicated teacher and an excellent scientist, has always encouraged us, all his three children, to follow the same path. My son, now in the twelfth grade, loved learning mathematics during his secondary education from his grandfather. Moreover, my father strives to instill good values in all his grandchildren. My brother and sister's children also seek knowledge from him. He is incredibly affectionate toward his sons-in-law and daughters-in-law. He was dearly loved by my maternal grandparents and, in return, treated them with the same respect and affection as his own parents.

Our father is a man who values family and relationships. He has helped many relatives in various ways and continues to support even those who do not belong to our family. His education at Ramakrishna Mission institutions has instilled in him many noble virtues.

Even now, whenever I visit a doctor in Kharagpur or Kolkata, my father accompanies me. This gesture gives me immense comfort and confidence.

From him, I have learned to recite some portions of Sri Sri Markandeya Chandi and hymns in praise (Stotras) of Goddess Durga. I have found that these recitations are incredibly helpful in maintaining mental peace. With my father's support, my wife and I were able to receive spiritual initiation from Srimat Swami Smarananda Ji of the Ramakrishna Math and Mission. My sister received initiation from Srimat Swami Bhuteshananda Ji, and my brother from Srimat Swami Gahanananda Ji.

I pray to Sri Sri Thakur that our father enjoys a long, healthy, and peaceful life. May he be always showered with divine blessings.

CHAPTER 66

A Dedicated Karma Yogi in the Eyes of the Eldest Daughter-in-Law

(Mrs.) Sulagna Misra
C-103, Faculty Apartments, IIT Kanpur, Uttar Pradesh

The date was November 23, 2006—the day of my wedding. Just seven days later, on November 30, my younger brother-in-law Sudip's wedding was scheduled. It was after my marriage that I first visited the IIT Kharagpur campus, where my father-in-law, the renowned Professor Jagadis Chandra Misra, was a distinguished mathematics professor.

I was raised in an environment that blended knowledge, humility, and devotion. My father used to stress upon the assertion, *"Vidya Dadati Vinayam"*—"Education bestows humility." At our home in Kharagpur, I witnessed that very day, after taking a bath and offering prayers in the shrine, my father-in-law would descend the stairs and bow down to his mother (my grandmother-in-law). My grandfather-in-law expired years before my marriage.

This simple yet profound act touched me deeply. In both my paternal and maternal grandparents' homes, parents were revered as living deities, and their sons were always eager to follow their commands.

One of the reasons my father deeply admired my father-in-law was his humility and politeness, despite being an exceptionally educated and highly respected individual. I have never once heard my father-in-law raise his voice. My father fondly referred to him as a "Ship of Knowledge."

My father treasured a mathematics book that my father-in-law had given him, which contained various research discussions on mathematics along with his biography and photograph. He kept it carefully in his bookshelf and would proudly show it to his friends while sharing stories about my father-in-law.

Despite his vast knowledge and achievements, my father-in-law has never been arrogant. Similarly, my own grandfather was a renowned doctor and had friendships with influential and elite individuals, including members of the royal Raja Rajen Mallik's family. Yet, my father always led a simple life. He would often say, "Your father-in-law may be highly educated, but he is an extremely humble and gentle man."

He also used to say, "Your father-in-law makes sacrifices for himself but ensures that his children, daughters-in-law, and son-in-law lack nothing. How much more can he possibly do?"

My mother was deeply impressed by the blend of devotion and education she saw in my in-laws. My mother-in-law's parental house, too, was a perfect example of this fusion—some were professors, others doctors, yet they were all deeply devoted and engaged in religious practices like Durga Puja and Kali Puja.

My own mother grew up in a similar atmosphere. The renowned spiritual leader Sri Sri Sitaram Das Omkarnath had visited my maternal grandfather's home multiple times and held my grandfather in great affection. He once placed his hand on my mother's head in blessing and pointing towards me, he said, *"This girl is truly special."*

When my mother recounted this, she told me that she felt as if an electric current passed through her body when the revered saint touched her. I told her, "A true devotee is always recognized by God."

My father-in-law begins his day with a morning walk and recitation of the Chandi Stavas (hymns dedicated to Goddess Durga). He has a keen interest in Sanskrit, which is quite extraordinary—mathematics and Sanskrit are often seen as poles apart, yet he excels in both.

The spiritual leader Omkarnath Thakur is also highly revered by my in-laws. My mother adored my mother-in-law, often saying, *"The mother in Kharagpur has divine blessings too."* She believed this, because all the three of her children had achieved great success in education, which she attributed to divine grace.

Perhaps the similarity in values between my maternal home and my in-laws' home is why I found so much comfort and ease in Kharagpur from day one. From the moment I entered my in-laws' house in IIT Kharagpur campus, I felt as if I had known this house and its people for a long time.

My father-in-law treats both me and my younger sister-in-law, Satamita (Sudip's wife), as his own daughters. He always makes sure that any issue we face is quickly resolved.

My sister-in-law (*Nanad*) and her husband (*Nandai*) are also like close friends to me. Being older, she cares for me like her younger sister.

It amazes me to think about how my father-in-law overcame so many obstacles in life to become such a distinguished professor. Even today, he is actively involved in educating and mentoring his grandchildren. He keeps a close eye on their studies, guiding them with the same dedication he showed towards his own students.

I often wonder—what is the source of his boundless energy and enthusiasm? Even now, he rejoices like a child when he receives an award. He still feels immense happiness when honored with a prize or recognition.

Even today, he stands as a pillar of strength for his children, shielding them from difficulties. Whenever he senses a challenge, he immediately jumps into action to resolve it.

And by his side, always, is my mother-in-law, his life partner and unwavering support. Perhaps this is the secret behind his unshakable determination and willpower.

I sincerely pray that they remain healthy and live long lives.

CHAPTER 67

Our Baba in My Eyes

(Mrs.) Satamita Misra
B-74, IIT Campus, Kharagpur-721302, West Bengal

I am the younger daughter-in-law of my father-in-law, Professor Jagadis Chandra Misra. On December 1, 2006, I entered this household as the youngest daughter-in-law. My first meeting with my father-in-law was when he came to my parental home to see me. Since he was a professor of Mathematics at IIT Kharagpur, I assumed he would be a strict and serious person. As a result, I felt quite nervous. However, from the very first meeting, he made the entire situation so easy and comfortable that my initial hesitation quickly disappeared. Soon after my marriage, he became a very dear and close figure in my life. Through his affectionate and fatherly demeanor, he transitioned from being just my father-in-law to becoming my 'father.'

Within two weeks of our marriage, my husband along with me moved to Canada. Before we left, Baba (father-in-law) meticulously advised me about every little detail to ensure I wouldn't struggle with the extreme cold. While we were in Canada, he frequently called to check on us and provided necessary guidance. Due to his research work, Baba often had to travel abroad. Once, we heard that he would be visiting Germany for a research project. Without hesitation, I requested that he visit us in Canada for 8-10 days while he was in Germany. Though traveling from Germany to Canada was quite expensive, Baba happily made the trip to Toronto just to meet his two daughters-in-law. Not only that, but he also brought along many things for us, fulfilling all our little wishes—such is his boundless affection for us!

Baba's presence in Canada filled our days with joy. Observing him closely, I realized how seamlessly he embodied a combination of intelligence, wisdom, simplicity, and values. He is indifferent to his own comforts and hardships, yet deeply attentive to our well-being.

In Ottawa, my elder brother-in-law (Dadamoni) and his wife (Didi) lived. To satisfy his daughters-in-law, Baba agreed to visit Niagara Falls with us.

He explored every aspect of Niagara Falls with the same enthusiasm as us and never seemed tired or inconvenienced. When I imagine the sages and scholars of ancient times, I find some similarities between them and Baba. He is present amidst all yet detached from everything, just like a true scholar. Whether dressed in a formal suit attending a seminar or draped in a traditional dhoti performing a religious ceremony, he perfectly embodies both roles.

To me, Baba is the ideal man. His calm, gentle, humble, patient, diligent, and courageous nature touches my heart. I have learned many things from him. He is a man with an incredibly positive attitude. When he left Canada to return to Germany, I felt immense sadness.

In December 2007, we returned to India, and my husband joined IIT Kharagpur as a faculty member. This gave me another opportunity to be close to Baba. Now that my son and daughter are growing up, Baba spends a lot of time with them, instilling good values in them from a young age. At the same time, he himself is bound by deep affection for them. It used to be amusing when my daughter when she was in standard 3 skeptically told *Baba*, "You won't be able to solve these math problems, only Dadamoni (my elder brother) can explain them!" I feel that Baba thoroughly enjoyed those moments.

Baba shares a wonderful bond with everyone around him. His simple, sweet words make him dearly loved by all. In IIT Campus, many people know him as the "Genius of Mathematics." Since I live in B-74 of the IIT Campus, I have the privilege of being closest to Baba. Despite being globally renowned for his research and academic contributions, one can never guess his stature from his demeanor. Even today, to many people my first identity is that I am Prof. J.C. Misra's younger daughter-in-law.

Even at this age, Baba remains deeply involved in his research work. He is such a distinguished academician, yet he carries himself with remarkable humility. Let me share a couple of amusing incidents that highlight this.

Once, we were traveling in a Tata Sumo to our ancestral village, Bagmari, near Pratapdighi. When we reached Pratapdighi, we weren't sure which road would be best for the large vehicle to pass through, so we asked a passerby for directions to Bagmari. The man asked, "Whose house are you looking for?" Baba, who was sitting in the front seat, playfully replied, "Jagadis Chandra Misra's house." Not realizing he was speaking to the very man himself, the passerby responded, "Oh, you're going to Jagadis Babu's house! Let me show you the way."

On another occasion, a friend of mine visited our house to invite my children to her daughter's birthday celebration. At that time, I was upstairs, and Baba was staying in the living room on the ground floor. He welcomed my friend and conversed with her. Later, when I joined them, I introduced Baba by his name. What happened next was both surprising and amusing. My friend immediately stood up in shock, clasped her hands together, and exclaimed, "You are Professor J.C. Misra!" She then touched Baba's feet in reverence and said, "I am very familiar with your name! I saw you once years ago when I was a final-year M.Sc. (Mathematics) student at Kalyani University. Our Mathematics Department had organized a national conference, and you were the Chief Guest who inaugurated the event. Now I am a faculty at a college, and my husband is a professor at IIT."

These incidents exemplify how widely respected and renowned Baba is, both in India and abroad. Even though many people from the newer generations may not have seen him in person, they are well aware of his legacy.

While speaking about Baba, I must also mention my mother-in-law. She is the pillar of our household, holding everything together with care and devotion. My children lovingly call Baba "Bhaimoni" and Ma "Oma," treating them like their best friends. Behind Baba's immense success, along with the blessings of his parents, my mother-in-law's unwavering support has played an undeniable role.

We all take great pride in Baba. I have learned countless things from him, and I sincerely hope that the next generation of children will also be inspired by his ideals and academic excellence. I seek his blessings for a bright and prosperous future for them. May Baba and Ma always remain in good health and live a long, fulfilling life.

CHAPTER 68

Bhaimoni

Devarati Misra
First Year Student, Department of Computer Science & Engineering, Faculty of Engineering and Technology, Institute of Science and Technology, SRM University, Kattankulathur, Chennai-603203

My paternal grandfather, Dr. Jagadis Chandra Misra—whom we lovingly call '*Bhaimoni*'—is one of the most admirable people I know. A retired Professor of Mathematics from IIT Kharagpur, he is a man of profound intellect and remarkable humility. Despite his towering achievements, he remains deeply kind-hearted and grounded.

He was born in a serene village called *Bagmari* in the district of Purba Medinipur, West Bengal. Although the village is small, it is surrounded by natural beauty. There's an old saying—"Old is Gold"—which perfectly applies to him. Every time he visits us, he shares his vast experiences and life lessons, guiding us with wisdom and affection.

Even now, he remains energetic and active. Every morning, he rises early to practice yoga and physical exercises, maintaining a disciplined lifestyle. He encourages all of us to do the same—wake up early, stay active, and lead a healthy life. He often tells us that early rising and regular practice of yoga are essential for the wellness of both the body and the mind. Every day, he visits the temple twice—once in the morning and again in the evening. His spiritual routine includes *puja, japam, meditation*, and a daily recitation of the *Chandi Stavas* after his morning bath. His devotion and discipline are highly inspiring, and we all hold him in the highest regard.

Whenever he stays with us, he helps me with Mathematics, and I thoroughly enjoy learning from him. In August 2022, he visited us along with my grandmother. Though he originally planned to stay for a month, he extended his stay by six more months just to help me with Mathematics. Every day during that time, he patiently taught me for several hours. His support during that period was incredibly valuable, and I will always remain grateful for his time, effort, and love.

Sometimes he also helps me with English grammar. Whether it's a tricky math problem or a grammar doubt, Bhaimoni always has a clear and easy way of explaining things. I truly appreciate his style of teaching—calm, thorough, and encouraging.

He is a man who lives by the philosophy of *"simple living and high thinking."* His diet is modest—two chapatis, vegetables, dal, and small fish. One of his small joys is sipping tea prepared by my mother, which he always enjoys with a smile.

Whenever he visits Kanpur, he teaches my father *Chandi Path* and *Durga Stotra.* He emphasizes on the importance of discipline and encourages everybody to remain organized and focused in life.

On my birthday every year, he gives me wonderful gifts. During his visits, he brings clothes and a variety of food items for me and my brother. Sometime ago, he gifted me a beautiful bicycle, which I used for going to school, nearby shops, and even my friends' birthday parties. His gifts are always thoughtful and filled with love.

He has two sons and one daughter.He feels satisfied while talking about his children, saying that each of them possesses good human qualities. His eldest son is my father, *Dr. Subhas Chandra Misra*, a Professor in the Department of Industrial and Management Engineering at IIT Kanpur. His daughter—my *pisimoni, Dr. (Mrs.) Sumita Mukhopadhyay* is a faculty at the Indian Institute of Engineering Science and Technology (IIEST) Shibpur, Howrah. His younger son—my uncle, *Dr. Sudip Misra* is a Professor in the Department of Computer Science and Engineering at IIT Kharagpur.

From Bhaimoni, I have learned the true values of life—*kindness, love, humility, and self-discipline.* He has instilled in me a sense of confidence and has helped shape me into a better individual. He is like the *root of our family tree*, holding us all together with strength and unity.

My grandmother, whom we lovingly call *Thakuma,* is equally endearing. She is a devout and caring lady who always encourages my brother and me to visit the temple regularly. She lovingly shares stories, offers gentle guidance, and takes great interest in my music. Her warmth and devotion are a constant presence in our lives.

I feel truly blessed to have such affectionate and wise grandparents. I thank God for them every day and pray to the Almighty for their continued health, happiness, and long life.

CHAPTER 69

Our Bhaimoni, as I See Him

Devadeep Misra
Class XII, DAV Model School, IIT Campus,
Kharagpur-721302, West Bengal

My paternal grandfather, whom we lovingly call "Bhaimoni," is one of my most cherished people. Interestingly, we call each other by the same name. I must have picked it up as a toddler when he started calling me by that name, and it simply stayed with us both.

When I heard that his students, colleagues, and family were putting together a book of reflections and memories about him, I felt inspired to contribute an article on him. Writing about him gives me the opportunity to express how much I love and admire him.

I've heard from my mother that when I was born in a hospital in Asansol, Bhaimoni was at Santiniketan, delivering a lecture at Visva Bharati University. The moment he heard about my birth, he rushed straight to Asansol to see me. Since then, he has always been deeply affectionate and incredibly caring.

To me, Bhaimoni is a wonderful person with a heart of gold. As a child, whenever I got hurt, it was he who comforted me. He is always optimistic, calm, and remarkably fearless. He believes in facing life's challenges with a spiritual outlook—something I believe he developed during his early years as a student at Ramakrishna Mission institutions. He stays far away from negativity, and I've rarely heard him say a harsh word to anyone—or even listen to something negative.

One of my earliest memories goes back to when I was about three years old. My family and I were in Hamburg, Germany, where my father was working as an Alexander von Humboldt Research Fellow. We stayed there until the end of May 2011. In early May, Bhaimoni joined us—he was also a Humboldt Fellow, associated with the Hamburg University of Technology.

We stayed together in an apartment in the Hasselbrook area of Hamburg. I remember the day my father and I went to the airport to receive him. He was thrilled to see me, and I was equally happy to see him. We traveled together on the S-Bahn, chatting all the way.

Even after spending long hours at his office, he never failed to play with me in the nearby park. Despite his osteoarthritis and the pain in his knees, he would join me on the merry-go-round, just to make me smile. He would also push me on the swings and share cups of fruit yogurt with me—something we both loved. Grocery trips always began with buying yogurt and ended with pastries and baked goodies.

That year, we returned to India together, carrying gifts and memories. We visited Germany again in 2013, 2016, and 2019.

The 2019 trip was extra special. This time, we visited Nuremberg, and the whole family came—my parents, my sister Phul, and also my grandmother, *Omma*, who was visiting abroad for the first time. With his usual confidence and wisdom, Bhaimoni made me co-in-charge of the trip, along with my father.

We visited many places—Garmisch-Partenkirchen in the Alps, the historic town of Bamberg, and European cities like Prague, Venice, Pisa, Rome, and Paris. In Venice, we explored the canals by boat, visiting the islands of Murano (famous for glasswork) and Burano (renowned for handwoven fabrics). In Pisa, we took playful photos pretending to hold up the Leaning Tower. We tasted delicious Italian ice creams and pizzas, wandered through the Vatican in Rome, visited the Colosseum, and collected souvenirs for our cousins Tuktuki, Tultuli, and Govinda—whom we consider our siblings.

A funny and memorable incident happened on a trip to our ancestral village, Bagmari, with Bhaimoni. We were driving a big rented car and stopped to ask for directions. My grandfather asked someone, "Which road is better to reach Bagmari village with this large car?" The man asked, "Whose house are you visiting?" When Bhaimoni said, "Jagadis Babu's house," the man immediately exclaimed, "Oh, you should've said it earlier! Jagadis Babu's house—of course!" Little did he know he was actually speaking to Jagadis Babu himself!

This story reminds me of a famous anecdote about Albert Einstein, who once forgot the address of his own house in Princeton and had to ask a cab driver for directions. The driver, not recognizing him, proudly replied, "Everyone in Princeton knows where Einstein lives!" And Einstein replied, "I'm Einstein.

I forgot my home address. Can you take me there?" The amused driver gladly took him home and didn't even charge a fare.

Bhaimoni is a master of Mathematics, English, and Sanskrit. Whenever I have doubts—especially in these subjects—he's the first person I turn to. He always insists on being well-rounded: good in academics, disciplined, physically active, and polite. He encourages me to play outside, practice yoga daily, and adopt healthy habits like drinking water on an empty stomach, washing my eyes frequently, and eating lots of fruits and vegetables.

During Saraswati Puja, he guides me in chanting the mantras and explains their meanings. He encourages me to memorize Sanskrit shlokas and always reminds me that character and values matter more than anything else. He wants me to grow into a responsible, compassionate citizen.

As for *Omma*, she is incredibly kind-hearted. She feels deeply for others—sharing their joys and sorrows alike. She is closely attached to all her children and grandchildren, and constantly looks after everyone's health and wellbeing. She prepares delicious, healthy meals and shares stories from the Ramayana, Mahabharata, and other mythological tales with us.

Together, Bhaimoni and Omma are pillars of love, wisdom, and support in my life. They care deeply about my studies, my health, and my future. I consider myself incredibly lucky to have such wonderful grandparents.

CHAPTER 70

My Paternal Grandfather

Devapratim Misra
Class IX, Kendriya Vidyalaya, IIT Campus, Kanpur-208016, Uttar Pradesh

My paternal grandfather, Prof. Jagadis Chandra Misra, whom we lovingly call "Bhaimoni," is a retired Professor of Mathematics from IIT Kharagpur. Currently he is living on the IIT Kharagpur campus with my uncle, his younger son.

Whenever Bhaimoni visits us at IIT Kanpur, he brings a lot of love, joy—and many gifts—for me and my sister. He is a very disciplined and hardworking person. Every day, he wakes up by 6 a.m., goes for long walks twice a day—once in the morning and once in the evening—and practices yoga regularly. His daily routine reflects his commitment to fitness of the body and a healthy lifestyle.

He believes in simple living and high thinking. At home, he wears a traditional *dhoti*, and when stepping out for walks, he wears a shirt and trousers. Despite his academic achievements, he remains incredibly down-to-earth. What I admire most is how effortlessly he connects with me—explaining complex mathematical problems in ways that I can easily understand. His knowledge of English grammar is equally strong, and I always enjoy learning from him when he is with us.

Once, he took us on a memorable trip to our ancestral village in the district of Purba Medinipur, West Bengal. There, he showed us the high school he had attended, where his father had also been a teacher. We walked through lush paddy fields and met many villagers. To our amazement, even people who had never seen him personally knew him by name and held him in high esteem. The affection and respect the villagers have for him touched our hearts.

Being a simple man, Bhaimoni prefers simple food—chapatis, dal, vegetables, and small fish are enough to satisfy him. Along with academic knowledge, he teaches us valuable life lessons—good manners, healthy habits, and the importance of becoming responsible and kind citizens of our country.

Recently, my thread ceremony (Upanayan) was held at our uncle's residence—Quarter No. B74, IIT Campus, Kharagpur. It was a grand and meaningful occasion, lovingly organized by my uncle Prof. Sudip Misra and aunt Shrimati Satamita Misra. My elder cousin, Devadeep Misra (Gopal Dada), also played a major role in planning the event with enthusiasm and care.

My parents, grandparents, and even my maternal uncle and aunt were fully engaged in every aspect of the Upanayan and the Kali Puja held on the occasion of my Upanayan. All our relatives were invited. Kaku and Kakima (uncle and aunt) made comfortable arrangements for their stay and meals. Several experienced priests were invited to conduct the rituals, including the havan (sacred fire ceremony), with great devotion and precision.

Both my grandfather and grandmother are honest, gentle, and kind-hearted people. When my grandmother stays with us, she lovingly prepares delicious meals for the whole family. She always worries about the health and well-being of every family member and becomes deeply moved by the suffering of others. Her compassion is truly touching.

I am truly blessed to have such loving grandparents. They mean the world to me, and I pray to God for their continued good health and long life.

CHAPTER 71

Bhaimoni

Devadrita Misra
Standard VI, DAV Model School, IIT Campus, Kharagpur, West Bengal

It is Bhaimoni (our beloved grandfather), Prof. Jagadis Chandra Misra who had suggested the name, Devadrita. Out of love and deep affection, he has also assigned another name to me—'Chandramukhi' (Moon-faced). However, most others in the house call me 'Phul'.

Bhaimoni loves me a lot, and I love him very dearly. He made up a small rhyme for me when I was a small child, while holding me on his lap and showering me with affection:

"Chandramukhi, my dear little sister, with a smile like the moon,
That's why I love her so much, more than anyone could assume.
Chandramukhi, my little sister, always so busy in her play,
Dropping all the clothes from the rack, making things look messy!"

He composed this rhyme, as I heard from my parents, when I was just a baby.

He also wrote another rhyme for me:

"Chandramukhi—Chandramukhi,
Where are you dancing away?
Stop for a moment, dear sister,
Let me have a word, I pray..."

Bhaimoni and Oma (our grandma) love not just me, but all their five grandchildren very dearly. We are all the apples of the eyes of our Bhaimoni and Oma both. Whenever Bhaimoni travels abroad, he brings lots of toys, chocolates, and treats for all of us.

I pray to God, may our Bhaimoni and Oma live a healthy life and in our midst for many, many years to come and shower their blessings on all of us.

With love and respect, I offer my pranaam (obeisance) to both of them.

Section V

Appendices

APPENDIX 1

Authors (in alphabetical order)

1. **Dr. Achintya Mukhopadhyay**: Professor of Mechanical Engineering, Jadavpur University, Kolkata-700032
2. **Dr. Aniruddha Sinha** : Assistant Professor, Department of Mathematics, Yogoda Satsanga Palpara Mahavidyalaya, Purba Medinipur
3. **Ashish Panda** : Assistant Labour Commissioner (Retired), Government of West Bengal
4. **Ashok Bhowmik** : Former Principal, (Recipient of President's Award), Sodepur Higher Secondary School, Kolkata
5. **Balai Lal Das** : Retired Teacher, Panchagram Shiksha Niketan Higher Secondary School, Fazelpur, Patashpur, East Medinipur
6. **Binod Bihari Jana** : Headmaster (Retd.), Majna Primary School, Pratapdighi, Purba Medinipur-721440
7. **Dr. Bijay Kumar Sahu** : Senior Lecturer, Gandhi Mahavidyalaya, Rourkela, Odisha
8. **Dr. Biswajit Mallick** : Assistant Professor, Department of Mathematics, University of Allahabad, Uttar Pradesh
9. **Dr. Biswanath Das** : Head, Department of Statistics (Retd), Presidency University (formerly, Presidency College, Kolkata
10. **Dr. Bishnupada Nanda** : Professor and Head, Department of Education, Jadavpur University, Kolkata
11. **Devadeep Misra** : Class XII, DAV Model School, IIT Campus, Kharagpur-721302, West Bengal

12. **Debiprasad Dutta** : Assistant Teacher (Retd.), Bolpur Vivekananda Vidyapith, Birbhum, West Bengal
13. **Devarati Misra** : First Year Student, Department of Computer Science and Engineering, Faculty of Engineering and Technology, Institute of Science and Technology, SRM University, Katlankulathur, Chennai-603203
14. **Devadrita Misra** : Standard VI, DAV Model School, IIT Campus, Kharagpur, West Bengal
15. **Devapratim Misra** : Class IX, Kendriya Vidyalaya, IIT Campus, Kanpur-208016, Uttar Pradesh
16. **Dr. Dhiman Ganguly** : MBBS, MD, MRCP(UK), FCCP(USA), Professor, Department of Medicine, Vivekananda Institute of Medical Sciences and Hon.Visiting Consultant, Ramakrishna Mission Seva Pratishthan, Kolkata
17. **Dharanidhar Gayen** : Former Teacher, Dashagram M.B.K.B. Girls' School, Dashagram, Sabang, Paschim Medinipur
18. **Durgarani Bhattacharya** : Ward No. 1, Vivekananda Sarani, Digha More, Egra, Purba Medinipur-721429.
19. **Dyutiprava Bhattacharya Mahapatra** : Sumangalam, Gonara, Manglamaro, Purba Medinipur-721434
20. **Dr. G. Radhakrishnamacharya**: Professor of Mathematics & Dean (Retd.), N.I.T. Warangal, Andhra Pradesh
21. **Gita Misra** : Wife of Shri Tarapada Misra, Chand Sarak, Sarat Sarani, Krishnanagar-741101
22. **Dr. Gopal Chandra Bera** : Principal, Midnapore College
23. **Dr. Gopal Chandra Shit** : Professor, Department of Mathematics, Jadavpur University, Kolkata-700032

24. **Dr. G.P. Bhattacharjee** : Professor and Head (1995-1998), Mathematics Department, IIT Kharagpur (Currently in USA)

25. **Dr. Haripada Maity** : Former Principal, Mugberia Gangadhar College, Mugberia, Purba Medinipur

26. **Dr. Kamalesh Bhowmik** : Professor (Retired), Saha Institute of Nuclear Physics, Kolkata-700064, and Former Registrar, West Bengal State University, Barasat, Kolkata-700126.

27. **Manasi Nanda Raut** : Retired Teacher, Belda Prabhati Balika Vidyapith, Belda, Paschim Medinipur

28. **Manmatha Nath Das** : Former Teacher, Mugberia Gangadhar High School (Higher Secondary), Bhupatinagar, Purba Medinipur-721425

29. **Dr. Mrityunjay Kumar Patra** : Associate Professor (Retd.), Pingla Thana Mahavidyalaya, Paschim Medinipur

30. **Dr. Motahar Reza** : Associate Professor and Head, Department of Mathematics, GITAM University, Hyderabad, Telangana

31. **Dr. Namita Mahapatra** : Former Visiting Professor, Medinipur Homeopathy Medical College and Hospital & Former Medical Officer, B.C. Roy Technology Hospital, IIT Kharagpur

32. **Dr. Narayan Chandra Chattopadhyay** : Associate Professor (Retd.) Department of Mathematics, Seva Bharati Mahavidyalaya, Jhargram

33. **Prof. Nitya Niranjan Kundu** : Formerly, Head of the Department of History, Ramakrishna Mission Vidyamandira, Belur Math, Howrah

34. **Paresh Manna** : Retired Inspector, Food and Supply, Government of West Bengal

35. **Parames Misra** : Section Manager, Ontario Power Generation, Canada

36. **Pranabesh Jana** : Former Head of Mathematics Department, Kalyani Government Engineering College, Kalyani, Nadia

37. **Dr. Purnendu Sekhar Das** : Professor (Retd.), Vidyasagar University, Medinipur and Former Professor of Economics, Humanities Department, IIT Kharagpur

38. **Prof. Ranajit Kumar Nayek** : Ex-Lecturer in English, Mugberia Gangadhar Mahavidyalay, West Bengal

39. **Saktipada Giri** : Head Teacher, Ramakrishna-Sarada Shiksha Sadan, Pratapdighi, Purba Medinipur-721440, West Bengal

40. **Dr. Saktipada Nanda** : Associate Professor (Retd.), Department of Mathematics, Sree Chaitanya College, Habra, North 24 Parganas, West Bengal

41. **Dr. Sanchita Dandapat** : 110/22C, B.T. Road, Kolkata-700108

42. **Dr. Santwana Mukhopadhyay**: Professor, Department of Mathematical Sciences & Associate Dean (Academic Affairs), IIT (BHU), Uttar Pradesh

43. **Saroj Narayan Misra** : Assistant Headmaster (Retd.), Tikrapara Higher Secondary School, Pariharpur, Pratapdighi, East Midnapore-721440.

44. **Dr. Sachindra Kumar Baksi** : Professor and Head of the Department of Mathematics (Retd.), Ramakrishna Mission Vidyamandira, Belur Math, Howrah

45. **Satamita Misra** : B-74, IIT Campus, Kharagpur-721302, West Bengal

46. **Shyamal Chowdhury** : Retired Manager, United Bank of India, Kolkata

47. **Sibabrata Bagchi** : Retired General Manager, India Government Mint, Kolkata.

48. **Dr. Somnath Maiti** : Assistant Professor, Department of Mathematics, Rajendra College, J.P. University, Bihar-841301

49. **Dr. Soumyadeep Mahapatra** : Associate Professor, ESI-PGIMSR, Joka, Kolkata

50. **Srabani Sengupta** : Recipient of President's Award, Headmistress, Belgharia Mahakali H.S. School (Retd.), Kolkata

51. **Dr. Subhash Chandra Mahapatra** : Retired Professor, Department of Rural Development, IIT Kharagpur
Current Residence: Sumangalam, Gonara, Manglamaro, Purba Medinipur

52. **Dr. Subhas Chandra Misra** : Professor, Department of Industrial and Management Engineering, Indian Institute of Technology, Kanpur, Uttar Pradesh

53. **Dr. Subhash Chandra Samanta** : Professor, Department of Physics, Midnapore College

54. **Dr. Sudarsan Nanda** : Former Professor & Head, Department of Mathematics, IIT Kharagpur and Former Vice-Chancellor, North Orissa University, Baripada, Odisha

55. **Dr. Sudip Misra** : Professor, Department of Computer Science and Engineering & Associate Dean, Indian Institute of Technology, Kharagpur-721302, West Bengal

56. **Sukdeb Chakraborty** : Superintending Engineer (Retired), Eastern Coalfields Limited, Parbelia, Purulia

57. **Dr. Sukhendu Bikash Kar** : Former Headmaster, Tikrapara Ambikamayi Higher Secondary School, Pratapdighi, Purba Medinipur

58. **Dr. Sumita Mukhopadhyay** : Assistant Professor, School of Advanced Materials, Green Energy and Sensor Systems, Indian Institute of Engineering Science and Technology (IIEST), Shibpur

59. **Dr. Sushil Kumar Ghosh** : Associate Professor, Garhbeta College, Paschim Medinipur

60. **Swami Devarajananda**	: Joint Convenor, Ramakrishna-Vivekananda Bhava Prachar Committee, Ramakrishna Math and Ramakrishna Mission, Belur Math-711202
61. **Swapan Bhadra**	: Retired Manager, Central Bank of India, Kolkata
62. **Swapan Bhattacharya**	: Retired Acting Principal, Government College, Kailashahar, Tripura
63. **Dr. S.K. Pandey**	: Professor and Head, Department of Mathematical Sciences, IIT (BHU), Varanasi, U.P.
64. **Dr. Sukumar Chandra**	: Principal, Pingla College, Paschim Medinipur
65. **Sulagna Misra**	: C-103, Faculty Apartments, IIT Kanpur, Uttar Pradesh
66. **Dr. Tapas Chatterjee**	: MBBS, MS, MCh, FRCS (SN) Consultant Neurosurgeon, Kolkata, India

Appendix 2

Personal Details of Prof. Jagadis Chandra Misra

Birth	: 7th October, 1943 (20 Ashwin, 1350 B.S., Thursday)
Caste/Community	: Brahmin, Vatsya gotra, Capricorn
Place of Birth	: Bagamari, P.O.: Pratapdighi, P.S.: Patashpur, District: Purba Medinipur, West Bengal, India
Current Residence	: Qrs No. B74, I.I.T. Campus Kharagpur, Pin-721302
Contact Details	: Phone (Mobile): 8373843896
Father	: Ganes Chandra Misra (Former Teacher: Tikrapra Higher Secondary School)
Mother	: Pramila Devi
Grandfather	: Girish Chandra Misra, Kavyatirtha
Grandmother	: Gouri Devi
Great Grandfather	: Ramdhan Tarkaralankar
Great Grandmother	: Kailasi Devi
Second Great Grandfather	: Umarkanta Tarkabagish
Second Great Grandmother	: Bhabani Devi
Third Great Grandmother	: Kenaram Sarvabhouma
Fourth Great Grandfather	: Ayodhya Nath Vidyabagish
Marriage	: 28th May, 1969 (14th jaishta, 1376 B.S.)
Wife	: Shrimati Shorasi Misra

APPENDIX 3

Children

1. Eldest Son: **Dr. Subhas Chandra Misra**
B.E., M.Tech (IIT Kharagpur), M.S. (Canada), Ph.D. (Canada), P.D.F. (Harvard University, USA), FIET (UK), FRSPH (London), FRSA (London)
Professor, Dept.of Management Sciences, IIT Kanpur

Daughter-in-law: **Smt. Sulagna Misra,** *M.A.*
Grand Daughter: Devarati Misra (Tultuli)
Grand Son: Devapratim Misra (Govinda)

2. Daughter: **Dr. (Mrs.) Sumita Mukhopadhyay,**
M.Sc., M.Tech. (IIT Kharagpur), Ph.D. (IACS), FIET (UK), FIETE (India), FRSA (London)
Asst. Professor, School of AMEG Sensor Systems, I.I.E.S.T Shibpur

Son-in-law: **Dr. Achintya Mukhopadhyay**
B.E,M.E., PDF (Humboldt Fellow, Germany)
Professor of Mechanical Engineering, Jadavpur University
Grand Daughter: Supurna Mukhopadhyay (Tuk Tuki)

3. Youngest Child: **Dr. Sudip Misra**
B.Sc. Hons. (IIT Kharagpur), M.S. (Canada), Ph.D. (Canada), PDF (USA), Humboldt Fellow (Germany), ACM Fellow (USA), FIEEE (USA), FNASc, FNAE (New Delhi),
Professor of Computer Science and Engineering & Associate Dean, IIT Kharagpur

Daughter-in-law: **Smt. Satamita Misra,** *M.Sc.*
Grand Son: Devadeep Misra (Gopal)
Grand Daughter: Devadrita Misra (Phul)

APPENDIX 4

Curriculum Vitae

1. Name: **Dr. Jagadis Chandra Misra**

   E-mail: misrajc@gmail.com Mobile: +91-8373843896

   Address for Communication:

   Qrs. B-74, IIT Campus, Kharagpur-721302, West Bengal

2. **Present position and official address:** Honorary Visiting Professor, Department of Mathematics, Ramakrishna Mission Vidyamandira (Autonomous Postgraduate Institution), Belur Math, Howrah-711202, West Bengal, India

3. **Areas of Specialization:**

   Applied Mathematics, Biomathematics, Modelling and Simulation, Physiological Fluid Dynamics, Mechanics of Fluids and Solids

Prof. J.C. Misra figures in the List of Top 2% Scientists in the world for six consecutive years from 2020 to 2025, according to studies conducted by a team of scientists at Stanford University, USA led by Prof. John P. A. Loannidis. The list is based on the assessment of scientists from across the globe for the research carried out during their career span.

4. **Fellowships of National/International Academic/Professional Bodies:**
    - Was elected a **Fellow of West Bengal Academy of Science & Technology,** 2025.
    - Was elected a **Fellow of the Indian National Academy of Engineering** in (INAE) 2000 in recognition of the valuable impact of his research contribution in Engineering & Technology.
    - Was elected a **Fellow of the National Academy of Sciences, India (NASI)** in 1987.
    - Was elected a **Fellow of the Institute of Mathematics and its Applications (U.K.)** in 1988.
    - Was elected a **Fellow of the Institution of Engineering and Technology (IET), UK** in 2019.
    - Fellow of the Institute of Theoretical Physics, Calcutta.
    - Was elected a **Fellow of the Royal Society of Medicine, London** in 1989 in recognition of the significant impact of his research contribution in the field of Biomedical Engineering.
    - Was elected a **Fellow of the Royal Society of Public Health, London** 2019 in recognition of impact of his research contributions in Physiology and Medicine.
    - Was elected a **Fellow of the Royal Society of Biology, London** 2020 in recognition of his research contributions in Physiological Fluid Dynamics.

5. **Awards, Distinctions and Recognition:**

    (a) Prof. J.C. Misra figures in the **global list of Top 2% scientists**, during the last six consecutive years from 2020 to 2025 as per the study conducted by Stanford University, USA.

    (b) Was among the few 'eminent retired faculty members' honoured during the Platinum Jubilee celebrations of IIT Kharagpur on 18th August 2025.

    (c) Was one of the two recipients of '**INAE Outstanding Teachers Award-2013**', Indian National Academy of Engineering, New Delhi.

    (d) Received the prestigious Award '**Ram Mohan Puraskar**' in 2004 **for 'Outstanding Contributions in the Field of Mathematics'**. The

Award consisted of a cash prize of **Rs. five lakhs, a memento,** and a **citation.**

(e) Recipient of the prestigious award, 1984 IIT Kharagpur **Silver Jubilee Research Award,** the research publications submitted by him having been adjudged by a **National Level Committee** to be **outstanding** (He was the only recipient of this award in 1984). This award consisted of a cash prize and a certificate. It was awarded by IIT Kharagpur.

(f) Recipient of **Dr. A.P.J. Abdul Kalam Award for Lifetime Contribution in Science,** Panama Labs, Chennai, 2017.

(g) Recipient of EET CRS **Award for Research Excellence,** Mumbai, 2017.

(h) Recipient of EET CRS "Best Scientist Award-2014", Bangalore.

(i) **Recipient of CEGR Shiksha Gourav Purskar-2014,** New Delhi.

(j) **Recipient of Lifetime Achievement Award-2015,** VENUS International Foundation, awarded in Chennai on 5th July 2015

(k) Recipient of '**Rashtriya Gaurav Award**' in 2004 by India International Friendship Society, New Delhi for meritorious services and remarkable research contributions in Mathematics (along with nuclear physicist Padma Shri Dr. Bikash Sinha, Director of Saha Institute of Nuclear Physics, Calcutta).

(l) Received the coveted **Alexander von Humboldt Fellowship,** Germany in 1975.

(m) Delivered the prestigious **Indian Science Congress Platinum Jubilee Lecture** 2005 in the Section of Mathematical Sciences (including Statistics). Past lecturers include Prof. C.R. Rao, FRS, and Prof. C.S. Seshadri, FRS.

(n) Was nominated as an Active Member of the **New York Academy of Sciences** in 1996.

(o) Was elected a Member of **Biomechanical Engineering Society, USA** in 1989.

(p) Was elected a Member, **International Society of Biorheology, New York,** 1981.

(q) Was elected a Member, **Society for Applied Mathematics and Mechanics (GAMM), Germany,** 1982.

(r) Life Member, **Indian Science Congress Association.**

(s) Life Member, **Indian Society of Theoretical and Applied Mechanics.**

(t) Life Member, **Indian Society of Technical Education.**

(u) He has been described as **"a true pioneer in human biodynamics"** by the authors, V. Ivancevic and T. Ivancevic (University of Adelaide, Australia) in their book entitled "Natural Biodynamics", World Scientific, 2005 (London/USA/Singapore), who have very extensively referred to Misra's research contributions in the book.

(v) He was appointed by the **National Science Foundation of USA, Imperial Press (UK) and World Scientific, Singapore** as a Member of their Expert Committees.

(w) Was elected in 2006 **President of the Mathematical Sciences Section** (including Statistics), **Indian Science Congress.**

(x) Was awarded the highly coveted **D.Sc.** (Doctor of Science) degree by the University of Calcutta.

(y) His appointment to the post of Professor was a special offer from IIT Kharagpur, **'in recognition of his academic excellence'.**

6. **Positions held (in chronological order)**

(a) Lecturer, Dept. of Mathematics, Indian Institute of Technology Kharagpur: 1971–'78

(b) Asst. Professor, Dept. of Mathematics, Indian Institute of Technology Kharagpur: 1978–'85

(c) Professor, Dept. of Mathematics, Indian Institute of Technology Kharagpur: 1985–2009

(d) Head, Dept. of Mathematics, Indian Institute of Technology Kharagpur: 1998–2001

(e) Professor & Pro Vice-Chancellor, Institute of Technology Education and Research/SOA University, Bhubaneswar: 2009–'14.

(f) Adjunct Professor, Center for Healthcare Science and Technology, Indian Institute of Engineering Science and Technology, Shibpur, West Bengal: 2015–Till date

(g) Honorary Guest Professor of Mathematics, R.K. Mission Vidyamandira

(Autonomous Postgraduate college), Belur Math, Howrah: 2020–Till date

7. **Visiting Positions held**
   (a) Visiting Professor Friedrich-Alexander University of Erlangen-Nuremberg (FAU), Germany, 2019.
   (b) Visiting Professor, Institute of Mechanics and Ocean Engineering, Technical University of Hamburg, Germany, 2016.
   (c) Visiting Professor, Institute of Thermo-fluid Dynamics, Technical University of Hamburg (Germany), 2012.
   (d) Visiting Professor, Leibniz University, Hannover (Germany), 2009.
   (e) Visiting Professor, University of Bremen, Bremen (Germany), 2006.
   (f) Visiting Scientist, University of Calgary, Calgary (Canada), 1981.
   (g) Visiting Fellow, Technical University of Hannover, Hannover (Germany), 1982.
   (h) Humboldt Fellow, Technical University of Hannover, Hannover (Germany), 1975–77.
   (i) Visiting Fellow, Technical University of Hannover, Hannover (Germany), 1982.
   (j) Visiting Professor, Hong Kong University of Science & Technology, 2002.
   (k) Visiting Professor, Malay University, Kuala Lumpur, Malaysia, 2007.

8. **Short Visits Abroad**

   Prof. Misra paid short visits to many distinguished institutions abroad, delivered seminar lectures, including:

   - Universities of Oxford and Cambridge,
   - University of Scotland,
   - Universities of Kobe and Osaka in Japan,
   - Courant Institute of Mathematical sciences, New York;
   - Cornell Medical Center of the New York Hospital,
   - Universities of California, San Diego and Los Angeles in USA,
   - University of Alberta, Edmonton in Canada,

- Graz University in Austria,
- Ecole Polytechnique Institute in France,
- Technical University of Berlin,
- University of Kassel,
- University of Stuttgart in Germany,
- University of Malay, Malaysia, etc.

9. **Academic Qualifications**

   (a) S.F.: W.B.B.Sec. Edn., First Division with credit marks in Mathematics, 1959.

   (b) I.Sc.: Ramakrishna Mission Vidyamandira, Belur Math, Calcutta University, First Division with credit marks in Mathematics, 1961.

   (c) B.Sc. (Hons.): Honours in Mathematics, Ramakrishna Mission Vidyamandira, Belur Math, Calcutta University, 1964.

   (d) M.Sc. (Applied Mathematics): Calcutta University, 1st Class, 1966.

   (e) Ph.D.: Applied Mathematics, Jadavpur University, 1971

   (f) D.Sc.: Applied Mathematics, Calcutta University, 1984.

10. **A. Achievement of Former Students**

    His Undergraduate/Masters/Ph.D. students are well-placed in India and abroad. Some of them occupied responsible positions like Directors of IITs, Managers in Industries, Deans, HoDs and Professors at IITs/NITs/Universities, while several of them have turned out to be distinguished researchers.

    B. Places where work has been referred/cited in Reviews

    His work has been extensively referred/cited in Mathematical Reviews, Applied Mechanics Reviews, Citation Index and in a large number of research papers published by other researchers.

    C. Sponsored Research Projects

    (a) Principal Investigator of a Research Project on Mathematical Modelling of the effects of wall deformation on blood flow in arteries, **CSIR**, New Delhi, 1985–1988.

    (b) Principal Investigator of a Major Project on the Network Environme nt, sponsored by **MHRD**, New Delhi, 1999–2000.

(c) Principal Investigator of a Major Project on Modelling and Computer Graphics Simulation for the Analysis of DNA, **MHRD**, New Delhi, 2000–2003.

(d) Principal Investigator, Research Project entitled "Effects of non-linearity and viscoelasticity of wall tissues and blood viscoelasticity on magnetohydrodynamic flow in arteries in normal and pathological states, **CSIR**, New Delhi, 2006–2009.

(e) Principal Investigator, Research Project entitled "Problems on Heat and Mass Transfer in Physiological Fluid Dynamics: Modeling and Simulation", **SERB**, DST, New Delhi, 2015–2018.

All these projects were already completed successfully.

11. **Some of the Invited lectures delivered in India/Abroad.**

(a) **Courant Institute of Mathematical Sciences,** June 1981 New York. Topic of Lecture: Deformation and Stresses in arterial walls under normal physiological loading.

(b) **Cornell Medical Center of the New York Hospital,** June 1981. Topic of Lecture: Fracture and remodeling of bones.

(c) **Euromech Colloquium held at Paris,** December1976. Topic of lecture: Propagation of cracks in thermally stressed solids.

(d) **Fourth International Congress of Biorheology Tokyo (Japan),** May 1981. (He was delegated to by the Indian National Science Academy, New Delhi). Topic of lecture: Deformation and flow in arteries.

(e) Was invited to deliver a lecture and to chair a session at the **Fifth International Congress of Biorheology held in Baden Baden, Germany.**

(f) Delivered the prestigious **P.L. Bhatnagar Memorial Lecture, NIT Hamirpur, Himachal Pradesh,** 2001.

(g) Delivered an invited lecture and chaired a Plenary Session at the **International Congress on Computational and Applied Mathematics, Brussels, Belgium,** 2002.

(h) Delivered an invited lecture at the **National University of Singapore,** 2002.

(i) Delivered an invited lecture at the **Hong Kong University of Science and Technology,** 2002. Delivered a keynote address on Mathematical

Modelling and chaired a Plenary Session at the International Conference of Applied Mathematics and Mathematical Physics, **SUST, Sylhet, Bangladesh**, 2003.

(j) Delivered an invited lecture in Bio-informatics at the **International Conference on Information Technology, Kathmandu**, 2003.

(k) Delivered an invited lecture on Mathematical Modelling in the Mechanics of Blood Flow at the **University of Hamburg-Harburg, Germany**, 2005.

(l) Delivered an invited lecture on Mathematical Models in Cardiovascular System Dynamics at the **University of Kassel, Germany**, 2006.

(m) Delivered an invited lecture on Blood flow in arteries in pathological states, **University of Alberta, Edmonton, Canada**, April 2006.

(n) Delivered an invited lecture on Challenges in Biofluid Dynamics, **University of Hamburg-Harburg, Germany**, 11 June 2007.

(o) Delivered an invited lecture on Mechanics and Biology: Past and Present at the Institute of Mechanics, **Technical University of Berlin, Germany**, 14 June 2007.

(p) Delivered an invited lecture on Mathematics, Mechanics and Medicine at the **Institute of Mechanics, University of Stuttgart, Germany**, 18 June 2007.

(q) Delivered an invited lecture on Biomechanics: Past and Present at the **University of Bremen, Germany**, 21 June 2007.

(r) Delivered an invited lecture on Biomedical Mathematics: Prospects and Challenges at **Leibniz University of Hanover, Germany**, 25 June 2007.

(s) Delivered an invited lecture on "Origin and current status of Biomedical Engineering" at the **University of Malay, Kuala Lumpur**, 19th September 2007.

(t) Delivered an invited lecture on "Modeling the Dynamical Behaviour of the Cardiovascular System" at the **University of Malay, Kuala Lumpur**, 20 September 2007.

(u) Mathematics in Medicine and Biology, National Conference on Advances in Mathematics, **Guwahati University**, September 4–7, 2008.

(v) Computational Biology: Prospects and Challenges, National Workshop of Mathematical Modelling in Biology, **SPM University, Tirupati**, AP, February 23–27, 2008.

(w) Non-Newtonian Flow of blood Through Arteries in Normal and Pathologic a l States, National Workshop on Mathematical Modelling in Biology, **SPM University, Tirupati**, AP, February 23–27, 2008.

(x) Mathematics in Medicine and Biology, National Conference on Advances in Mathematics, **Guwahati University**, September 4–7, 2008.

(y) Mathematics and Spirituality, Fourth All India Students' Conference on Science and Spiritual Quest, **NIT Tiruchirapalli**, December 27–29, 2008.

(z) Leonhard Euler and his contributions in Mathematics, Invited lecture at National seminar Emerging areas in Mathematics and Applications, **Burdwan University**, February 18–20, 2009.

(aa) Non-linearties in Biology and Medicine, invited lecture delivered at National Seminar on Advances in Nonlinear Systems, **Visva-Bharati, Santiniketan**, February 21–23, 2009.

(ab) Delivered an invited lecture on "Blood flow in arteries in a vibratio n environment" at **Institute of Dynamics and Vibration, Leibniz University of Hanover, Germany**, May 28, 2010.

(ac) Delivered an invited lecture on "Flow of non-Newtonian fluids in channels: Application to blood flow in arteries" at **Institute of Thermo-fluid Dynamics, Technical University of Hamburg-Harburg (Germany)** on 23rd May 2011.

(ad) Chief Guest at National Symposium on Mathematical Sciences, National Mathematics Year 2012, held at **Calcutta Mathematical Society, Salt Lake, Kolkata,** April 21–22, 2012. Topic of the lecture: Mathematical Physiology.

(ae) Chief Guest at the National Conference on Computational Mathematics and Nonlinear Dynamics, 19–21 February 2016 held at **Visva-Bharati University, Santiniketan**; Topic of the lecture: Application of Mathematics in Life Sciences.

(af) Keynote speech "Mathematical modelling of Physiological fluid flows" (two lectures) delivered at National Workshop on Recent Advances in

Fluid Dynamics and Applications in Science and Technology, **MITS, Andhra Pradesh**, 25–26 May 2018.

(ag) Keynote speech "Mathematical Modeling of Electro-osmotic Flows in Physiological Systems" delivered at International Conference on Mathematical Modelling and Scientific Computing (ICMMSC 2018), **IIT Indore,** 19–21 July 2018.

(ah) Keynote Speech "Modelling in Physiological Fluid Dynamics, October 24–26, 2019", International Conference on Applied Mathematics in Science and Technology, **SOAU, Bhubaneswar.**

(ai) Keynote Speech "Use of Mathematics in Biology", **Ramanujan Memorial Lecture, Mugberia College, Vidyasagar University, West Bengal**, 2020.

(aj) Invited Lecture "Impact of Heat Transfer on Electro-osmotic Flows in Micro-vessels: Modelling of Blood Flow in the Micro-circulatory System", 1st International Conference on Applied Analysis, Computation and Mathematical Modelling in Engineering (AACMME-2021)" **National Institute of Technology Rourkela, Odisha**, February 24–26, 2021.

(ak) Was invited for delivering an Invited Lecture at the 2nd International Conference on Recent Advances in Applied Mathematics, **IIT BHU**, July 03–05, 2024.

Details of Books Published

Sl No.	Title	Authors/ Editors	Publishers	Year of Publi-cation	ISBN Number
1.	Mathematical Modelling of Nonlinear Systems, Vol. I: Nonlinear Systems and Mathematical Models	**J.C. Misra and S.B. Sinha**	IIT Kharagpur	1999	
2.	Mathematical Modelling of Nonlinear Systems, Vol. II: Mathematical Techniques and Application Areas	**J.C. Misra and S.B. Sinha**	IIT Kharagpur	1999	
3.	Applicable Mathematics: Its perspectives and Challenges	**J.C. Misra**	Narosa Publishing House, New Delhi	2001	8173194068
4.	Recent Trends in Mathematical Sciences	**J.C. Misra and S.B. Sinha**	Narosa Publishing House, New Delhi	2001	817319405 X, 9788173194054
5.	Uncertainty and Optimality	**J.C. Misra**	World Scientific	2002	9789812380821
6.	Applicable Mathematics in the Golden Age	**J.C. Misra**	Narosa Publishing House, New Delhi	2003	8173194874
7.	Mathematics and Mathematicians at IIT Kharagpur	**J.C. Misra**	Allied Publishers, New Delhi	2003	8177644653
8.	Computing and Information Sciences: Recent Trends	**J.C. Misra**	Narosa Publishing House, New Delhi	2003	8176463612, 9788176463614
9.	Computational Mathe-matics, Modelling and Algorithms	**J.C. Misra**	Narosa Publishing House, New Delhi	2003	8173194904, 9788173194900
10.	Industrial Mathematics and Statistics	**J.C. Misra**	Narosa Publishing House, New Delhi	2003	8173194882, 9788173194887
11.	Mathematical Models for Bioengineering and Probabilistic Systems	**J.C. Misra**	Narosa Publishing House, New Delhi	2005	8173194939
12.	Modern Applied Mathematics	**J.C. Misra**	Narosa Publishing House, New Delhi	2005	8173194920
13.	Biomathematics: Modeling and Simulation	**J.C. Misra**	World Scientific, Singapore/London/ USA	2006	9812381104
14.	Achinpurer ak Pathik (in Bengali)	**J.C. Misra**	Kabitika Publishing House, Kolkata	2023	9788119564897
15.	A Traveller in an Unknown Land (Autobigraphy)	**J.C. Misra**	Allied Publishers, Noida	2025	9789348699541 (PB) 9789348699350 (HB)

Books on Prof. J.C. Misra

1.	Nana Chokhe ak Barenya Ganit-Sadhak (in Bengali)	**M.P. Maity, M.N. Das and B.L. Das**	Kabitika Publishing House, Kolkata	2023	9788119564439
2.	A Mathematics Wizard in Different Eyes	**Dr. Haripada Maity Shri Manmatha Nath Das Prof Ranajit Kumar Nayek Shri Balailal Das**	Allied Publishers, Noida	2025	9789348699688 (PB) 9789348699435 (HB)

Summary of Relevant Contributions

1. Total number of papers published (in refereed journals): 241
2. Total citation record and h-index:

   h-index: 41;

   i-10 index: 112

   Total citations: 5325

   (Database used: Google Scholar)
3. Number of books published: 15
4. Number of completed Research Projects as Principal Investigator: 5
5. Number of research students guided and awarded doctoral degrees: 30

   Number of invited lectures delivered in Distinguished Institutions/ Universities in India and Abroad, as well as in National/International conferences: 37

Some Selected Research Publications

1. **J.C. Misra**, C. Hartung and O. Mahrenholtz (1977). Effect of Pulse Loading on Brain Injury, **Mechanics Research Communications** (UK), Vol. 4, 297–302 (Springer).
2. **J.C. Misra** (1978). Axisymmetric Vibration of Human Skull-brain System, **Ingenieur Archiv.** (Germany), Vol. 47, 11–19.
3. **J.C. Misra** and S. Samanta (1987). Effect of Material Damping on Bone Remodelling, **Journal of Biomechanics** (Oxford), Vol. 20, 241–249.
4. **J.C. Misra** and S. Chakravarty (1986). Flow in Arteries in the Presence of Stenosis, **Journal of Biomechanics** (Oxford), Vol. 19, 907–916.
5. **J.C. Misra** and S. Chakravarty (1984). A Study on Rotational Brain Injury, **Journal of Biomechanics** (Oxford), Vol. 17, 459–466.
6. **J.C. Misra** and S.K. Pandey (2001). A Mathematical Model for Oesophageal Swallowing of a Food-bolus, **Mathematical and Computer Modelling** (U.K.), Vol. 33, 997–1009.
7. **J.C. Misra** and S.K. Pandey (2002) Peristaltic Transport of Blood in Small Vessels-study of a Mathematical Model, **Computers and Mathematics with Applications**, (U.K.) 43, 1183–1193.
8. **J.C. Misra**, G.C. Shit and H.J. Rath (2008). Flow and Heat Transfer of a MHD Viscoelastic Fluid in a Channel with Stretching Walls: Some Applications to Haemodynamics, **Computers & Fluids** (Elsevier),

Vol. 37, No. 1, 1–11. [**Occupies The 6th Position in the List of Top 25 Hottest Articles Published by Science Direct.**]

9. **J.C. Misra** and G.C. Shit (2006). Blood Flow through Arteries in a Pathological State: A Theoretical Study, **International Journal of Engineering Science** (UK). Vol. 44, 662–671.
10. **J.C. Misra** and S.I. Singh (1988). Study on The Mechanics of Aneurysms in the left Ventricle of the Heart, **Computers and Mathematics with Applications** (UK), Vol. 15, 17–27.
11. S. Maiti and **J.C. Misra** (2011). Peristaltic flow of a fluid in a porous channel: A study having relevance to flow of bile within ducts in a pathological state, International Journal of Engineering Science (Elsevier), Vol.49, 950–966.
12. **J.C. Misra** and S. Maiti (2012). Peristaltic Pumping of Blood Through Small Vessels of Varying Cross-section, ASME **Journal of Applied Mechanics**, Vol. 79, No. 6, 061003: 1–19 (19 pages), DOI: 10.1115/1.4006635.
13. **J.C. Misra** and A. Sinha (2013). Effect of thermal radiation on MHD flow of blood and heat transfer in a permeable capillary in stretching motion, **Heat and Mass Transfer**, Germany (Springer), Vol. 49, 617–628, DOI 10.1007/s00231-012-1107-6.
14. **J.C. Misra**, S. Chandra, and H. Herwig (2015). Flow of a micro-polar fluid in a micro-channel under the action of an alternating electric field: Estimates of flow in bio-fluid ic devices, **Journal of Hydrodynamics**, vol. 27, 350–358 (Elsevier).
15. **J.C. Misra,** B. Mallick, P. Steinmann (2020), Temperature distribution and entropy generation during Darcy-Forchheimer-Brinkman electrokinetic flow in a microfluidic tube subject to a prescribed heat flux, **Meccanica,** 55, 1079–1098.
16. B. Mallick, **J.C. Misra** (2022), Interplay of steric factor and high zeta potential on entropy generation during nanofluid slip flow in a microfluidic tube, **The European Physical Journal Plus,** 137, 868, https://doi.org/10.1140/epjp/s13360-022-03069-9 S
17. R. Prodhan, M. Ferdows, **J.C. Misra**, E. Tzirtzilakis, MG Murtaza (2024) Non-Similar Analysis of Mixed Convection Biomagnetic Boundary Layer Flow Over a Vertical Plate with Magnetization and Localized Heating/ Cooling, **European Journal of Computational Mechanics** Vol. 33(2), 91–120 doi: 10.13052/ejcm2642-2085.3321

18. M. Dhange, G. Sankara, U. Bhujakkanavar, K.K. Das, **J.C. Misra** (2024) Hemodynamic characteristics of blood flow in an inclined overlapped stenosed arterial section, **Partial Differential Equations in Applied Mathematics**, Vol. 11, 2024, 100829 https://doi.org/10.1016/j.padiff.2024.100829

APPENDIX 5

New Findings in Biomechanics

Gone are the days when engineering and medicine were the two mutually exclusive branches of science. Progress of technological know-how has led to the development of a number of interdisciplinary subjects. The Department of Science & Technology, Govt. of India, is spending crores of rupees every year in sponsoring specialised research in such higher institutions of learning as the IITs, the IISc and ISI.

Anyone heard of the near preposterous suggestion of applying differential equations to determine the aberrations in the cranial structure of humans? Or equating mass/heat transfer and motion of vibrating ions to discern the heart tissue pattern? Or even using stress distribution geometry to explore the cardiovascular system? Yet the eyes of the usually different Dr. J.C. Misra (of Mathematics Dept., IIT-Kharagpur) emit a strange glow as he gets carried away in his almost childlike enthusiasm while describing some of his fantastic findings in the newly emerging field of Biomechanics, which roughly seeks to explore a soup of medicine, mathematics and physics. "For any organism, biomechanics helps us to understand its normal function, predict changes due to alterations and propose methods of artificial intervention." Before commencing his postdoctoral research in West Germany in 1975 as Humboldt Fellow, he was initially concerned with continuum mechanics, where he put forward mathematical analysis of conventional structural mechanics problems.

During an inspiration from the essential similarity of the structural aspects to the human/living organs, he immediately formulated several mathematical models for the physiological problems of brain injuay, fracture and remodelling of the bones and blood flow through arteries and ventricular stress. Among his models, the ones that deserve special mention are, the dynamical response of heart and blood vessels in a state of physiological leading, flow in stenosed arteries, propagation of pulse waves through aortic wall and stress concentration in the neighbourhood of cracks in the bone specimens. His studies on wave propagation in arteries have important bearings on prosthesis in selecting the materials for construction of artificial blood vessels. Some of these models are of special significance to clinicians in their detection of cardiovascular diseases, for prescribing medicines. His work has till now attracted world renowned neural scientists concerned with cerebral concussions. Eagerly envisaging many industrial applications, he says, further research will help design better artificial restores and life support systems-prosthetic heart valves, implantable artificial materials, artificial limbs and internal organs to wheelchairs and beds, for instance. Greater safety equipment in flying and swimming are only a step away for the accent is now on the greater significance of the individual and his relationship to nature.

(The Amrita Bazar Patrika, 24 January, 1989
Reporter: Bhaskar Majumdar)

Citation of INAE Outstanding Teacher Award 2013

Indian National Academy of Engineering, New Delhi

Prof. Jagadis Chandra Misra obtained his B.Sc. (Hons.) in Mathematics and M.Sc. in Applied Mathematics Degrees from Calcutta University. He then obtained his Ph.D. Degree from Jadavpur University and D.Sc. from Calcutta University. He has served the cause of education for nearly five decades, the major portion being at Indian Institute of Technology Kharagpur. He joined the Siksha O Anusandhan University, in 2009 as a Pro Vice-Chancellor. He is known as a dedicated teacher and a brilliant researcher. In addition to achieving excellence in classroom teaching both at undergraduate and postgraduate levels, Prof. Misra is well-known as a committed researcher and a motivated supervisor of Doctoral students. He built up an active school of research in Biomechanics and Structural Mechanics and is one of the pioneers in research in these fields. Prof. Misra has received several prestigious awards and honours including the Humboldt Fellowship, Germany; IIT Kharagpur Silver Jubilee Research Award; Rashtriya Gaurav Award, Rammohan Puraskar and Indian Science Congress Platinum Jubilee Lecture Award in Mathematical Sciences.

Glimpses of His Journey

Attested
1908.2003
Head
Department of Electrical Engineering
Indian Institute of Technology
Kharagpur-721 302

Jadavpur University

Certified that **Jagadishchandra Misra** was admitted to the Degree of Doctor of Philosophy (Science) of this University on 17.4.71 and that the degree was conferred on him at the Convocation held in 1971 with all the Rights and Privileges thereto appertaining.

Given at Jadavpur, Calcutta, this Fourth day of July in the year Nineteen Hundred and Seventy One. In Witness whereof the Signatures of the Chancellor and the Vice-Chancellor of Jadavpur University are hereunto affixed.

A. K. Majumdar
Vice-Chancellor

S. K. Chakravarti
In exercise of the duties of
Chancellor

INDIAN INSTITUTE OF TECHNOLOGY
KHARAGPUR

SILVER JUBILEE RESEARCH AWARD

This is to certify that the research paper(s) published by Dr. Jagadis Chandra Misra a member of faculty of the Institute, in the field of Bio-mechanics and submitted in support of his application, has/have been adjudged to have made a valuable contribution to the knowledge in the field and the author has been awarded the IIT Kharagpur Silver Jubilee Research Award in Group I for the year 1984 on approval by the Board of Governors.

The award carries a cash prize of Rs. 2,500/-

Given this day, the 30th May, 1986

Registrar

Director

Chairman
Board of Governors

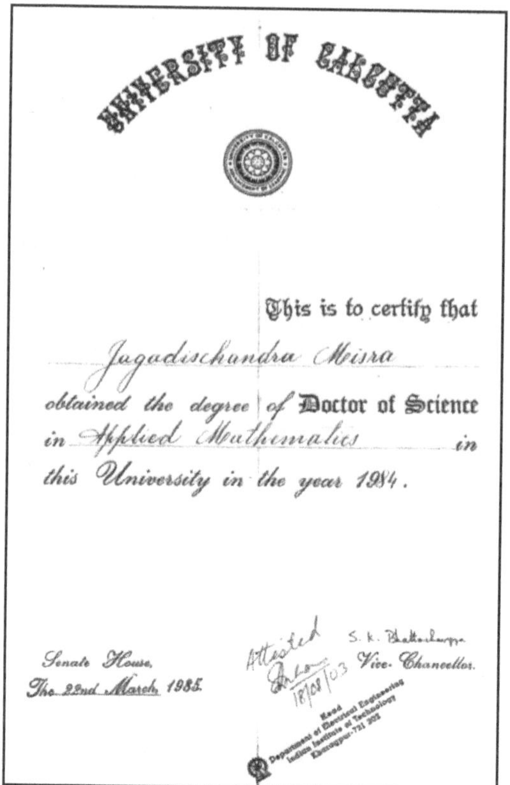

UNIVERSITY OF CALCUTTA

This is to certify that

Jagadischandra Misra

obtained the degree of **Doctor of Science**

in Applied Mathematics in

this University in the year 1984.

Senate House,

The 22nd March 1985.

S. K. Bhattacharyya
Vice-Chancellor.

Attested 18/08/03

Head, Department of Electrical Engineering, Indian Institute of Technology, Kharagpur-721 302

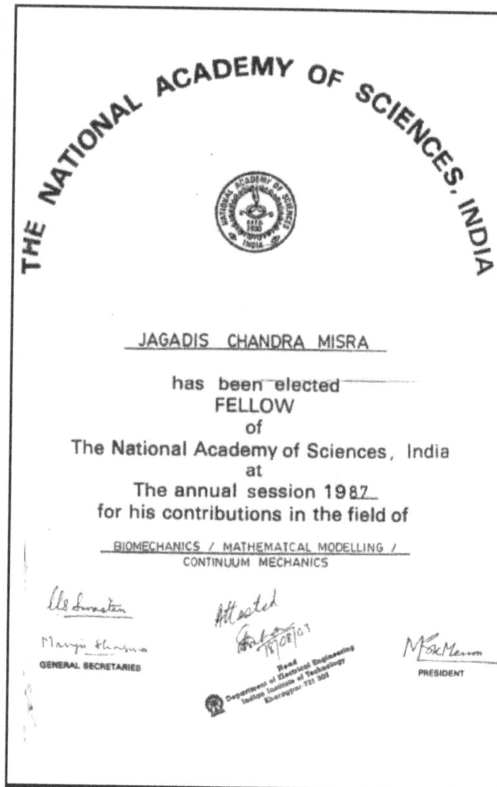

THE NATIONAL ACADEMY OF SCIENCES, INDIA

JAGADIS CHANDRA MISRA

has been elected

FELLOW

of

The National Academy of Sciences, India

at

The annual session 1987

for his contributions in the field of

BIOMECHANICS / MATHEMATCAL MODELLING / CONTINUUM MECHANICS

GENERAL SECRETARIES

PRESIDENT

Attested 18/08/03

Head, Department of Electrical Engineering, Indian Institute of Technology, Kharagpur-721 302

The Institute of Mathematics and its Applications

IMA

This is to certify that

JAGADIS CHANDRA MISRA

was elected a

Fellow of the Institute

on the 29TH day of MARCH 1988

Given under the Common Seal of the Institute by resolution of the Council

President

Members of Council

Secretary & Registrar

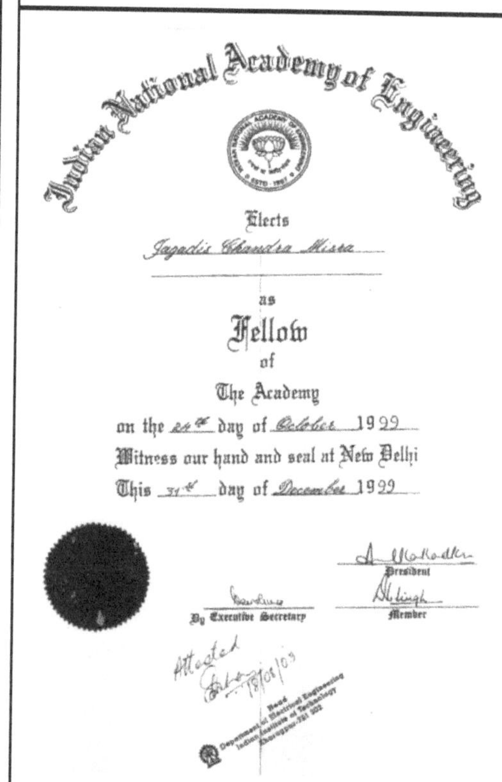

Indian National Academy of Engineering

Elects

Jagadis Chandra Misra

as

Fellow

of

The Academy

on the 24th day of October 1999

Witness our hand and seal at New Delhi

This 31st day of December 1999

President

By Executive Secretary

Member

Attested 18/08/03

Head, Department of Electrical Engineering, Indian Institute of Technology, Kharagpur-721 302

The Royal Society of Medicine

Pursuant to the powers vested in it by Royal Charter the Society has in general meeting assembled this day elected

PROFESSOR DR JAGADIS C MISRA MSc PhD DSc

A Fellow of The Royal Society of Medicine to be entitled to enjoy such privileges as shall be [in a]ccordance with and subject to the By-Laws of the said Soci[ety]

Executive Director Robert N. Thomson

INDIAN INSTITUTE OF TECHNOLOGY KHARAGPUR

भारतीय प्रौद्योगिकी संस्थान खड़गपुर

Sanjiv Goenka
Chairman
Board of Governors

October 25, 2004.

Dear Prof. Mishra,

What an achievement! What an oustanding contribution to science and technology! Absolutely brilliant.

My congratulations to you on your receiving this prestigious Rashtriya Gaurav Award.

With regards.

Yours sincerely.
Sanjiv Goenka

Prof. J.C. Misra
Department of Mathematics
Indian Institute of Technology
Kharagpur 721 302.

CESC House, Chowringhee Square, Kolkata - 700 001
Telephone : (033) 2254861/0163 Telefax (33) 2256790 E-mail sgoenka@rpgnet.com

---

RAM MOHAN MISSION

162/69, LAKE GARDENS, KOLKATA - 700 045

awards

"RAMMOHAN PURASKAR 2004"

worth Rupees Five Lacs to

Dr. Jagadis Chandra Misra

Professor, Indian Institute of Technology, Kharagpur for his outstanding contributions in Mathematics.

Date : 22nd May, 2004

Place : Kolkata

Sankar Biswas
SANKAR BISWAS
PRESIDENT

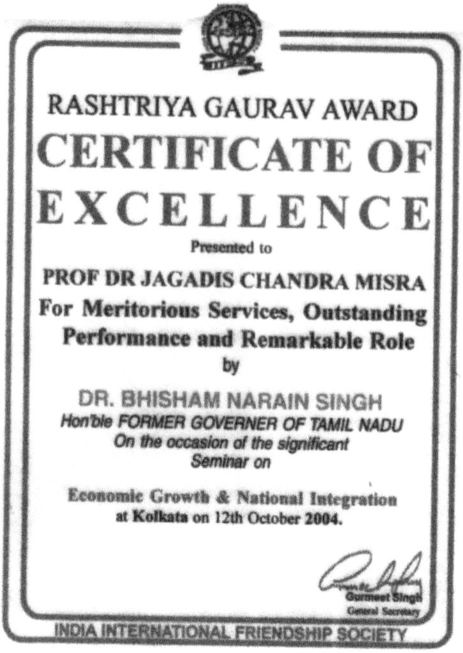
RASHTRIYA GAURAV AWARD

CERTIFICATE OF EXCELLENCE

Presented to

PROF DR JAGADIS CHANDRA MISRA

For Meritorious Services, Outstanding Performance and Remarkable Role

by

DR. BHISHAM NARAIN SINGH

Hon'ble FORMER GOVERNER OF TAMIL NADU

On the occasion of the significant Seminar on

Economic Growth & National Integration at Kolkata on 12th October 2004.

Gurmeet Singh
General Secretary

INDIA INTERNATIONAL FRIENDSHIP SOCIETY

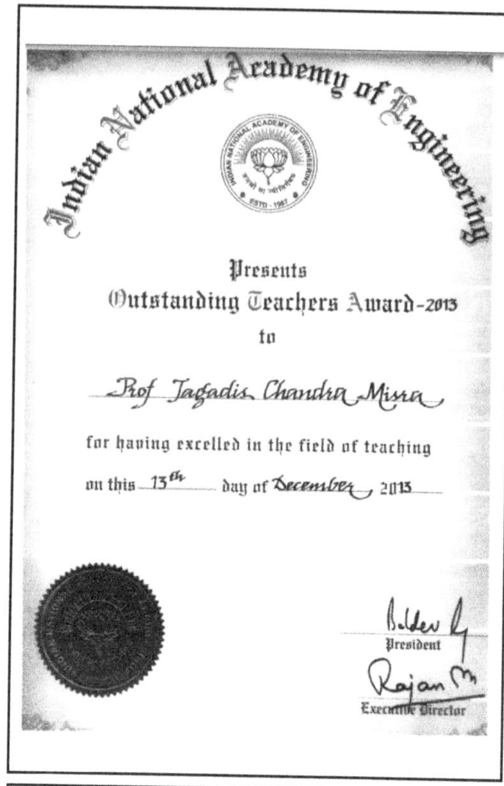
Indian National Academy of Engineering

Presents

Outstanding Teachers Award-2013

to

Prof Jagadis Chandra Misra

for having excelled in the field of teaching

on this 13th day of December, 2013

President

Executive Director

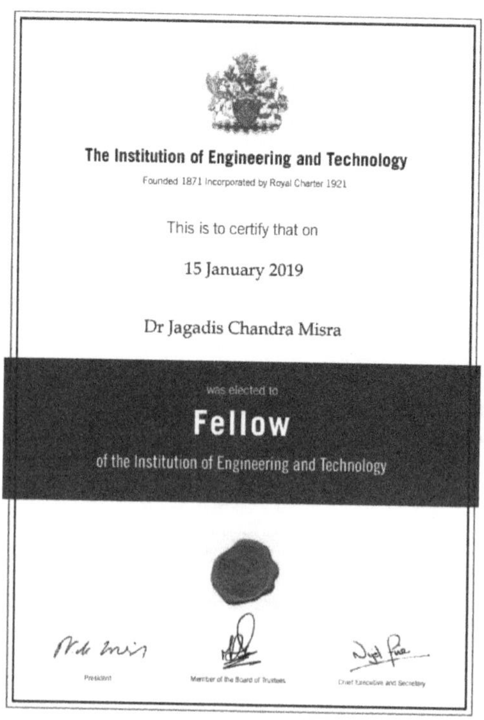
The Institution of Engineering and Technology

Founded 1871 Incorporated by Royal Charter 1921

This is to certify that on

15 January 2019

Dr Jagadis Chandra Misra

was elected to

Fellow

of the Institution of Engineering and Technology

President

Member of the Board of Trustees

Chief Executive and Secretary

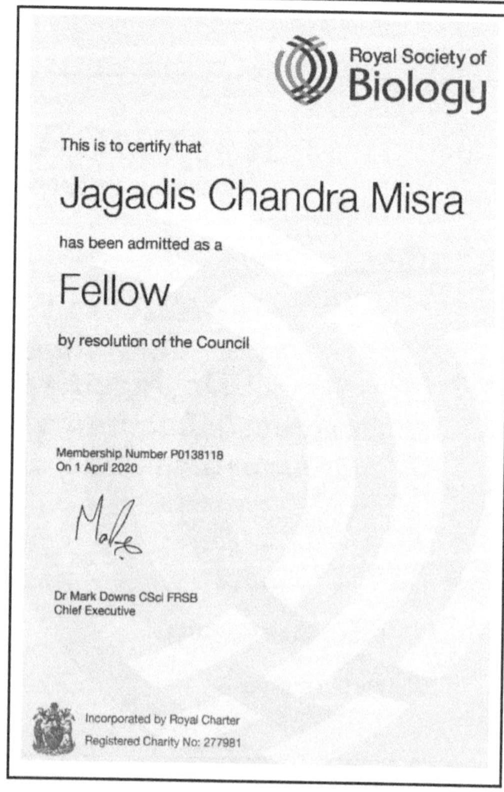
Royal Society of Biology

This is to certify that

Jagadis Chandra Misra

has been admitted as a

Fellow

by resolution of the Council

Membership Number P0138118
On 1 April 2020

Dr Mark Downs CSci FRSB
Chief Executive

Incorporated by Royal Charter
Registered Charity No: 277981

টিকরাপাড়া অম্বিকাময়ী উচ্চতর মাধ্যমিক বিদ্যালয়ের

প্রাক্তন ছাত্র;

খড়গপুর আই. আই. টি. এর গণিত বিভাগের
প্রধান অধ্যাপক ডঃ জগদীশ চন্দ্র মিশ্র মহাশয়ের
' রামমোহন ' পুরস্কার ও ' রাষ্ট্রীয় গৌরব ' প্রাপ্তিতে বিদ্যালয়ের ছাত্র,
শিক্ষক, শিক্ষাকর্মী ও পরিচালক মণ্ডলীর ---

০ঃ সম্বর্ধনা ও শ্রদ্ধাঞ্জলি ঃ০

হে জ্ঞান তপস্বী, বরেণ্য অধ্যাপক,

আপনার আগমনে আমাদের বিদ্যালয়ের সমস্ত ছাত্র, শিক্ষক, শিক্ষাকর্মী ও পরিচালক মণ্ডলী আজ আনন্দে আপ্লুত। গণিতবিদ্ হিসাবে আপনার ' রামমোহন ' পুরস্কার, ' রাষ্ট্রিয় গৌরব ' প্রাপ্তি , আপনার আই. আই. টি. – এর প্রধান অধ্যাপকের গৌরব তথা আমাদের বিদ্যালয়ের গৌরবকে করেছে শত সহস্র গুনে বর্ধিত। এই বিদ্যালয়ের অতীত দিনের সুযোগ্য ছাত্র পরিচয়ে আজ আমাদের হৃদয় শতগুনে স্ফীত। আন্তর্জাতিক গবেষণা পত্রিকায় আপনার রচিত দেড় শতাধিক প্রবন্ধের প্রকাশ আপনাকে বহুগুনে করেছে পল্লবিত ও বিকশিত। হে - নীরব - বিজ্ঞান সাধক, আপনার সৃষ্টি-সফল প্রতিভার অবদানে আমাদের এনে দিয়েছে যে গৌরবানুভবের দুলর্ভ সুযোগ, সেই জন্যে আপনাকে জানাই আমাদের হৃদয়-স্পন্দিত সশ্রদ্ধ অভিনন্দন।

হে কর্মযোগী,

পাশ্চাত্য বিশ্ববিদ্যালয়গুলির লোভনীয় হাতছানি আপনাকে দেশমাতৃকার সেবা থেকে বিরত করতে পারেনি। আপনার " আজন্ম সাধন ধন " উপহারে দীন ভারত মায়ের স্নেহাঞ্চল আজ পরিপূর্ণ। সারস্বত মণ্ডলী আজ পেয়েছেন পথ চলার আলোকবর্তিকা। অফুরন্ত জ্ঞানের অধিকারী হয়ে আজ ও আপনি প্রবেশ করে চলেছেন বিষয় থেকে বিষয়ান্তরে – বিজ্ঞানের অতল সাগরে।

হে সৌম্য,

আপনার সংস্কৃতি , কৃষ্টি , চিন্তাভাবনা ও [illegible] পদ্ধতি সারস্বত সমাজে এনেছে মহিমময় উজ্জ্বলতা। পত্র পত্রিকার মাধ্যমে আপনি স্পর্শিত হয়েছেন সবার হৃদয়ে। আমাদের সকলের [illegible] হৃদয় নিঃসৃত বিনম্র শ্রদ্ধা আপনার প্রতি জাগরূক থাকুক।

হে ক্ষণজন্মা,

পার্শ্ববর্তী গ্রাম বাগমারী, একদিন যা ছিল অখ্যাত, যেখানে ষাট বছর আগে আপনার জন্মলগ্নের শঙ্খধ্বনির সাথে সাথে খ্যাতির সূচনা হয়েছিল সূচিত, আজ তা খ্যাতির শীর্ষে। আপনার প্রয়াত পিতা ও এই বিদ্যালয়ের প্রাক্তন শিক্ষক গণেশ চন্দ্র মিশ্র মহাশয়ের সেদিনের ' জগদীশচন্দ্র 'নামকরণ আজ স্বার্থকতায় সমুজ্জ্বল। জাপান, জার্মান, আমেরিকা, গ্রেট ব্রিটেন প্রভৃতি বিদেশের বহু সাম্মানিকে আজ আপনি বিভূষিত। ভাবীকালে আপনি আপনার স্বীয় সৃষ্টির মধ্যে কর্মে চিরভাস্বর হয়ে থাকবেন। দেশ বিদেশের অগণিত ছাত্র, শিক্ষক ও গবেষক আপনার দ্যুতিতে আলোকিত হতে থাকবেন।

হে বন্ধু,

আজ আপনাকে নিবেদিত আমাদের অন্তরের শ্রদ্ধা, ভালবাসার বিনম্র নিবেদন আমাদেরই গর্বিত করেছে। ছাত্র, শিক্ষক, শিক্ষাকর্মী ও পরিচালক মণ্ডলীর পক্ষ থেকে তাই জানাই আমাদের অকুণ্ঠ – অভিনন্দন। আপনার অকৃত্রিম আপনত্ব বোধের প্রকাশে আমরা সকলে মুগ্ধ। জন্মভূমির স্মৃতি পথে এই বিদ্যালয়ে আপনার পুনরায় শুভাগমন আমাদের আনন্দবর্ধন করুক। এই লব্ধ প্রতিষ্ঠ প্রাক্তন কৃতী ছাত্রকে পেয়ে আমরা ও আমাদের বিদ্যাভবন আজ সম্মানিত। আপনাকে আজ আমরা হৃদয়-প্লাবিত সম্বর্ধনা জানাতে পেরে আনন্দিত ও গৌরবান্বিত।

ইতি

বিনয়াবনত,

ছাত্র-ছাত্রী, শিক্ষক, শিক্ষাকর্মী, ও পরিচালক মণ্ডলী।
টিকরাপাড়া অম্বিকাময়ী উচ্চতর মাধ্যমিক বিদ্যালয়,
পোঃ- প্রতাপদীঘি ❖ জেলা ঃ- পূর্ব মেদিনীপুর
পশ্চিমবঙ্গ

টিকরাপাড়া
তাং ঃ- ১৮ - ১০ - ২০০৪

RSPH
ROYAL SOCIETY FOR PUBLIC HEALTH
VISION, VOICE AND PRACTICE

The Royal Society for Public Health is an independent, multi-disciplinary organisation dedicated to the promotion and protection of collective human health and wellbeing. Through advocacy, mediation, empowerment, knowledge and practice we advise on policy development, provide education and training services, encourage scientific research, disseminate information and certify products, training centres and processes. The Chairman and Council of the Royal Society for Public Health do hereby affirm that

Jagadis Chandra Misra

has submitted proof of academic professional achievements and has agreed to abide by The Code of Conduct of the Royal Society for Public Health and has accordingly been elected

A Fellow OF THE ROYAL SOCIETY FOR PUBLIC HEALTH

and is hereby entitled to use the designation FRSPH and to enjoy all the benefits which apply thereto.

Chief Executive of the Royal Society for Public Health

Membership Number: 128932

Valid until: 31/01/2021

Patron Her Majesty The Queen
RSPH John Snow House 59 Mansell Street London E1 8AN
RSPH Incorporated by Royal Charter Registration Number RC000828 Charity Registration Number 1125949

১৬ই জানুয়ারী ২০০৭, রোহিনী চৌধুরানী রুক্মিনীদেবী উচ্চ বিদ্যালয় (উঃমাঃ) এর হীরক জয়ন্তী বর্ষবরণ অনুষ্ঠানে বিশিষ্ট শিক্ষাবিদ ডঃ জগদীশ চন্দ্র মিশ্র

মহোদয়ের শুভাগমনে আমাদের

~শ্রদ্ধাঞ্জলী~

শ্রদ্ধাস্পদ হে জ্ঞানযোগী,

তোমার জ্ঞানালোকের দ্যুতিতে অজ্ঞানতার কালো আঁধার আজ হার মানিয়াছে। তোমার অক্লান্ত ও নিরলস সাধনায় গনিতের মত কঠিন বিষয় আজ সহজ হইয়া দেশ বিদেশে কত কৃতিছাত্র গড়িয়াছে তাহার হিসাব কষা নিতান্তই কঠিন,

শুধু বিদ্যায়তনের গন্ডীবদ্ধ পরিসরে নয় তাহার বাহিরেও প্রাচ্যে-পাশ্চাত্যে তোমার হৃদয় সৌন্দর্যের অনির্বচনীয় প্রকাশে আমরা সবাই বিমুগ্ধ অভিভূত।

হে পন্ডিতপ্রবর নীরব সাধক! যে দুর্লভ সম্মানে তোমার সৃষ্টি প্রতিভা সম্মানিত মেদিনীপুরের জেলা বাসী হিসাবে আমরাও সম্মানিত।

তোমার উপস্থিতিতে আমরা ধন্য ও কৃতার্থ। তুমি চিরজীবি হও, তোমার জ্ঞান ভান্ডার আরও দীপ্যমান হইয়া আলোক বিকীরন করুক — এই প্রার্থনা করি।

শ্রদ্ধাবনত

ছাত্র-ছাত্রী, শিক্ষক-শিক্ষিকা-শিক্ষাকর্মী
ও সদস্য বৃন্দ।

টিকরাপাড়া অম্বিকাময়ী হাইস্কুলের প্রাক্তন শিক্ষক স্বর্গীয় গণেশ চন্দ্র মিশ্রের সুযোগ্য পুত্র ও খড়গপুর আই.আই.টির গণিত বিভাগীয় প্রাক্তন প্রধান অধ্যাপক ডঃ জগদীশ চন্দ্র মিশ্র মহাশয়ের সরকারী "রামমোহন" পুরস্কার পাওয়া উপলক্ষ্যে *প্রতাপদীঘি রামকৃষ্ণ সারদা শিক্ষা সদনের ছাত্র- ছাত্রী, শিক্ষক-শিক্ষিকা, পরিচালন কমিটি ও ট্রাস্টিবোর্ডের পক্ষ হইতে—*

সংবর্ধনা জ্ঞাপন

হে জ্ঞান তপস্বী,

সারাজীবন ধরে জ্ঞানের তপস্যা করে বিশ্ববাসীর কল্যাণ সাধন করেছেন। আপনার পরম শান্তিপূর্ণ এই যোগ সাধনা, পরমার্থ লাভে সহায়তা করে আপনাকে যশের শীর্ষে উন্নীত করুক এই শুভ কামনা করে আমরা সার্থক হই, ধন্য হই, কৃতার্থ হই।

হে বরেণ্য ও শ্রদ্ধেয় অধ্যাপক,

আপনার শিক্ষাধারার ক্ষীরোদাম্বুরাশিতে আজ অবগাহিত হয়েছে অগণন শিষ্যকুল। তাদের অমেয় দীপ্ত পুন্ডরীক আপনাকে নবতর সৃষ্টির আনন্দে উদ্বোধিত করুক।

হে জ্ঞানযোগী বিজ্ঞানী,

আপনার বিশিষ্ট বৈজ্ঞানিক কর্মকাণ্ডের অজস্র মহার্ঘতা ও দানসত্র আমাদের সংস্কৃতিকে করেছে ঋদ্ধ, চিরনবীন ও ভাস্বর। সুদূর ভবিষ্যতের দৃষ্টিতে আপনি স্পর্শিত হবেন ভাবী পুরুষের আননে, মননে, ভবিষ্যৎ কর্মধারায়। তাই আত্মার আত্মীয় আপনাকে জানাই সশ্রদ্ধ অভিনন্দন।

হে মহান নাগরিক,

কোন নক্ষত্রলোকের শান্ত সমাহিত রূপদ্যুতি নিয়ে মাটি মায়ের কোলে সুসন্তান হিসাবে জন্মলাভ করেছিলেন। আগামী অপরাজেয় কাল আপনার মনের কস্তুরীমালার সৌরভ নিয়ে অবিনশ্বর হয়ে থাকবে।

হে মেদিনীপুরের সুসন্তান,

অনুর্বর মৃত্তিকায় জ্ঞানের অমৃত ফসল ফলিয়ে আমাদের মাতৃভূমির পবিত্র মৃত্তিকায় উর্বরতার নূতন দিগন্ত উন্মোচন করেছেন। সকলের ভাগ্যে এমনটি ঘটেনা। তাই আমাদের পক্ষ থেকে আপনাকে উষ্ণ অভিবাদন রইলো।

হে মানবতার শ্রেষ্ঠ পথপ্রদর্শক,

আপনাকে নমস্কার। আপনার সৃষ্ট বৈজ্ঞানিক কর্মের জন্য অভিনন্দন মিছিলের শেষভাগে সুধাসিক্ত কনকাঞ্জলি হস্তে দণ্ডায়মান আমাদের শিক্ষাসদনের সদস্যবৃন্দ। তাঁদের শ্রদ্ধা গ্রহণ করে সকলকে ধন্য করুন। পরম করুণাময় পরমেশ্বরের আশীর্বাদ আপনার উপর বর্ষিত হোক।

বিনয়াবনত—

রামকৃষ্ণ সারদা শিক্ষা সদনের ছাত্র-ছাত্রী,
শিক্ষক-শিক্ষিকা, পরিচালন কমিটির সদস্য বৃন্দ ও
রামকৃষ্ণ সারদা সেবাশ্রমের ট্রাস্টি বোর্ডের সদস্য বৃন্দ
প্রতাপদীঘি ঃঃ পূর্ব মেদিনীপুর
দূরভাষ ঃ (০৩২২০) ২৪৬-০৪২

প্রতাপদীঘি
তাং- ২৬/৬/২০০৪

অশেষ গুণালংকৃত বিজ্ঞান সাধক

ডঃ জগদীশচন্দ্র মিশ্র মহোদয়ের প্রতি

শান্তিশ্বরী কালীমাতা ট্রাস্টের

সানন্দ সংবর্ধনা শ্রদ্ধাঞ্জলি

পুণ্যবান জনক-জননী
শিক্ষক ও সমাজসেবী বাবু গণেশচন্দ্র,
স্নেহময়ী প্রমীলা দেবী
জন্মঃ- ১৯/০৪/১৯৪৪

পুণ্য জন্মভূমি
বাগমারী, পটাশপুর, পূর্ব মেদিনীপুর
সংবর্ধনা মঞ্চ ঃ মাতা শান্তীশ্বরী মন্দির প্রাঙ্গণ
প্রতাপদীঘি, পূর্ব মেদিনীপুর

বহুমানভাজন হে বিজ্ঞানীসাধক,
সকল বিজ্ঞানের ভিত্তিভূমি যে মৌলিক বিজ্ঞান, সেই গণিত শাস্ত্রকে আত্মস্থ করে বিশ্বের বিজ্ঞানী সমাজে সম্মানের প্রথম সারিতে আসীন হয়েছ তুমি। সেই প্রজ্ঞায় প্রোজ্জ্বল তোমাকে দেশ-বিদেশের বহু বিজ্ঞান প্রতিষ্ঠান সাদরে গ্রহণ করেছেন তাঁদের 'ফেলো'-রূপে। তুমি ভূষিত হয়েছ ভারত সরকার সহ নানা বুধ-সমাজের 'রাষ্ট্রীয় গৌরব', 'রামমোহন সম্মান' প্রভৃতি নানাবিধ উপাধি-ভূষণে। বিশ্বব্যাপ্ত পণ্ডিত মণ্ডলীর সঙ্গে তোমার স্বদেশবাসী আমরাও তোমার উদ্দেশে নিবেদন করি সসম্ভ্রম শ্রদ্ধার অঞ্জলি।

বরেণ্য হে শিক্ষাব্রতী প্রাজ্ঞ প্রশাসক,
এ দেশের অন্যতম বিশ্বসেরা শিক্ষাসত্র আই আই টি-র বিভাগীয় প্রধান ও কীর্তিমান অধ্যাপক তুমি। পিতার আদর্শে স্নেহশীল শিক্ষার্থীবৎসল। আন্তর্জাতিক স্তরে গবেষণাপত্র বিচারক। টেকনিক্যাল বিশ্ববিদ্যালয়ে প্রশাসনে কর্মতৎপর ছিলে প্রো-ভাইস চান্সেলের রূপে। নানা স্তরে বিদ্যাভারতীর তুমি ক্লান্তিহীন একাত্র তাপস, তোমাকে প্রণাম।

হে স্বদেশ গৌরব,
বিশ্বব্যাপী খ্যাতি আর অভ্রভেদী পণ্ডিত্যের দ্যুতি তোমাকে করেছে বড়ো, অনন্য চিন্ময়। তবু জানি, তুমি আমাদেরই লোক। এই বাগমারী গ্রাম, প্রাথমিক বিদ্যালয়ে বসন্তবাবুর ব্রতচারী, টিকরাপাড়া অম্বিকাময়ী গুণাকরবাবু কিংবা অনিলবাবুর পাঠদান, প্রতাপদীঘির কোলে শৈশবের লীলাখেলা- কিছুই ভুল নাই তুমি, ভুল নাই তুমি আমাদের মতো গ্রামবাসী স্বজন বান্ধবদের। 'আচার্য জগদীশ চন্দ্রের' পাশে তুমি আর এক বিজ্ঞানসাধক— এ তো বড়ো! এ গৌরব আমাদেরও। আমাদের অহংকার তুমি। সেই অহংকারে পটাশপুরের এই ঐতিহ্যের জনপদবাসীদের হয়ে তোমার উদ্দেশ্যে রচি আনন্দের সংবর্ধনা অর্ঘ্য আমাদের, উপচারে অতি দীন, তবু হৃদয়উত্তাপে উষ্ণ ভালোবাসা ভরা।

সতত প্রার্থনা করি, শত শরতের সূর্যে আরও দীপ্তিবন্ত হোক তোমার জীবন। সুস্থ ও সুন্দর থাকো। মাতা শান্তীশ্বরী দিন নিরন্তর কল্যাণ-আশিস।

নম্রনত,
প্রতাপদীঘি শান্তীশ্বরী মন্দির ট্রাস্ট কমিটির সদস্যবৃন্দ।

তাং- ০৫/১১/২০২১

নম্রনত,
প্রতাপদীঘি শান্তীশ্বরী মন্দির ট্রাস্ট কমিটির সদস্যবৃন্দ
প্রতাপদীঘি ঃঃ পূর্ব মেদিনীপুর

WEST BENGAL ACADEMY OF SCIENCE AND TECHNOLOGY

WEST BENGAL
TECHNOLOGY
W A
S T
ACADEMY
SCIENCE

Jagadis Chandra Misra

has been elected Fellow of the

West Bengal Academy of Science and Technology

in the Year 2024

for notable contributions

in the field of

Physiological Fluid Dynamics

Maitrayee DasGupta
Secretary

Sivaji Chakravorti
President

Slideshow

Prof. Jagadis Chandra Misra's Parents: Ganes Chandra and Pramila Devi

Parents-in-law: Phani Bhusan and Bijaya Devi

Uncle Jnanada Charan

Prof. Misra after being Awarded Ph.D. degree, 1971

Felicitation by Final Year Mathematics (Hons.) Students of Uluberia College, 1971

Prior to Leaving for Germany, 1975

Prof Jagadis Chandra's Mother with Next Three Generations

Mother with her Eldest son and Daughter-in-law

Jagadis Chandra and his Wife in the Living Room of IIT Residence

At the Golden Temple of Amritsar, Punjab, India

After Receiving IIT Silver Jubilee Research Award, 1984

Jagadis Chandra and his Wife at Pratapdighi

Mrs. Shorasi Misra in the Vicinity of House C1-63, IIT Quarters

With Children, Sudip and Sumita during an Educational Tour

At Assam University, Silchar during the Inaugural Session
of a National Conference, 2017

At the Annual Convention of INAE, 2013

With Astrophysicist J.V. Narliker and Cricketer Sourav Ganguly

With Dr. G. Sarojamma, Head of Maths Dept. (later Vice Chancellor), Tirupati Women's University

Inaugural Session of International Conference ICRAMS 2000 at Maths Dept. IIT Kharagpur

At the Centre for Education Growth and Research New Delhi

At Berlin Technical University, Germany

With Sudip's Family during Tour to Europe

Mother and Mother-in-law performing Pre-Wedding Ritual of Daughter Sumita

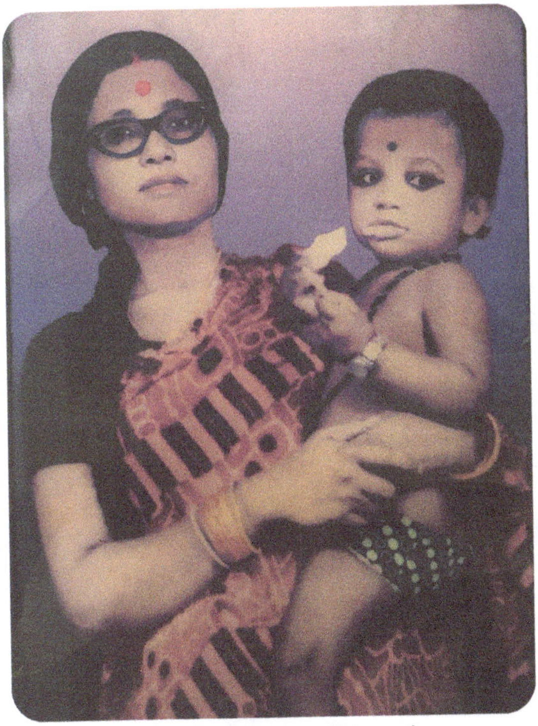

Infant Sudip in the lap of his mother

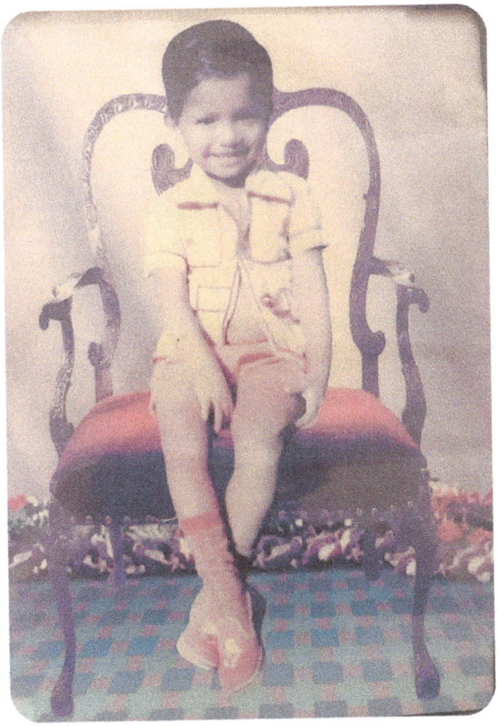

Sudip in his childhood

At Engineer's Conclave LPSO-ISRO, Thiruvananthapuram, Kerala, 2022

Son Subhas receiving "Excellence in Teaching Award" at IIT Kanpur, Teachers' Day, 2022

Son Sudip receiving "Faculty Excellence Award" on IIT Kharagpur Foundation Day 2017

Sudip receiving Career 360 Outstanding Faculty Award from MHRD Minister, Mr. Prakash Javadekar, 2018

Sudip receiving the Chair Professor Award at Platinum Jubilee Inaugural Session, IIT Kharagpur, 2025

With Mr Rajiv Agarwal, Prof Misra's Student (2008-11).
Rajiv Won Young Alumni Achievers Award, 2025

Being Awarded "Siksha Gaurav Puraskar", 2014, CEGR, New Delhi

Daughter Sumita being Felicitated on her Election as a Fellow of Institution of Engineering and Technology (IET), UK

Prof. Misra with his family at a Wedding Ceremony, Contai, 2025

Parames with his family and with Swami Kripamayananda, Head of Vedanta Society of Toronto

Mother Pramila Devi with her Great Grandchildren

With Grandchildren in Germany

Grandson Devadeep and his Playmates in Hamburg, Germany

Granddaughter Supurna performing a Dance Recital

Grand daughter Devarati as a Student of CSE at SRM University, Kattankulathur, Chennai

With Grandson, Devadeep in a Children's Park at Hamburg, Germany

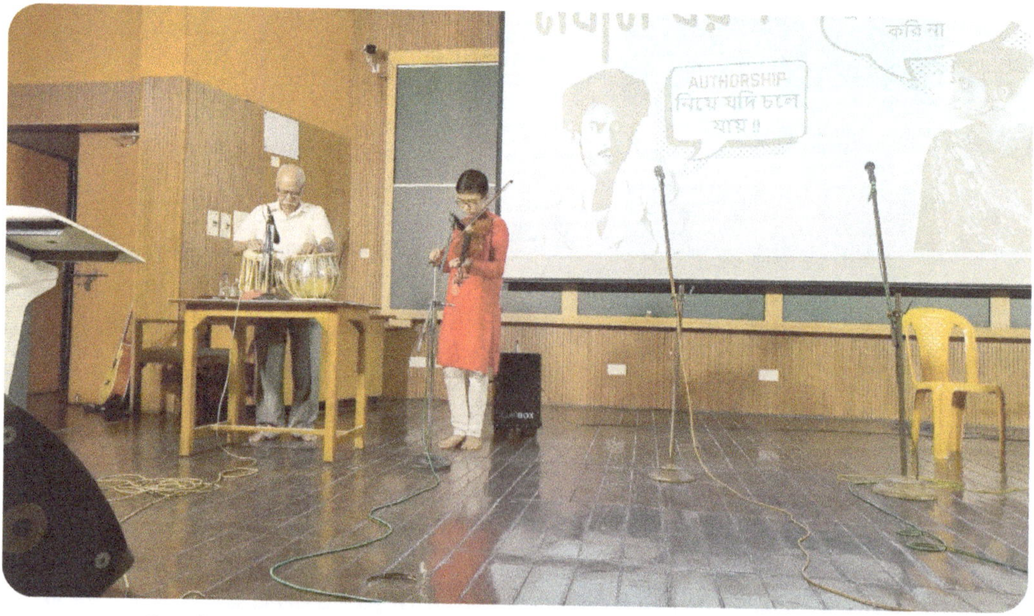

Grandson Devapratim Playing Violin in a Cultural Programme, IIT Kanpur 2022

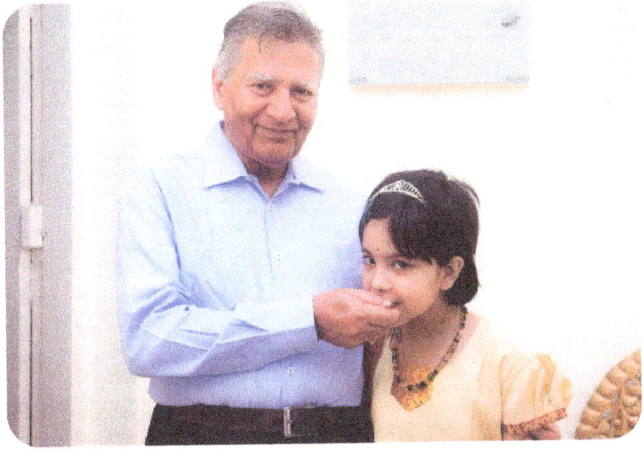

With Youngest Granddaughter, Devadrita

Prof. Misra and his Wife with their Family Members at IIT Kanpur

At the Aerospace Engineering Laboratory, SRM University, Kattankulathur, Chennai 2025

Daughter Sumita's Family

With Daughter Sumita and her family during a Trip to Bakkhali and Frasergunj, 24 Parganas, 2025

With Family Members at Nuremberg, Germany, 2019

With Grand Children in Europe

During an Annual Meeting of Humboldt Fellows at Technical University Berlin, 2016

Brothers engaged in Intimate Conversation

Birthday Celebration on Durga Puja Mahashtami Tithi, 7 October, 2023

During Sacred Thread Ceremony of Grandson Devapratim at IIT Campus, Kharagpur

With Journalist Prof Kumaresh Ghosh

With Swami Bhadratmananda, Asst. Secretary, Ramakrishna Mission Vidyarthi Ashram, Belgharia

Son Sudip being Felicitated by ACM India for winning 'Outstanding Contribution to Computing Education (OCCE) Award - 2023', at its Annual Meeting, NISER Bhubaneswar. Prof. Misra was also invited to the dais.

With Swami Suparnananda, Secretary, R.K. Mission Institute of Culture, Golpark, Kolkata, 17 October, 2025

Shantiswari Kali Temple Inauguration, Pratapdighi, East Midnapore 2025

Jagannath Temple Inauguration, Pratapdighi, East Midnapore 2025

After Joining the Faculty of IIT Kharagpur, 1971

Prof. J.C. Misra, Head, Maths. Dept.

Prof. J.C. Misra at a Conference

Prof. J.C. Misra in a Wedding Ceremony, Durgapur, 2017

During INAE Trip to Kanyakumari, 2022

Worshipping River Yamuna at Ayodhya in Sacred Memory of Parents and Dines, 13.10.2025

Evening Aratrikam at Assi Ghat, Varanasi, 11 October, 2025

At Dhakeswari Temple, Dhaka, Bangladesh, 25 April, 2022

Beside Statue of Dr. Mahendra Lal Sircar, Physician of Lord Sri Ramakrishna & Founder Secretary of IACS Kolkata

During Visit to Vivekananda Rock Memorial Kanyakumari, 2022

Yoga at IIT Kanpur Park-67

Morning Walk at IIT Kanpur Park-67

At Mumbai Airport

During Christmas In Mumbai

During a Visit to Aizal, Mizoram, March 2025

Diamond Jubilee Celebration at Paharpur H.S. School, Purba Medinipur, 2020

Lighting the Lamp in the Inaugural Ceremony of Diamond Jubilee at Paharpur School, West Bengal

At the Inaugural Session of a Conference, Mugberia College, East Medinipur, West Bengal

Receiving Rashtriya Gaurav Award, 2004

With Family Members after Receiving Rashtriya Gaurav Award

Inauguration of Ramanujan Lecture Series, Gangadhar Mahavidyalaya, Mugberia, Purba Medinipur, Feb. 11, 2020

Felicitation by Sixty Plus Golden Life Association Members, Santoshpur, Kolkata-700075, 7th September, 2025

Plantation at Santoshpur Lake-Park, August 03, 2024, in presence of Ms. Nandita Roy, Ward Councillor

পশ্চিম মেদিনীপুর ■ ঝাড়গ্রাম

আনন্দবাজার পত্রিকা

কৃতিকথা

গণিত সাধক ৩

ছোটদের গণিত চর্চায় উৎসাহদাতা

নিজস্ব সংবাদদাতা

■ আইআইটি-র সিলভার জুবিলি পুরস্কার মঞ্চে। *ছবি সংগৃহীত*

খড়্গপুর: আন্তর্জাতিক স্তরে পরিচিত তাঁর গণিত সাধনা। উৎসাহ পেয়েছিলেন বাবার কাছ থেকে। গণিতে শিক্ষার্থীদের উৎসাহ দেওয়ার সেই ধারা নিজেও বহন করে চলেন। গণিতের প্রতি উৎসাহ বাড়াতে জগদীশচন্দ্র মিশ্রের অবদান আজ স্বীকৃত।

খড়্গপুর আইআইটিতে গণিত বিভাগের প্রধান হিসাবে দায়িত্ব পালন করার সময় থেকেই শিক্ষার্থীদের উৎসাহ দেওয়ার শুরু। ১৯৯৮ সাল থেকে ২০০১ সাল পর্যন্ত তিনি দায়িত্বে ছিলেন। জাতীয় ও আন্তর্জাতিক নানা সম্মেলনের আয়োজন করেছিলেন আইআইটিতে। তার অঙ্গ হিসাবে পর পর তিন বছর স্কুল স্তরের পড়ুয়াদের গণিতে উৎসাহ দিতে আয়োজন করেন আলোচনাসভার। সঙ্গে ছিল গণিত বিষয়ক ক্যুইজ। হাজির করেছিলেন রাজ্যের বিভিন্ন স্কুলের পড়ুয়াদের।

জীবনের তিনটি পর্যায় তাঁর মোড় ঘুরিয়ে দিয়েছিল বলে মনে করেন জগদীশচন্দ্র। প্রথম পর্যায়ে বেলুড় রামকৃষ্ণ মিশন বিদ্যামন্দির। যেখানে শিক্ষার সঙ্গে চরিত্র গঠনে তিনি অনেকটা এগিয়েছিলেন বলে মনে করেন। দ্বিতীয় পর্যায় আইআইটিতে অধ্যাপনার সুযোগ। তাঁর কাজের পরিধি অনেক বাড়িয়ে দিয়েছিল। শেষ পর্যায়ে রয়েছে জার্মানিতে পাওয়া 'হামবোল্ট' ফেলোশিপ। জার্মানিতে দু'বছর বায়ো মেকানিক্স নিয়ে কাজের সুযোগ পেয়েছিলেন। সেই কাজ পরে অধিকাংশ গবেষণায় তাঁকে পরিচিতি দিয়েছিল বলে মনে করেন জগদীশচন্দ্র।

গণিত-সাধক বলেন, "শুধু সুযোগ নয়, তার ব্যবহারও জানতে হবে। অনেক পরিশ্রমও করেছি। এখনকার প্রজন্মের ছেলে মেয়েদের মধ্যেও যদি সেই সততা, অধ্যাবসায় ও ধৈর্য থাকে তা হলে কেউ তাঁকে রুখতে পারবে না। সাফল্য অর্জন নিশ্চিত।" আরেকটি বিষয় তিনি মনে করিয়ে দিয়েছেন, "দেশের জন্য কাজ করার মানসিকতা থাকতে হবে। আমি বিদেশে সুযোগ পেয়েও যেমন দেশেই ফিরে এসেছি তেমন আমার ছেলে-মেয়েরাও বিদেশের অনেক হাতছানি উপেক্ষা করে দেশে থেকেই তাঁদের কাজ করে যাচ্ছেন।"

পারিবারিক বন্ধনকে গুরুত্ব দেন। বাবার অণুপ্রেরণা কথা যেমন স্বীকার করেন তেমনই গুরুত্ব দেন স্ত্রী ষোড়শী মিশ্রের আত্মত্যাগও। ১৯৬৯ সালে পটাশপুর থানার অমরপুরের মেয়ে ষোড়শীর সঙ্গে বিয়ে হয় জগদীশচন্দ্রের। সাম্মানিক স্নাতক ও বিএড ষোড়শী বাগমারি গ্রামের একটি হাই স্কুলের শিক্ষিকা ছিলেন। বিয়ের পরে চাকরি ছেড়ে জগদীশচন্দ্রের সংসারের দায়িত্ব নেন। জগদীশচন্দ্র বলেন, "আমি অনেকবার বিদেশে গিয়েছি। কিন্তু উনি এখানেই থাকতেন। আমার মায়ের সেবার জন্য। কিন্তু কখনও রাগ করেননি। মায়ের মৃত্যুর পরে ২০১৬ সালে গবেষণার কাজে জার্মানি গিয়েছিলাম। উনি সঙ্গে ছিলেন।"

পশ্চিম মেদিনীপুর ▪ ঝাড়গ্রাম

আনন্দবাজার পত্রিকা

কৃতিকথা
গণিত সাধক

কৃতিকথা

ইউরোপ আমেরিকায় খ্যাত পটাশপুরের গণিত সাধক

প্রত্যন্ত গ্রামে জন্ম। বাবার প্রেরণায় অঙ্ক সাধনায় মগ্ন হয়েছিলেন ছোট থেকেই। সেই অঙ্কই তাঁকে পৌঁছে দিয়েছে গবেষণার শীর্ষস্থানে। আইআইটি-র অধ্যাপকের কাজ স্বীকৃত বহু নামী প্রতিষ্ঠানে। গণিতজ্ঞ জদীশচন্দ্র মিশ্রের সাধন-কথায় **দেবমাল্য বাগচী**

প্রশ্ন: গ্রামীণ এলাকায় জন্ম। আপনি কি চাষি পরিবারের সন্তান?

উত্তর: ঠিক তা নয়। আমার পূর্বপুরুষদের অনেকেই সংস্কৃত পণ্ডিত ছিলেন। অনেকে আয়ুর্বেদ চিকিৎসা, ওষুধও তৈরি করতেন। বাবা গণেশচন্দ্র ছিলেন পূর্ব মেদিনীপুরে টিকরাপাড়া হাই স্কুলের শিক্ষক। গণিত, সংস্কৃত ও ইংরেজি বিষয়ে পারদর্শী ছিলেন। ইউনিয়ন বোর্ডের সভাপতি ছিলেন। মা প্রমীলা। আমাদের যৌথ পরিবার। কিছু জমিও ছিল। ঘরসংসার জ্যাঠামশাই দেখাশোনা করতেন। তাঁর হোমিওপ্যাথি দাতব্য চিকিৎসালয় ছিল। আমার জন্ম অবিভক্ত মেদিনীপুর জেলার পটাশপুর থানার বাগমারি গ্রামে। ১৯৪৩ সালের ৭ অক্টোবর, দুর্গাপুজোর মহাঅষ্টমীতে। সেখানেই বাল্যকাল কেটেছে।

প্রশ্ন: বেলুড় রামকৃষ্ণ মিশনের ছাত্র আপনি?

উত্তর: প্রাথমিকের শিক্ষা পাশের গ্রাম প্রতাপদিঘি প্রাথমিক বিদ্যালয়ে। বাবার স্কুল থেকেই স্কুল ফাইনালে উত্তীর্ণ হই। আমাদের স্কুল থেকে দু'জন প্রথম বিভাগ পেয়েছিলেন। একজন আমি। অন্যজন ছিলেন অনাথ। যাঁকে বাবা আমাদের বাড়িতে রেখেই টিকরাপাড়া হাই স্কুলে ভর্তি করেছিলেন। বাবার ইচ্ছায় বেলুড় রামকৃষ্ণ মিশন বিদ্যামন্দিরে ভর্তি হই। কারণ সেখানে শুধু শিক্ষাদান নয়, চরিত্রগঠন ও শারীরবিদ্যায় শিক্ষিত করা হয়। ওখান থেকেই আইএসসি পাশ করি।

▪ জগদীশচন্দ্র মিশ্র। *নিজস্ব চিত্র*

প্রশ্ন: উচ্চ শিক্ষাও কি সেখানে?

উত্তর: আমরা যখন আইএসসি-র দ্বিতীয় বর্ষে বেলুড়েই তিন বছরের ডিগ্রি কোর্স চালু হল। আইএসসি পাশের পরে প্রেসিডেন্সি কলেজে সুযোগ এসেছিল। সেখানে দু'বছরেই ডিগ্রি অর্জন সম্ভব ছিল। ভাল পরিবেশে থেকে পড়াশোনার লক্ষ্যে বেলুড়েই ভর্তি হই। সেখানেই গণিতে সাম্মানিক স্নাতক। স্নাতকোত্তরে কলকাতা বিশ্ববিদ্যালয়ে ফলিত গণিত (অ্যাপ্লায়েড ম্যাথম্যাটিকস) বিষয়ে ভর্তি হই। থাকতাম বেলঘরিয়া রামকৃষ্ণ মিশন কলকাতার বিদ্যার্থী আশ্রমে। ১৯৬৬ সালে এমএসসি পাশ।

প্রশ্ন: গণিতের প্রতি টান কি বরাবর?

উত্তর: বাল্যকাল থেকেই। মূল কারণ বাবা। বিভিন্ন বই থেকে প্রচুর অঙ্ক করাতেন। সপ্তম শ্রেণিতেই অষ্টম শ্রেণির বই শেষ করে দিতেন। স্কুল ফাইনাল ও আইএসসিতে লেটার মার্কস পেয়েছিলাম গণিতে।

প্রশ্ন: কর্মজীবনের শুরু কি আইআইটি থেকেই?

উত্তর: না। স্নাতকোত্তর পাশের পরেই ১৯৬৭ সালের মার্চে পূর্ব মেদিনীপুরের নৈপুর শান্তিসুধা ইনস্টিটিউশনের গণিত শিক্ষক হিসাবে যোগদান করি। জুলাই পর্যন্ত শিক্ষকতার পরে উলুবেড়িয়া কলেজে অধ্যাপক হিসাবে যোগ দিই। যাদবপুর বিশ্ববিদ্যালয়ে স্বনামধন্য অধ্যাপক বিভূতিভূষণ সেনের অধীনে গবেষণার কাজ শুরু করি। ১৯৭১ সালে পিএইচডি অর্জন করি। ওই বছরেই আইআইটি

পশ্চিম মেদিনীপুর ■ ঝাড়গ্রাম

আনন্দবাজার পত্রিকা

১৪ কার্তিক ১৪৩২ শুক্রবার ৩১ অক্টোবর ২০২৫

কৃতিকথা
গণিত সাধক

খড়্গাপুরে গণিতের অধ্যাপক হিসাবে নিযুক্ত হই। ডিএসসি অর্জন ১৯৮৪ সালে কলকাতা বিশ্ববিদ্যালয় থেকে।

প্রশ্ন: আপনার গবেষণার মূল ক্ষেত্র কী ছিল?

উত্তর: আমি মূলত ফলিত গণিতের উপর ভিত্তি করে গাণিতিক মডেলিং নিয়ে কাজ করেছি। মানে কোনও কোনও গবেষণার ক্ষেত্রে তত্ত্বগত বিষয়ে গণিতের সাহায্য নিয়ে যে মডেল গড়ে গবেষণা হচ্ছে সেটা নিয়ে কাজ করেছি। ধরা যাক, ধমনিতে রক্তের প্রবাহ নিয়ে গবেষণার ক্ষেত্রে নলাকার কাঠামোর মাধ্যমে তরল বা রক্তের নিরীক্ষণ করার বিষয়টি গাণিতিক মডেলের মাধ্যমে হয়। তার উপর নির্ভর করেই আমার অধিকাংশ গবেষণা চলেছে।

প্রশ্ন: আপনার গবেষণার ক্ষেত্রটি তো বিস্তৃত?

উত্তর: আমি অ্যাপ্লায়েড ম্যাথম্যাটিকস, বায়ো ম্যাথম্যাটিকস, ফিজিয়োলজিক্যাল ফ্লুয়িড ডায়নামিক্স, মেকানিক্স অব ফ্লুইডস অ্যান্ড সলিডস ইত্যাদি ক্ষেত্রে গবেষণা করেছি। তবে মূল কাজ করেছি বায়ো মেকানিকসের উপরে। যেখানে কার্ডিয়োভাস্কুলার ডায়নামিক্স, ফ্র্যাকচার অ্যান্ড রিমডেলিং ডাইনামিকস অব বোনস-সহ নানা গবেষণা সাফল্য পেয়েছে। এই গবেষণার জেরে মস্তিষ্কে আঘাতের স্থান ও মাত্রা বিশ্লেষণ করে আঘাতজনিত সমস্যা নির্ণয়, রক্ত প্রবাহের গতিপ্রকৃতির রকমভেদ নির্ণয় করা গিয়েছে। আমার আন্তর্জাতিক জার্নালে প্রকাশিত গবেষণাপত্রের সংখ্যা আড়াইশোর বেশি।

প্রশ্ন: প্রথম বিদেশ পাড়ি কি গবেষণার সূত্রে?

উত্তর: সেটা ১৯৭৫ সাল। আমি জার্মানি থেকে 'হামবোল্ট' ফেলোশিপ পেয়েছিলাম। সেই প্রথম বিদেশ যাওয়া। কোনও কঠিন বস্তুতে তাপ প্রয়োগ করলে সেই বস্তুর যে বিক্রিয়া হয় তার পরিমাপ নিয়ে গবেষণা করায় এই সুযোগ পেয়েছিলাম। দু'বছর গবেষণার কাজ করি বায়ো মেকানিক্সে। ১৯৮১ সালে জাপান, সেখান থেকে ইউরোপ, আমেরিকা, কানাডা হয়ে ফের ইউরোপে ফিরি। নিউ ইয়র্কের ক্যুরান্ট ইনস্টিটিউট, কর্নেল মেডিক্যাল সেন্টার, জাপানের টোকিয়ো মেডিক্যাল ইউনিভার্সিটি ও কোবে ইউনিভার্সিটির মতো প্রতিষ্ঠানে গবেষণা ও আলোচনাসভায় যোগ দিয়েছিলাম।

প্রশ্ন: কাজের জন্য দেশ-বিদেশের বহু সম্মান পেয়েছেন তো?

উত্তর: ২০০৪ সালে গণিতশাস্ত্রে বিশেষ অবদানের জন্য পাওয়া 'রামমোহন পুরস্কার' পেয়ে সবচেয়ে আপ্লুত হয়েছিলাম। প্রথম জীবনে ১৯৮৪ সালে আমার নিজের প্রতিষ্ঠান আইআইটি থেকে যে 'সিলভার জুবিলি গবেষণা পুরস্কার' পেয়েছিলাম তার স্মৃতি ভোলার নয়। ২০১৩ সালে দিল্লির ইন্ডিয়ান ন্যাশনাল অ্যাকাডেমি অব ইঞ্জিনিয়ারিংয়ের পক্ষ থেকে 'আইএনএই আউটস্ট্যান্ডিং টিচার অ্যাওয়ার্ড' আমার কাছে যথেষ্ট উৎসাহের ছিল। বিভিন্ন দেশের নানা প্রতিষ্ঠান তাঁদের সর্বোচ্চ সম্মান 'ফেলো' হিসাবে নির্বাচিত করেছে।

প্রশ্ন: অবসরের পরেও কি শিক্ষকতা করেছেন?

উত্তর: আইআইটি থেকে অবসর নিয়েছি ২০০৯ সালের ৩০ এপ্রিল। তার পরের দিনই ভুবনেশ্বরে শিক্ষা ও অনুসন্ধান বিশ্ববিদ্যালয়ের সহ-উপাচার্য হিসাবে যোগ দিই। সেখানে মূলত গবেষণার কাজে উন্নতিসাধন করানো ছিল আমার কাজের মূল উদ্দেশ্য। ২০১৫ সালের শিবপুর ইন্ডিয়ান ইনস্টিটিউট অব ইঞ্জিনিয়ারিং সায়েন্স অ্যান্ড টেকনোলজিতেও গবেষণার কাজ করেছি। ২০১৯ সালে সেই কাজ শেষ হয়। তার পরে অবসর কাটাচ্ছি। তবে বিশিষ্ট শিক্ষানুরাগীদের উৎসাহে ও অনুরোধে আত্মজীবনী লিখছি। বাংলা ভাষায় 'অচিনপুরের এক পথিক' প্রকাশিত হয়েছে। এটির ইংরেজি অনুবাদ শেষ পর্যায়ে। কয়েকজন সাহিত্যিক ও ইতিহাসবিদ আমার সম্পর্কে 'নানা চোখে এক বরেণ্য গণিত সাধক' নামে সঙ্কলনগ্রন্থ করেছেন।

প্রশ্ন: ইংরেজি ভাষার এক বইয়ে আপনাকে 'অঙ্কের জাদুকর' হিসাবে অভিহিত করা হয়েছে? অন্য লেখায় 'এক বিস্ময়কর ব্যক্তি'র সম্মান দেওয়া হয়েছে। কী ভাবে দেখেন এই অভিধাগুলো?

উত্তর: কেন তাঁরা এ ভাবে বলছেন তা সঠিক ভাবে তো আমার পক্ষে বলা সম্ভব নয়। মনে হয় গবেষণার ভিন্ন ক্ষেত্রে, শারীরবৃত্তীয় ও চিকিৎসাশাস্ত্রে সফল ভাবে প্রভূত প্রয়োগের স্বীকৃতি হিসাবে তাঁরা হয়তো এ ভাবে অভিহিত করেছেন। এ সবের কতটা যোগ্য তা বিচার করা বিদ্বৎসমাজের বিষয়।

প্রশ্ন: এখন কি আইআইটির স্থায়ী বাসিন্দা?

উত্তর: আমার তিন সন্তান। বড়ছেলে সুভাষচন্দ্র আইআইটি কানপুরের ইন্ডাস্ট্রিয়াল ইঞ্জিনিয়ারিং ম্যানেজমেন্ট বিভাগের অধ্যাপক। মেয়ে সুমিতা মুখোপাধ্যায় শিবপুর আইআইএসটি-র অধ্যাপক। জামাই অচিন্ত্য মুখোপাধ্যায় যাদবপুর বিশ্ববিদ্যালয়ের মেকানিক্যাল ইঞ্জিনিয়ারিং বিভাগের অধ্যাপক। ছোট ছেলে সুদীপ আইআইটি খড়্গাপুরেরই কম্পিউটার সায়েন্স ইঞ্জিনিয়ারিং বিভাগের অধ্যাপক। সেই কারণেই অবসরের পরে আইআইটি ছেড়ে আর যেতে হয়নি। ছেলে-বৌমা, নাতি-নাতনি এবং সহধর্মিণীকে নিয়ে থাকছি। মাঝে মাঝে কলকাতা ও কানপুরেও থাকি।

আনন্দবাজার পত্রিকা সোমবার ৩ নভেম্বর ২০২৫

সম্পাদক সমীপেষু

দেশের জন্য ভাবা বিজ্ঞানী

গবেষণা ও অধিকতর সুযোগ-সুবিধার হাতছানিতে বহুদিন থেকেই এ দেশে শিক্ষালাভ করার পরে অন্যতম সেরা বিজ্ঞানী এবং প্রযুক্তিবিদদের বিদেশ যাত্রা অব্যাহত। অনেক ক্ষেত্রেই তাঁরা বিদেশি নাগরিকত্ব গ্রহণ করে সেখানে স্থায়ী ভাবে বসবাসও করেন। 'দেশ'কে একপ্রকার বিস্মৃত হয়ে। এমনকি বিদেশি হিসেবে নোবেলপ্রাপ্তির তালিকায় তাঁদের নামও দেখা যায়। আচার্য জগদীশচন্দ্র বসু, প্রফুল্লচন্দ্র রায়, সিভি রমন প্রমুখ বিজ্ঞানী অবশ্য এর ব্যতিক্রম। যাঁরা শত কষ্টের মধ্যেও বিজ্ঞান সাধনা করে দেশের সেবা করে গিয়েছেন। আনন্দবাজার পত্রিকার জেলা সংস্করণে, 'ছোটদের গণিত চর্চায় উৎসাহদাতা' প্রতিবেদনে (৩১ অক্টোবর) খড়্গপুর আইআইটির গণিত বিভাগের প্রাক্তন বিভাগীয় প্রধান জগদীশচন্দ্র মিশ্রের এক শিক্ষণীয় জীবন কাহিনি প্রকাশের জন্য ধন্যবাদ। তিনি শুধুমাত্র ছোটদের গণিত চর্চায় উৎসাহদাতা নন, শিক্ষার সঙ্গে চরিত্র গঠনেরও একজন উৎসাহদাতা। বিদেশে গবেষণা ও সুযোগ সুবিধা উপেক্ষা করে তিনি আজীবন দেশে থেকেই গণিত সাধনা করেছেন। চাকরি থেকে অবসরের পরেও যা অব্যাহত। তিনি বিদেশে সুযোগ পেয়েও দেশে ফিরে এসেছেন। 'আপনি আচরি ধর্ম' আপ্তবাক্য বাস্তবায়িত করতে তাঁর সন্তানেরাও বিদেশের অনেক হাতছানি উপেক্ষা করে দেশে থেকেই কাজ করে যাচ্ছেন, যা এখন বিরল। তিনি স্কুল স্তরের পড়ুয়াদের গণিতে উৎসাহ দিতে আয়োজন করেন আলোচনাসভা এবং ক্যুইজ। বেলুড় রামকৃষ্ণ মিশনের প্রাক্তন ছাত্র হিসেবে চরিত্র গঠনের শিক্ষা দেওয়ার অন্যতম কারিগরও তিনি। তাঁর মতে, 'শুধু সুযোগ নয়, তার ব্যবহারও জানতে হবে। এখনকার প্রজন্মের ছেলে মেয়েদের মধ্যেও যদি সততা, অধ্যবসায় ও ধৈর্য থাকে তা হলে কেউ তাকে রুখতে পারবে না। দেশের জন্য কাজ করার মানসিকতা থাকতে হবে'। আইআইটি খড়্গপুরের মতো উচ্চ শিক্ষা প্রতিষ্ঠানে যখন ছাত্র ছাত্রীদের মধ্যে একের পর এক আত্মহত্যার মতো দুর্ভাগ্যজনক ঘটনা ঘটছে তখন তাঁর মতো একজন উৎসাহদাতা গণিতজ্ঞ তথা মানুষ গড়ার কারিগরের খুবই প্রয়োজন।

নিকুঞ্জবিহারী ঘোড়াই
পাঁশকুড়া, পূর্ব মেদিনীপুর